IMAGES
of America

KINGSTON AND ULSTER TOWNSHIPS

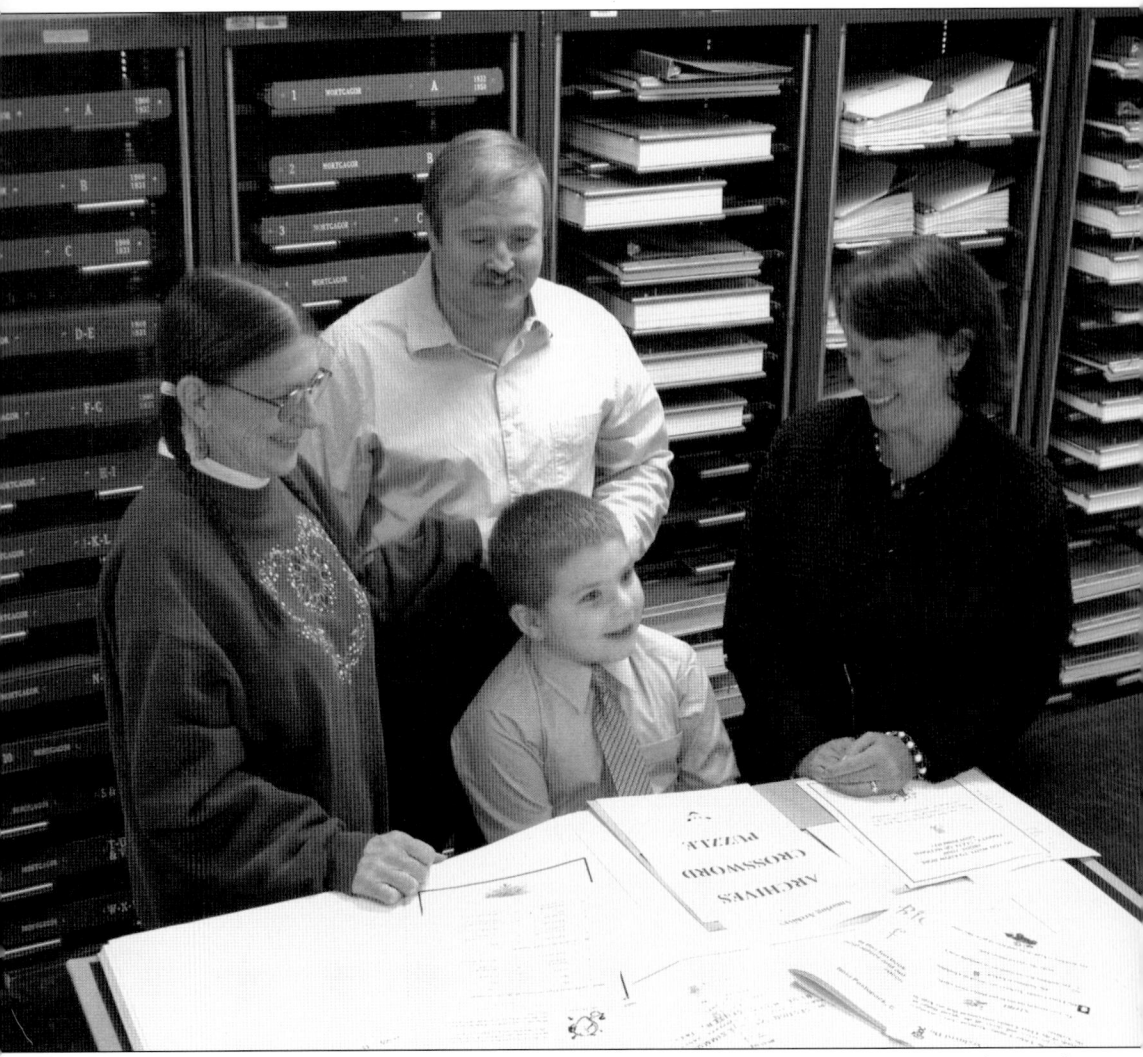

Joining the Ulster County clerk's staff in 1979, Nina Postupack rose through the ranks to take the helm in 2006. Postupack steers a course that, in addition to preservation, assures the rich local history is shared with future generations. Here she shows the authors and Kingston School District first-grader Tristan Boice some of the treasures of the record room. County archives not only house three and a half centuries of historical public records, they have developed a marvelous array of finding aids, exhibits, and tools for learning. This includes a series of archives for kids materials. (Photograph by Shirley Ann Moxham.)

On the cover: Please see page 26. (Town of Kingston.)

IMAGES
of America

KINGSTON AND ULSTER TOWNSHIPS

Susan B. Wick and Karl R. Wick

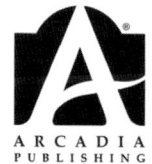

ARCADIA
PUBLISHING

Copyright © 2009 by Susan B. Wick and Karl R. Wick
ISBN 978-0-7385-6263-6

Published by Arcadia Publishing
Charleston SC, Chicago IL, Portsmouth NH, San Francisco CA

Printed in the United States of America

Library of Congress Control Number: 2008932696

For all general information contact Arcadia Publishing at:
Telephone 843-853-2070
Fax 843-853-0044
E-mail sales@arcadiapublishing.com
For customer service and orders:
Toll-Free 1-888-313-2665

Visit us on the Internet at www.arcadiapublishing.com

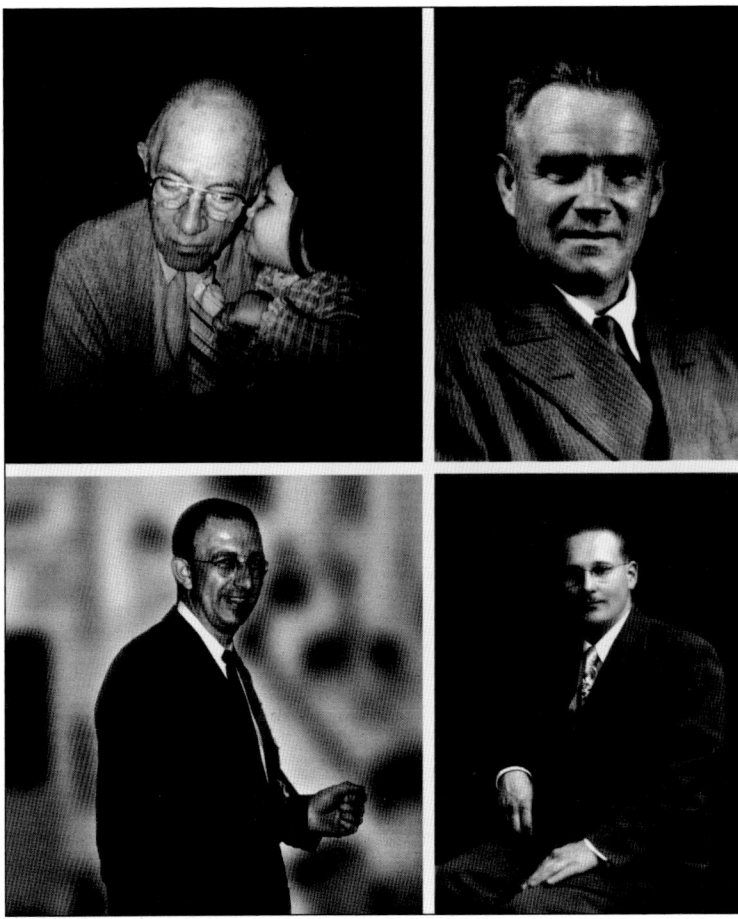

This book is dedicated to our dads and granddads, who helped build and maintain the Corridor of Commerce.

Contents

Introduction		7
Acknowledgments		6
1.	Beginnings	9
2.	The Blue Hills	19
3.	The Brabant and Dutch Settlement	29
4.	On the Rondout River in Eddyville	49
5.	Lake Katrine	59
6.	On the Hudson River in Flatbush and East Kingston	67
7.	Serving the Community	85
8.	Railroads Pass Through	107
9.	Corridor of Commerce	117

ACKNOWLEDGMENTS

The authors would like to extend a special thank-you to our friends and colleagues who assisted us with photographs, information, specialty documents, and artifacts. These people and places include Don and Shirley Briggs, Mr. and Mrs. Martin Jordan, Monika Kaufmann, Sean O'Connor, Raymond Krom, Matt Taggard, Joe Sinagra, Paul Watzka, Don Koeppen, Ed Molinaro, Bill Williams, Marty Cummins, Ted Jones, Jeremiah McDonough, Mike Campbell, Judge Alberstat, Laura Joy, Ernie Smith, Mac and Peg Tinnie, Gordon Quick, Ray Scheffel, Angie Buzzanco, Frank Rittie, Vince DeLuca, Pat Clausi, Bob Haines, Rob Sweeney, Jason Cosenza, Allyne Lange, Virginia Legg, Terry Ramsey, Harry Elder, the Ulster County Archives, Bill Walton, and CenturyHouse.org. The authors would also like to thank the local history section librarians at Ulster County Community College, Kingston Area Library, Ulster County Genealogical Society, and the Town of Ulster Library. Thank you all and thank you to everyone else for your encouragement and support.

Please see the authors' Web site at www.stremy.net for endnotes, expanded information, and additional images from the towns of Kingston and Ulster.

Unless otherwise noted, all images are from the collection of the authors.

Introduction

Snuggled between the Catskill Mountains and Henry Hudson's river, Kingston and Ulster Townships are bound with a common past, siblings borne of the 1667 Kingstowne patent. It was here before the beginning that Preuwamackan's clan tapped nature's resources. Hunting and trapping kicked it off, followed in short order by rows of corn. The arrival of European settlers added waving fields of winter wheat. These settlers learned techniques for farming native crops from their Lenape neighbors. In return, they taught their newfound friends that boundaries are elastic, a mile square is worth a loaf of bread, conveyance means forever, and a hardy draught of rum made it all much easier to swallow. On their own, the Europeans discovered other treasures, they wrestled stone and clay from hillside banks to lay up strong foundations and rubbed their hands in pure delight at the endless virgin forest just waiting for the saw.

As ambitions grew, water trails were sited for canal barges carrying cement and coal to tidewater and for sloops on-loading bluestone, bricks, and ice in their seasons from riverside docks and landings. And all the while bit-by-bit, Kingstowne was shrinking, whittled down as pieces of prosperity were handed out to Esopus, Saugerties, Wilbur, Rondout, and the city of Kingston. Each political adjustment sent the town center spinning on a leapfrog roundabout. Meanwhile, the railroads were making history of their own. Some proposed, some built, and some abandoned, during a tycoon's war waged around a real-life Monopoly board game. These scalawags realized impossible dreams at least for a little while, and took hundreds of working men along for the ride.

When the fat wore thin, many took the rails to greener pastures. Those who stayed played politics. Democratic Ring Party bosses loaded up the dice and sent Jockey Hill Molly Maguires to raise the dead and march them to the polls. After a bitter and violent election in 1879, the town underwent a final split by legislative decree. Thus, were born the townships Kingston and Ulster with a small piece pensioned off to Woodstock. Ulster secured the bulk of the land and populace, leaving Kingston with a few residents and businesses sprinkled about its meager holdings.

As the 19th century rolled to a close, trains, boats, and horseless carriages brought visitors looking for relaxation, creating a need for upgrades in accommodations and the transportation system. Hotels and boardinghouses rose to the occasion, providing vacation havens for the overworked and restless. Main roads were paved with crushed stone or macadam in an attempt to keep automobiles above the rutted mud. Predicted burgeoning of businesses along the road to Jericho did not materialize. Instead, growth settled on another front. The Saugerties Road, leading north out of town, made more sense. That thoroughfare passed through on its journey from Manhattan to the state capitol at Albany. Lined with disorderly roadhouses and speakeasies well before Prohibition, it was here during the Roaring 20s that Jack "Leggs" Diamond and a motley crew of his gangster pals entertained their local molls with bootleg hooch and hanky-panky.

The close of World War II brought home servicemen and servicewomen, sophisticated pioneers with dynamic ideas, bearing the standard of a new age. Ulster, enthused and energetic was determined to usher in this era of technology. And so, the 1950s saw the advent of IBM, bringing with it progressive-thinking individuals intent on developing infrastructure for the emerging computer industry. They did their stint then hurried on, fading into cyberspace, as once again the focus shifted to accommodate a changing landscape. What remains today is a corridor of retail merchants marketing amid the hustle and bustle of a permanent midway.

This Kingstowne 1716–1717 assessment roll was compiled under English rule. Its records combined values of personal and real property freeholds of some Kingstowne inhabitants. Kingstonians were assessed individually, not through landed gentry, and their quitrent was noted in English pounds. While the Crown preferred payment in winter wheat, they would accept furs, *sewant* (wampum), or silver coins. The list also served to determine voter eligibility and to draw from for jury duty. Eldest of Ulster County's sons and daughters, Kingstowne was incorporated by patent on May 19, 1667 and recognized as a town in 1702. A century later, settlement was such that it was time to survey and subdivide. Enter the Kingston Commons, 4 miles wide and more than 20 miles long, this major subdivision ran from Greene County to just south of Rifton. When parceled out, it made things grow. Ulster Township shares this history until 1879 when political growing pains caused "the Kingston riot cases," in which dead men tendered no tax, but got to vote and collect a pauper's paycheck. After a bitter election, Kingstowne was split by legislative decree. (Ulster County Archives.)

One
Beginnings

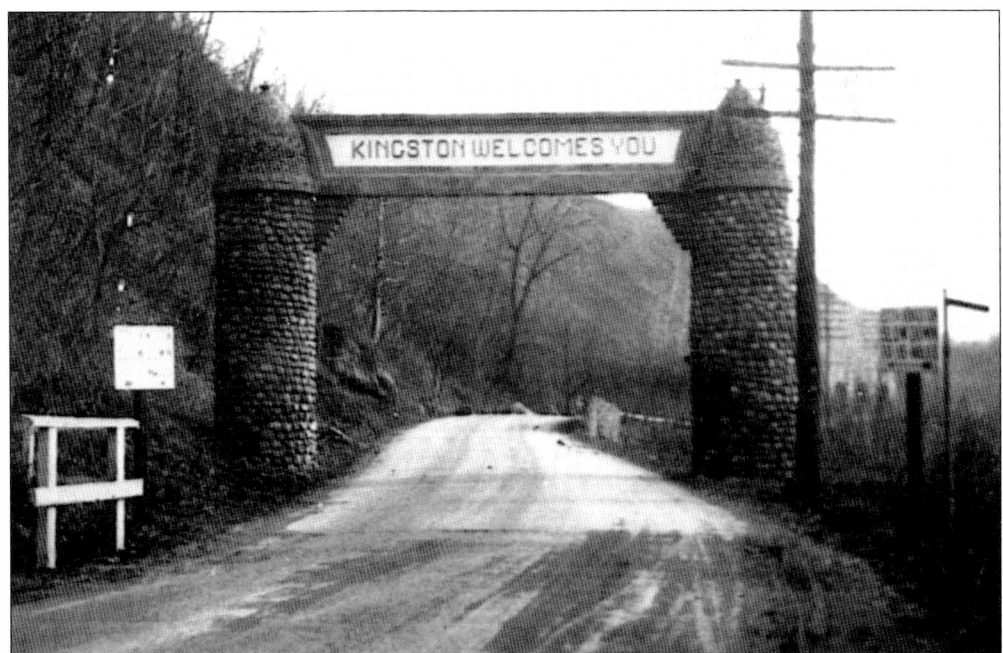

This Kingston gateway was down by the Rondout River, where it all began. Long before Henry Hudson journeyed past its shores, Kingston was a busy port teeming with Amerindians bent on trading salt and copper, flint and furs. In 1624, it became a portal for Europeans with pioneering spirits. (Martin Jordan.)

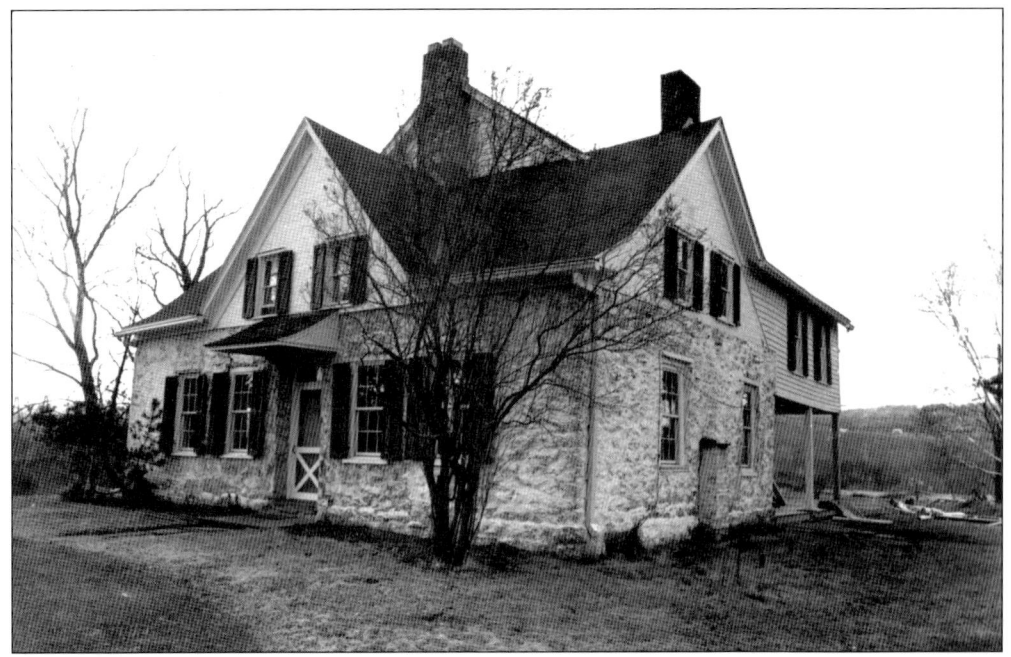

One of the first to settle outside the stockade's "curtains," T. C. DeWitt built this house and farmed the land on both sides of the road to Hurley. He raised corn and wheat and made butter and cheese. Being Dutch and stubborn, he kept Christmas by old Holland tradition and was fined and roundly scolded for his efforts by a stuffy English magistrate.

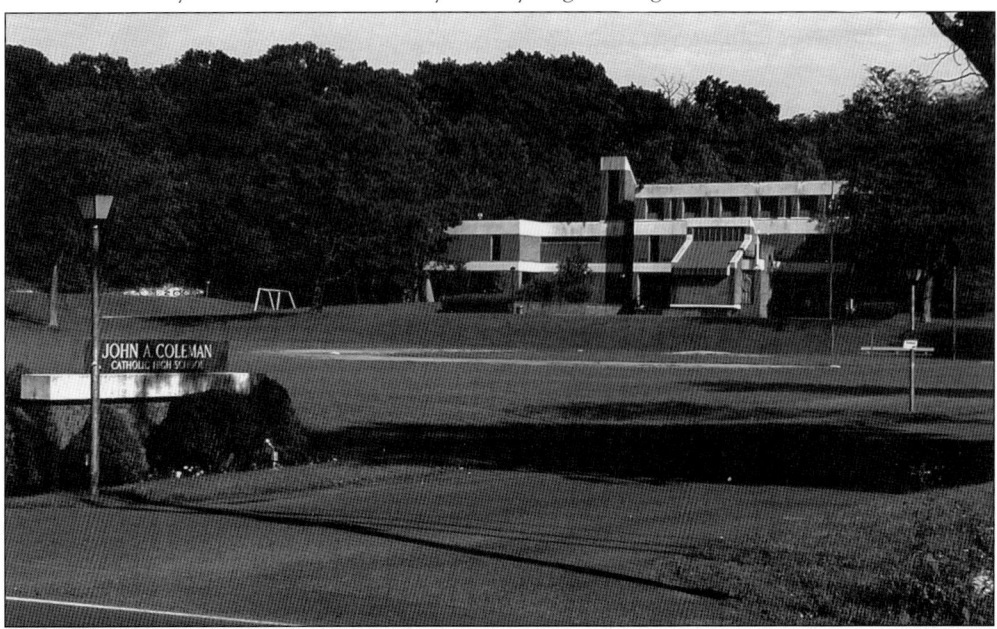

Sited where DeWitt once grew wheat to feed an army is John A. Coleman Catholic High School. Established in 1966, Coleman is dedicated to serving students of all faiths in grades 9–12. The school has a good sports program and an excellent theater department. A small school with a big heart, it provides a well-rounded education with an emphasis on college preparation. (John A. Coleman High School.)

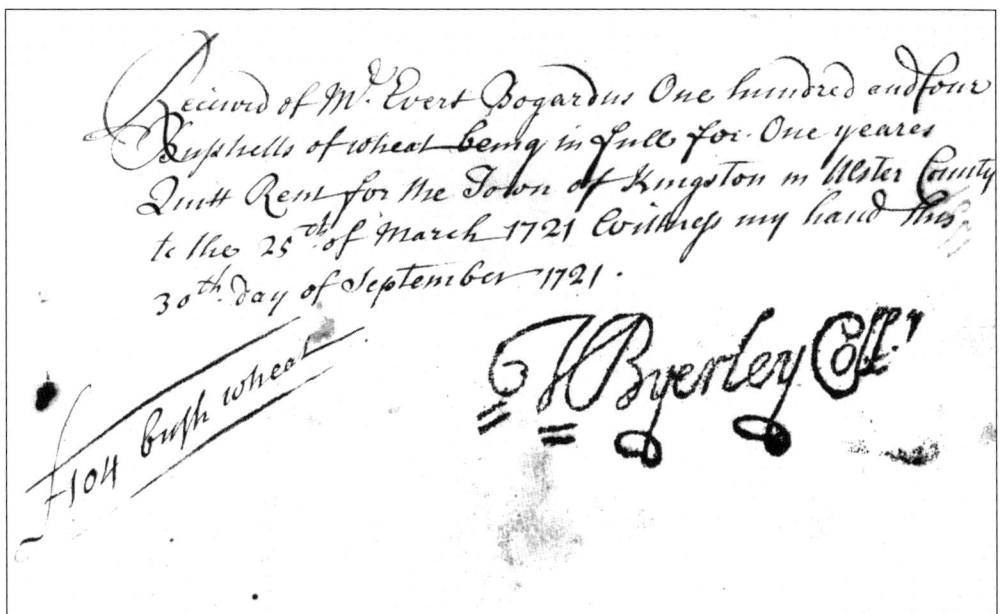

When this quitrent receipt was issued in 1721, Kingstowne was the heart of the breadbasket for England's New World colonies. Freeholds were assessed individually and their quitrent (another word for taxes) was payable in wheat at mills designated for that purpose. The grain was then sold and shipped worldwide. The proceeds of these sales belonged to the Crown and were supposed to be used for garrison and road maintenance. (Ulster County Archives.)

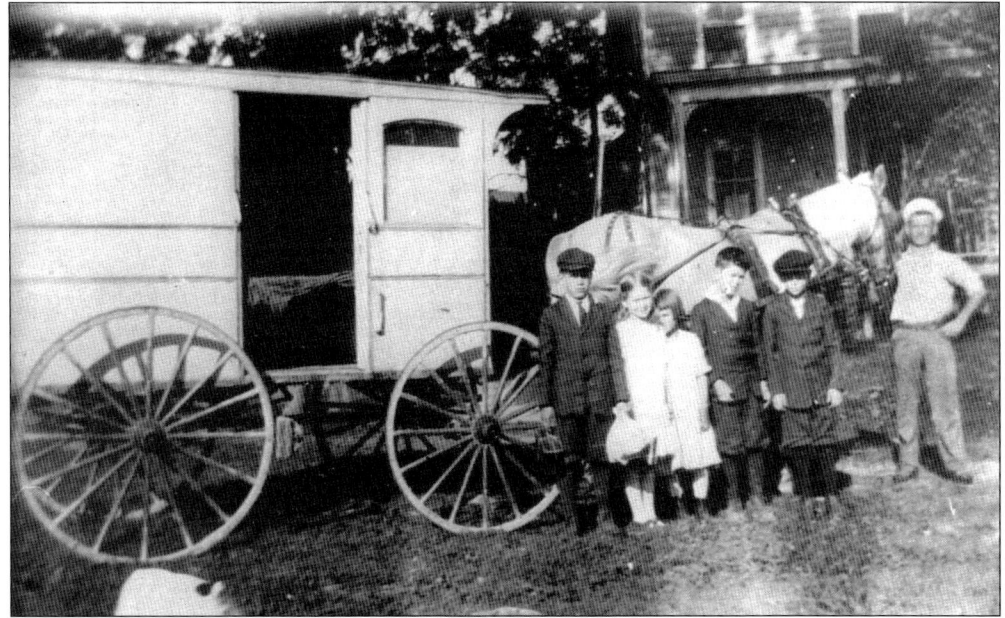

This was the school bus for the town of Kingston's 1920–1921 school year. After school No. 1 burned down in 1920, the district decided to temporarily bus the children to the Vandale School. Fred Beecher won the contract. The closed cab protected the children from winter winds and the wheels could be replaced with bobs. From left to right are Preston Herndon, Anna Beecher, Edwina Herndon, Thomas Herndon, George Beecher, and Fred Beecher. (Town of Kingston.)

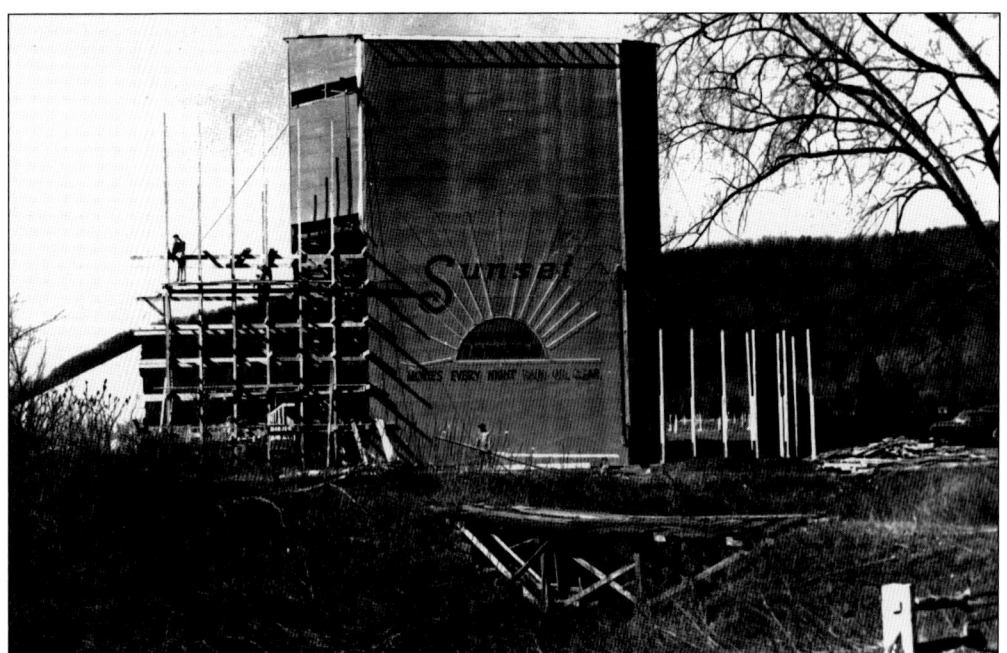

The Sunset drive-in theater on Route 28 (the old plank road) is receiving a 1957 retrofit to accommodate Cinemascope movies. The Ulster and Delaware Turnpike Road Company incorporated in 1802 to build a plank road along an ancient Amerindian salt trade route from Kingston to Jericho. The drive-in occupied the approximate location of the first tollhouse on the road. (Bob Haines.)

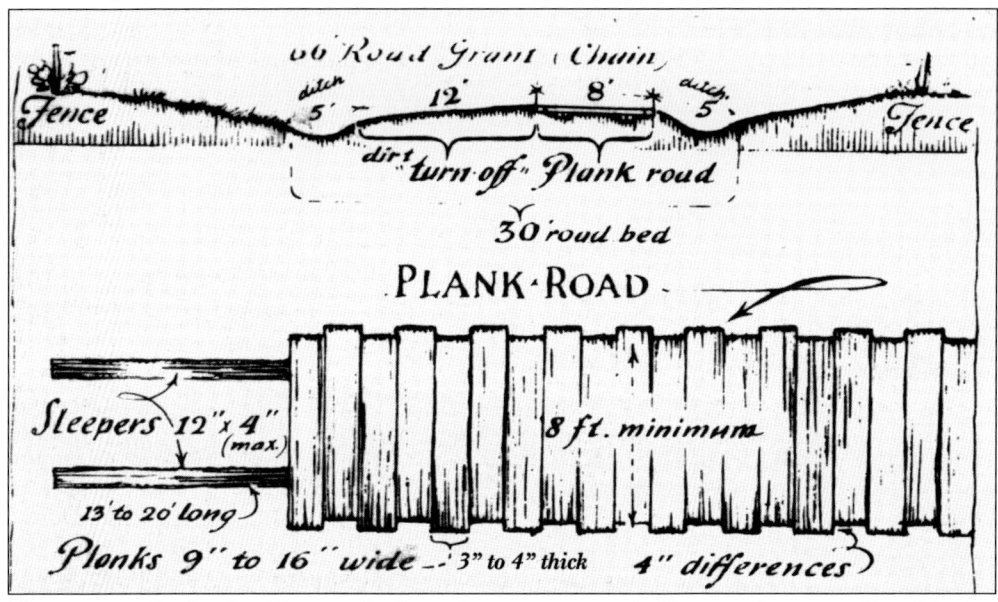

This is an early sketch of how a plank road was constructed. Very similar to a railroad bed, a plank road was slightly raised with a drainage ditch on each side. The sleepers kept the roadway planks off of the ground and relatively straight and level as well as providing a place to fasten them. Hemlock trees sans bark stripped for tanning were reclaimed to build these roadways. (Vera Sickler and Town of Olive.)

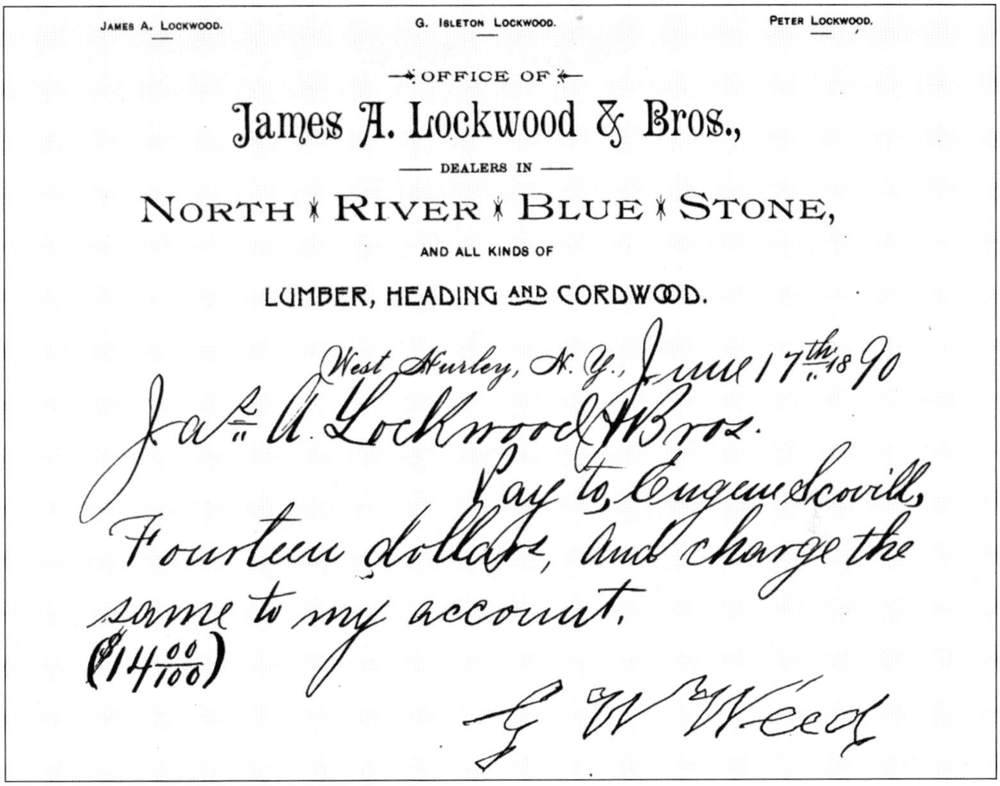

As well as being successful merchants, the Lockwood brothers had a farm just west of this first tollhouse and maintained a drovers' station there. Drovers herded meat on the hoof from outlying farms to the ports of Kingston. For a fee, the Lockwoods would house and feed them and their animals overnight. (Atkarton History Project.)

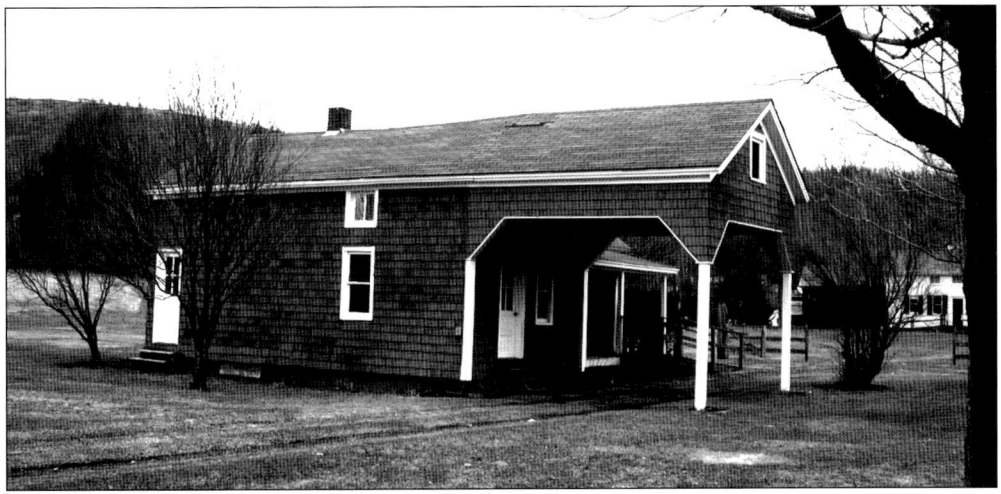

This typical large tollhouse was home to a small family as well as a stop on the turnpike. Some tollhouses were simple shanties, others like this one were far nicer. A toll board displaying rates would have been conspicuously placed. The larger stations sometimes offered services like blacksmithing and were collection points for the mail, which was carried by stagecoach. (Atkarton History Project.)

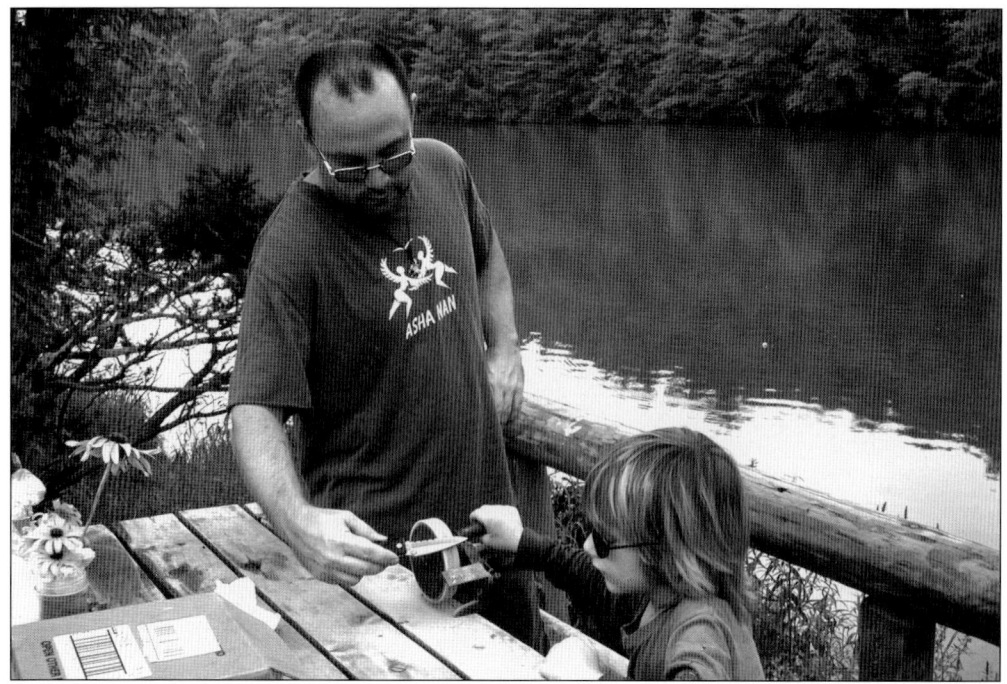

Levon Raacke and his dad, Karl, examine an artifact at Onteora Lake. The lake and surrounding 1,700 acres are available to the public for boating, biking, and exploring quarry site remains. Waughknok, an old Amerindian trail, runs parallel on the south. As late as 1920, there were Amerindians in the area. Meg Steward was noted for native baskets and her skills in helping birth the next generation.

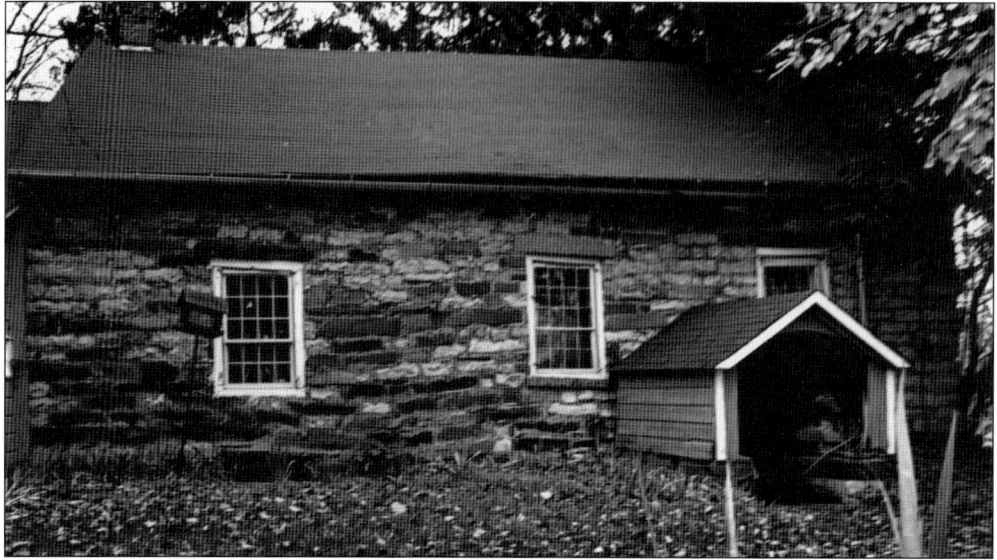

Late in the 1700s, the Myers family constructed a sawmill on Wintergreen Hill brook, which feeds into the Sawkill. The brook was not large and an undershot wheel was necessary even though a dam was used to create a millpond. This photograph is of the original Myers family homestead at Brabant near the Brabant or Chase Cemetery. In 1811, the family built a larger, two-family stone house near the mill. (Town of Kingston.)

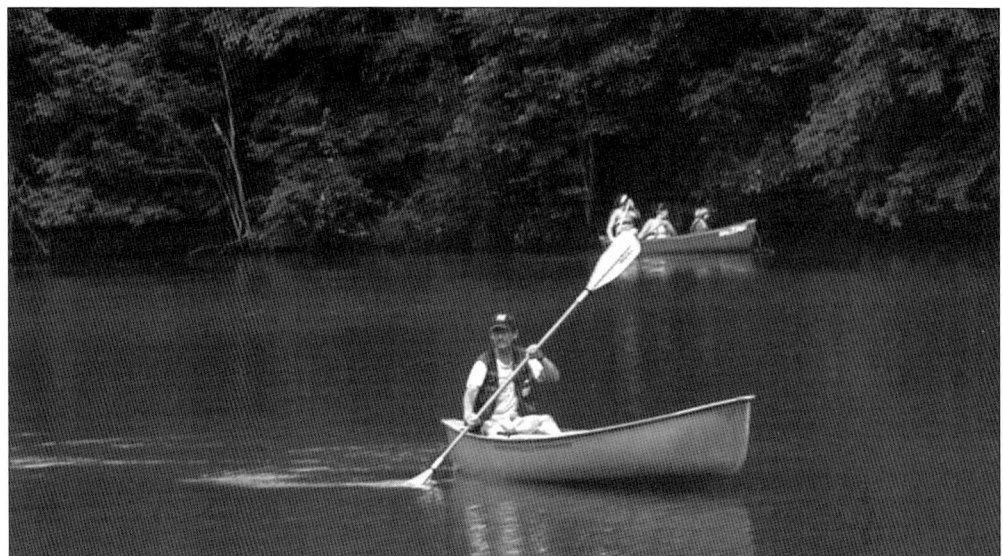

Identified on early maps as a binnewater (an interior, isolated pond), Onteora Lake is the headwaters of Preymaker Creek. Named for local Lenape leader and sachem Preuwamackan, this creek wanders through the bluestone hillside to the fertile Hurley corn flats where it merges with the Esopus Creek. John D. Briggs, Donna Wamsley, and Jen Raacke, descendants of Preuwamackan and the first Dutch settlers, endeavor to keep alive crafts and traditions of all their ancestors.

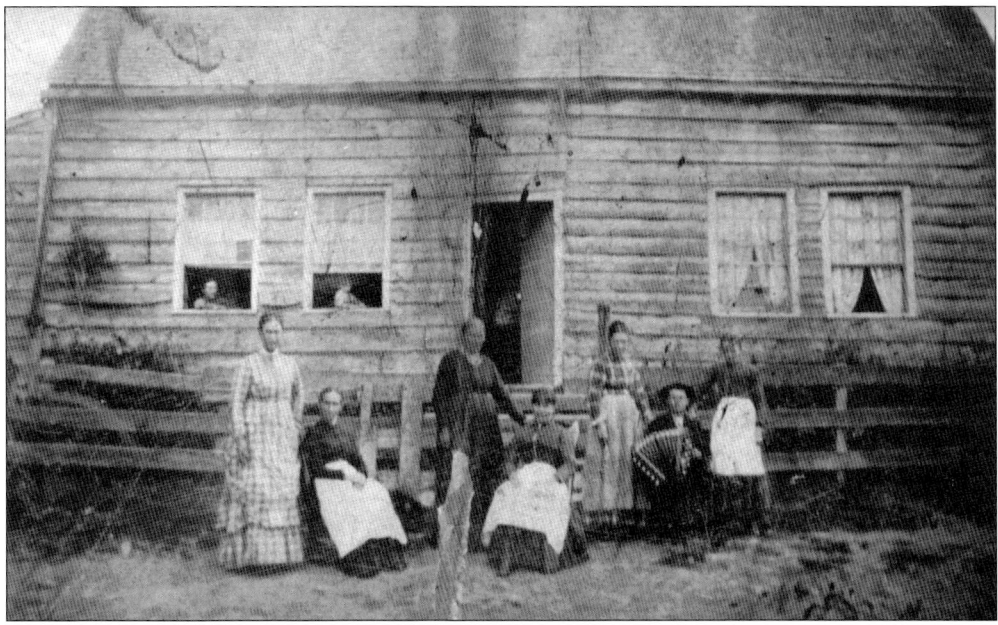

This rare 1885 linotype shows the McCaffrey home on Sawkill Road. Seen are, from left to right, Julia McCaffrey, Margaret McCaffrey, Granny McCaffrey, Mrs. Peppard, an unidentified McCaffrey, Charles McCaffrey on accordion, and Mrs. O'Brine. The house is a typical early-19th-century wood home with what appears to be an 1850s-era addition at the right side. It burned down in 1910. The property now holds a new home, constructed in a later century, around 1954. (Town of Kingston.)

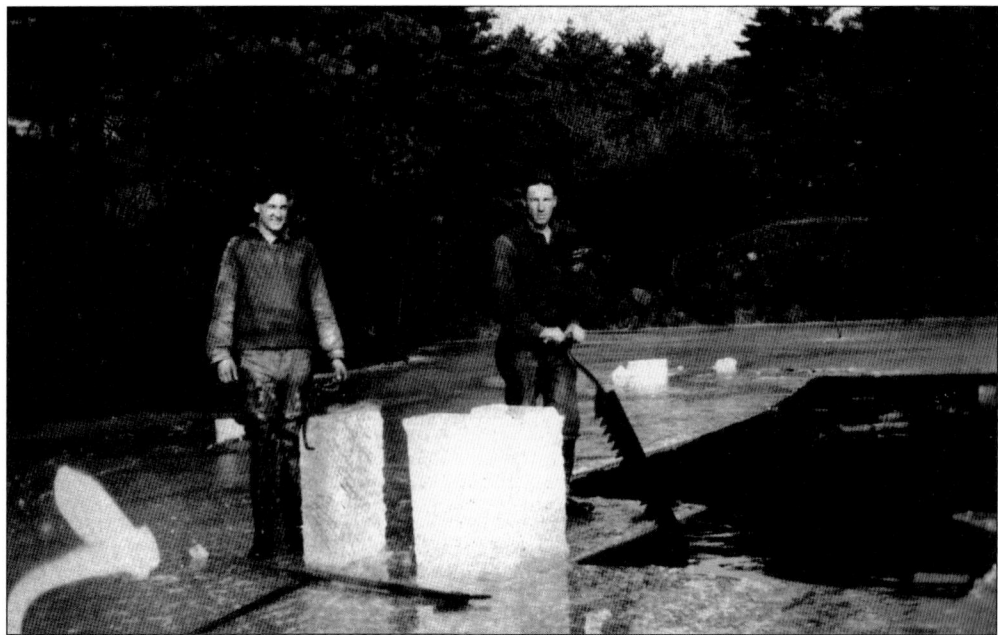

Harry Siemsen (right), town of Kingston historian, cuts ice in Sawkill in the 1940s. Born in Brooklyn, he came to Sawkill in 1906. Siemsen loved his new home and was active in town government, eventually becoming fire chief and town historian. Siemsen collected and transcribed nearly 200 folk songs written by local musicians. He learned and practiced many old-time skills including horseshoeing, hand harvesting grain, and hiving bees. (Town of Kingston.)

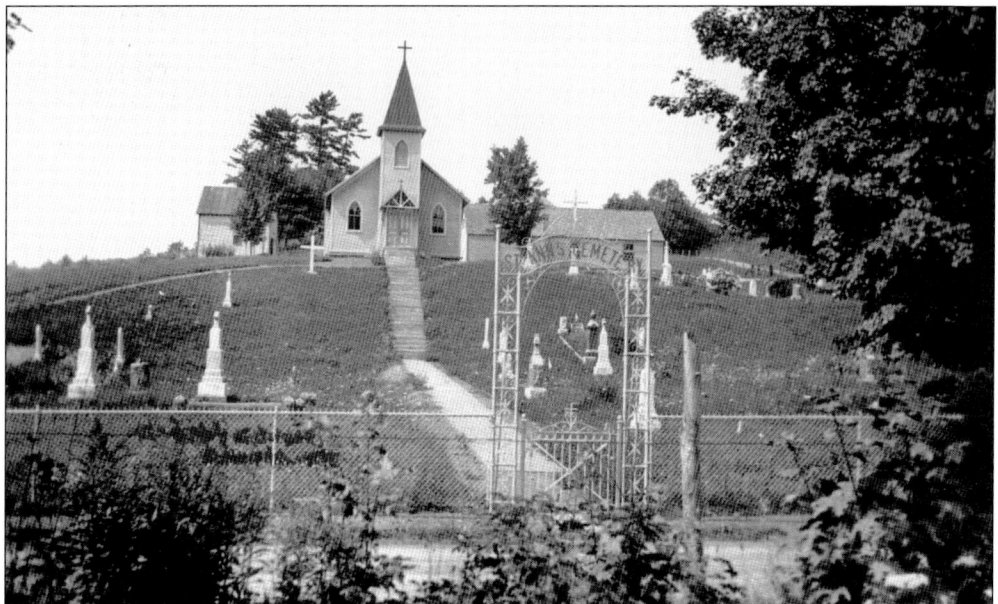

The St. Ann's Roman Catholic Church site was specifically purchased to provide a final resting place for local Catholics. According to several accounts, not all of its occupants took the word *final* seriously. Tales are told of feast day healing miracles and restless souls, such as the Lady in Black, haunting the burying ground. And there were the times the dead rose and marched to the polls, but that is another story. (Town of Kingston.)

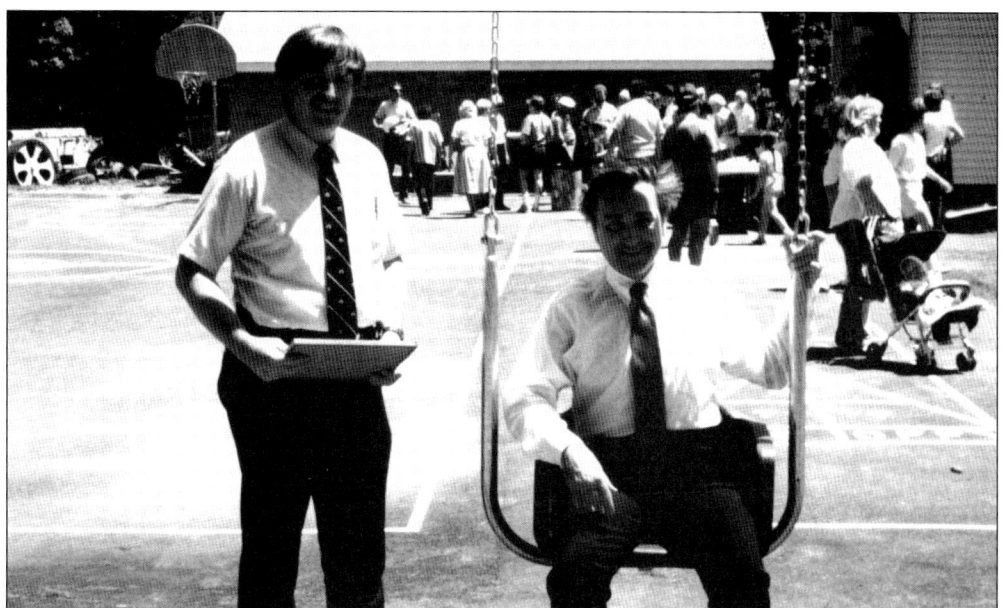

In this June 11, 1988, picture, popular New York State assemblyman (now congressman) Maurice Hinchey is ready to swing into action assisting supervisor Eugene McInnis at the dedication and grand opening of the play park during the town's 300th birthday celebration. Hinchey's attention to constituent service and his expertise in bringing home the bacon has assured him a warm spot in many hearts. (Town of Kingston.)

AN ACT to legalize and confirm the action of the board of supervisors of the county of Ulster in the division of the town of Kingston, in said county, by erecting the town of Ulster therefrom, and attaching a portion thereof to the town of Woodstock, in said county.

PASSED May 26, 1880; three-fifths being present.

The People of the State of New York, represented in Senate and Assembly, do enact as follows:

Action of board of supervisors legalized.

SECTION 1. An act entitled "An act to divide the town of Kingston, in the county of Ulster, and erect therefrom the town of Ulster and attach a part thereof to the town of Woodstock, in said county," passed by the board of supervisors of the county of Ulster at their annual meeting, the twenty-eighth day of November, in the year one thousand eight hundred and seventy-nine, two-thirds of all the members of said board voting in favor thereof, under and in pursuance of chapter three hundred and nineteen of the laws of eighteen hundred and seventy-two, is hereby, together with all the provisions thereof, in all respects legalized, and confirmed, and the action of the board of supervisors in the passage of said act hereby legalized and declared valid.

§ 2. This act shall take effect immediately.

In 1879, politics split Kingstowne as red shirted Molly Maguires raised the dead and stormed the polls to wrestle Dutch farmers for control. Calls for police protection were futile as the sheriff, in a fit of personal preservation, had taken himself elsewhere. After the Irishmen won, the stubborn Dutch petitioned the state for a town of their own, then they packed up their ports and farms and moved to Ulster. (Ulster County Law Library.)

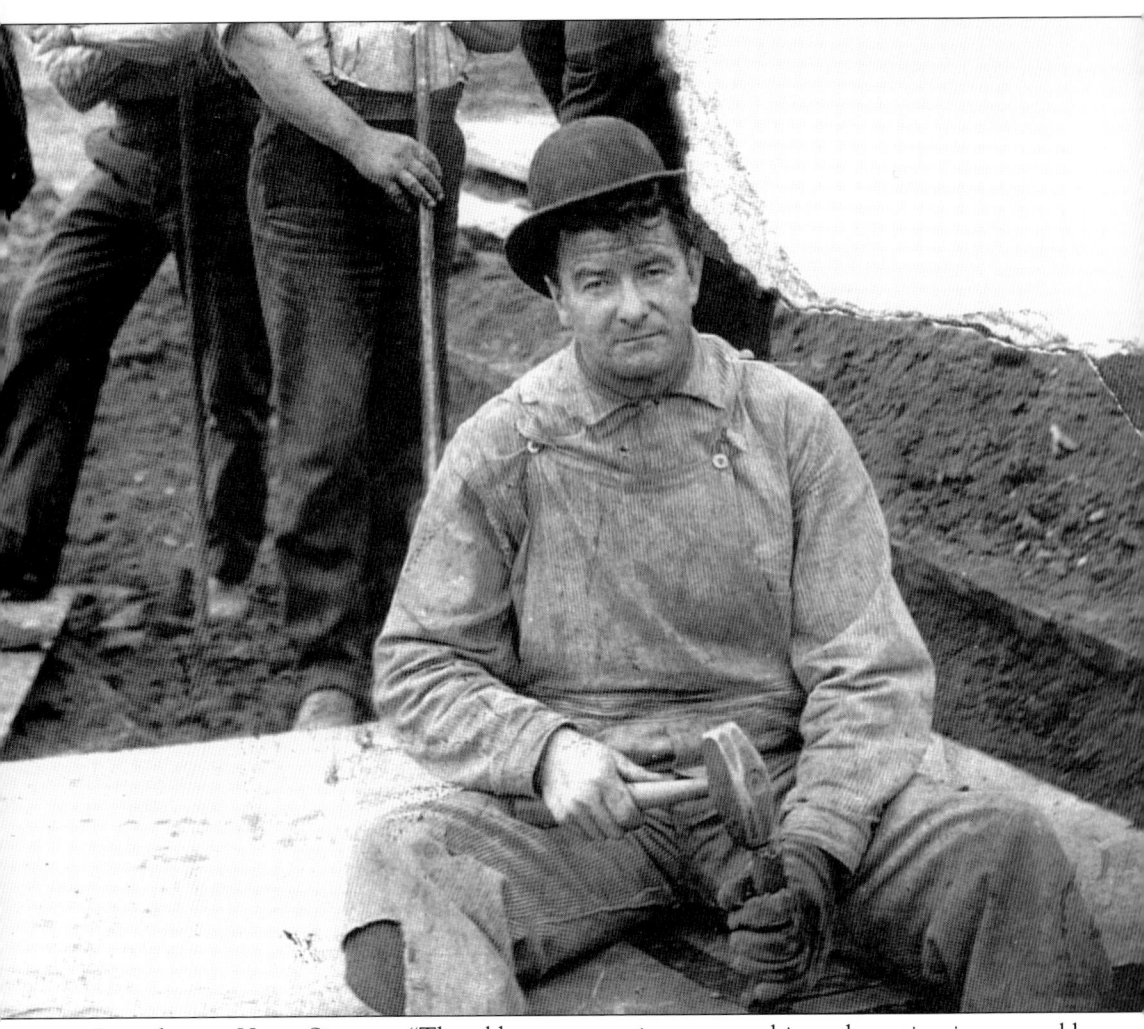

According to Harry Siemsen, "The old quarryman is gone . . . his tools rusting in some old barn or shed. His hoist and derrick stand where he left them one early winter evening, a marker to flag the place where men had worked hard and gambled with nature for a living." The early 1800s saw thousands of Irish immigrants travel up the Hudson River. Some made their way to the rocky hillsides of Kingston Township and found employment in the abundant bluestone quarries. Capped with Bowler hats and under-garbed with red union suits, these stone jockeys worked cheek by jowl along miles of the Ledge. For close to half a century the blue hills rang out with the sounds of a vibrant economy. Clanking hammers, whirling pumps and derricks, the deafening roar of blasting, clattering wagons hauling stone to market, and the stone jockeys plied their trade paving the streets of America. Life was good and high rolling, and then it crashed. Portland cement took over the paving market and an eerie quiet spread through the hills of Kingston as one by one the quarries closed. A thriving industry became a part-time cottage craft, supplementing the income of hillside farms tucked between the quarries where there are two stones for every dirt. (Peter Sinclair.)

Two

THE BLUE HILLS

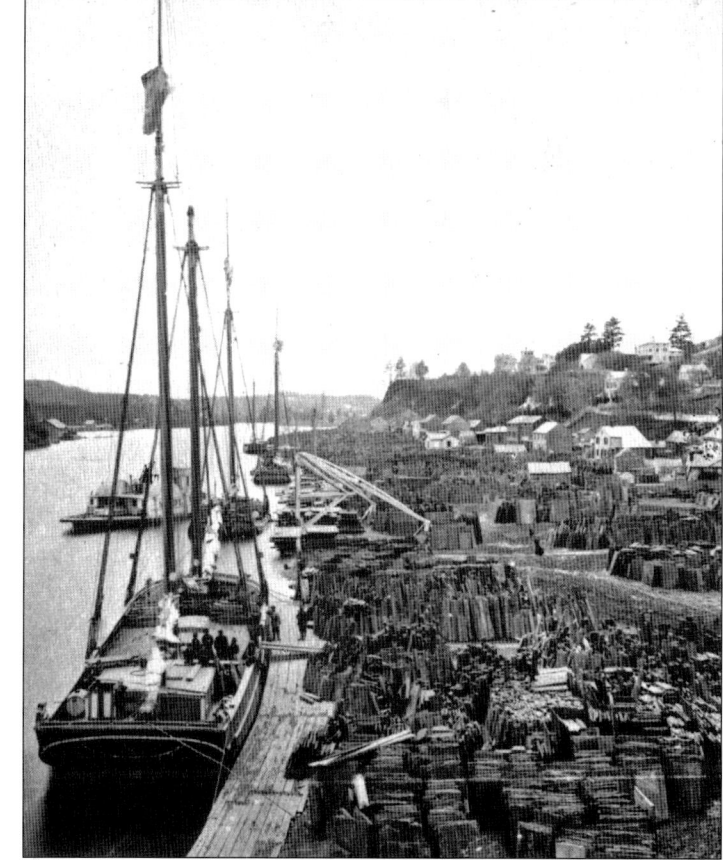

Hewitt Boice began quarrying in 1875. By 1898, he owned three stone yards with finishing mills, steam-powered derricks for loading, a blacksmith's shop, docks on the Rondout River, a schooner, five barges, and a string of quarries. In 1896, he won a contract to pave the sidewalks of New York City. He grossed $460,000 a year and employed 90 men. A leading wholesale dealer, he was dubbed "the Bluestone King." (Hudson River Maritime Museum.)

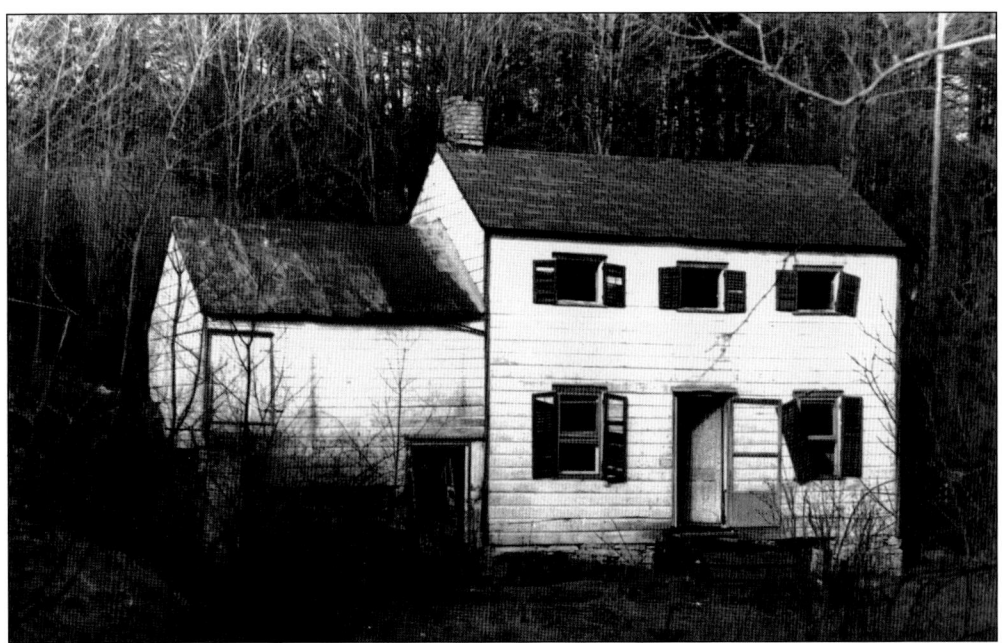

For many years, Peter Sinclair has been advocating for the stabilization and restoration of the Madden House. This quarryman's shanty sits beside the tracks of the Ulster and Delaware Railroad and represents a small, common working-class home of the mid-19th century. In a 2002 application for preservation, Sinclair says, "One great advantage in preserving the architecture of poverty is the low cost of its restoration." (Hudson Valley Vernacular Architecture.)

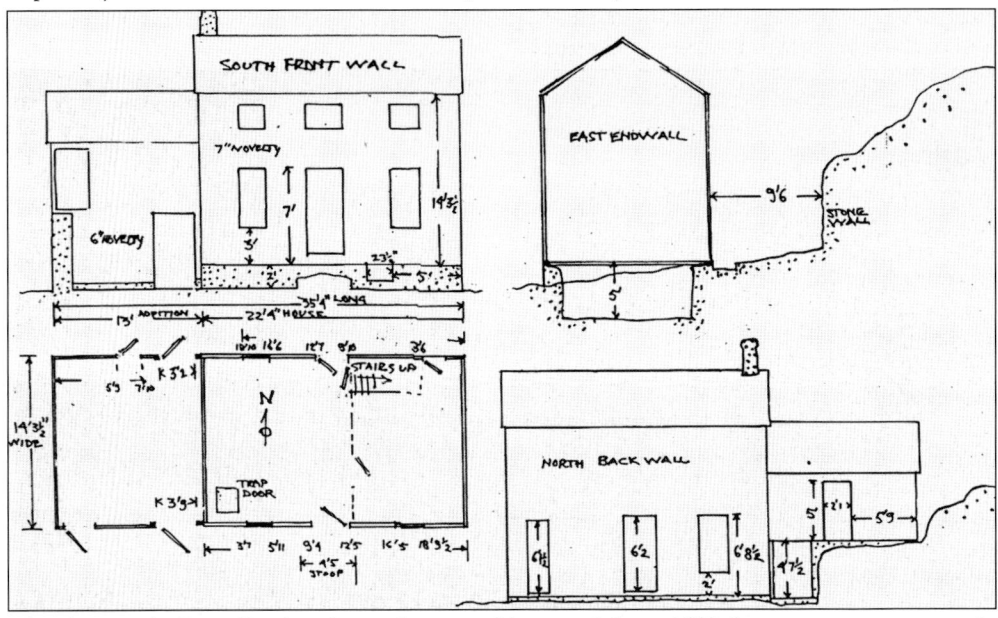

This drawing by Peter Sinclair shows the typical layout of the c. 1850 shanties run-up to provide company housing for quarrymen and their families. Sinclair believes architecture is like a regional language. "It's above ground archeology. It relates to the written and oral history in explaining the whole culture of an area." This house had been home to generations of Irish stone jockeys and their families. (Hudson Valley Vernacular Architecture.)

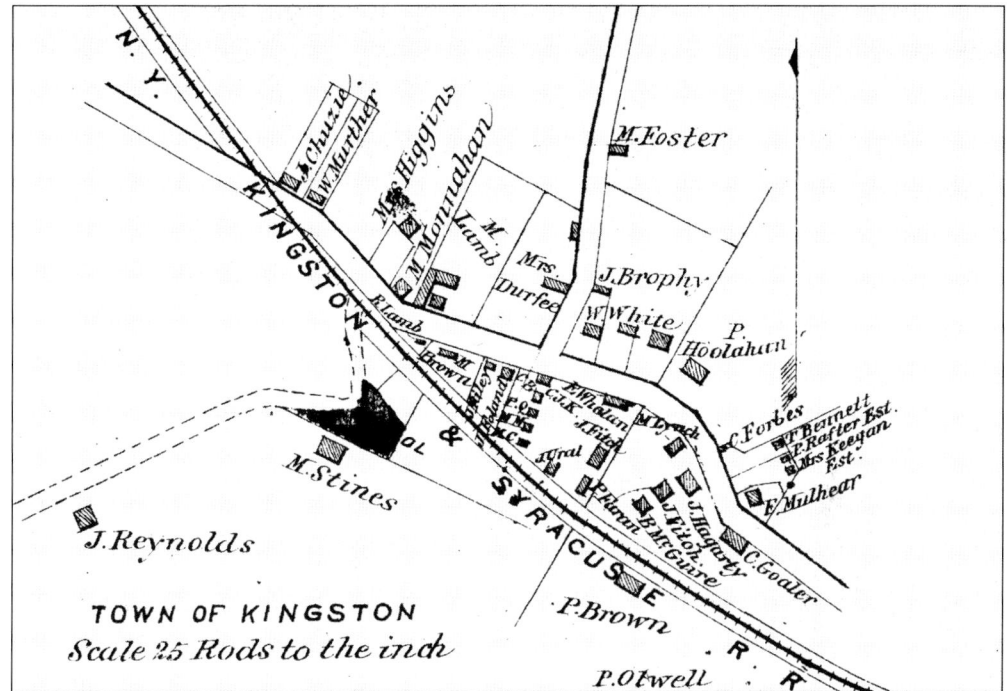

Stony Hollow was a quarry district served by the plank road and the Ulster and Delaware Railroad. Owen Grant ran a 12-man quarry equipped with dump carts and a horse-powered pump. Nearby, Mrs. McGieff hired two men to mine curb stone of a good blue color. The easy transportation these quarries enjoyed caused them to play out as the century turned from the 19th to the 20th. (Atkarton History Project.)

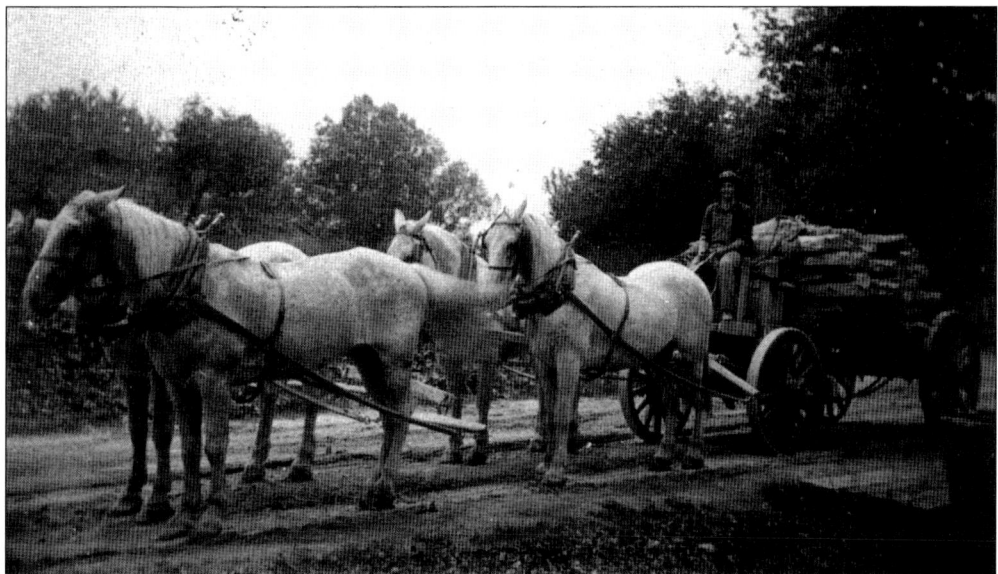

This Stony Hollow teamster is heading his team to the docks at Rondout. Four horses indicate a load of 12 to 16 tons. The fact that the road is all downhill is more of a hindrance than a help. The back wheels of a loaded wagon needed to be shoed or chained to help avoid accidents due to the cart getting before the horses. (Town of Kingston.)

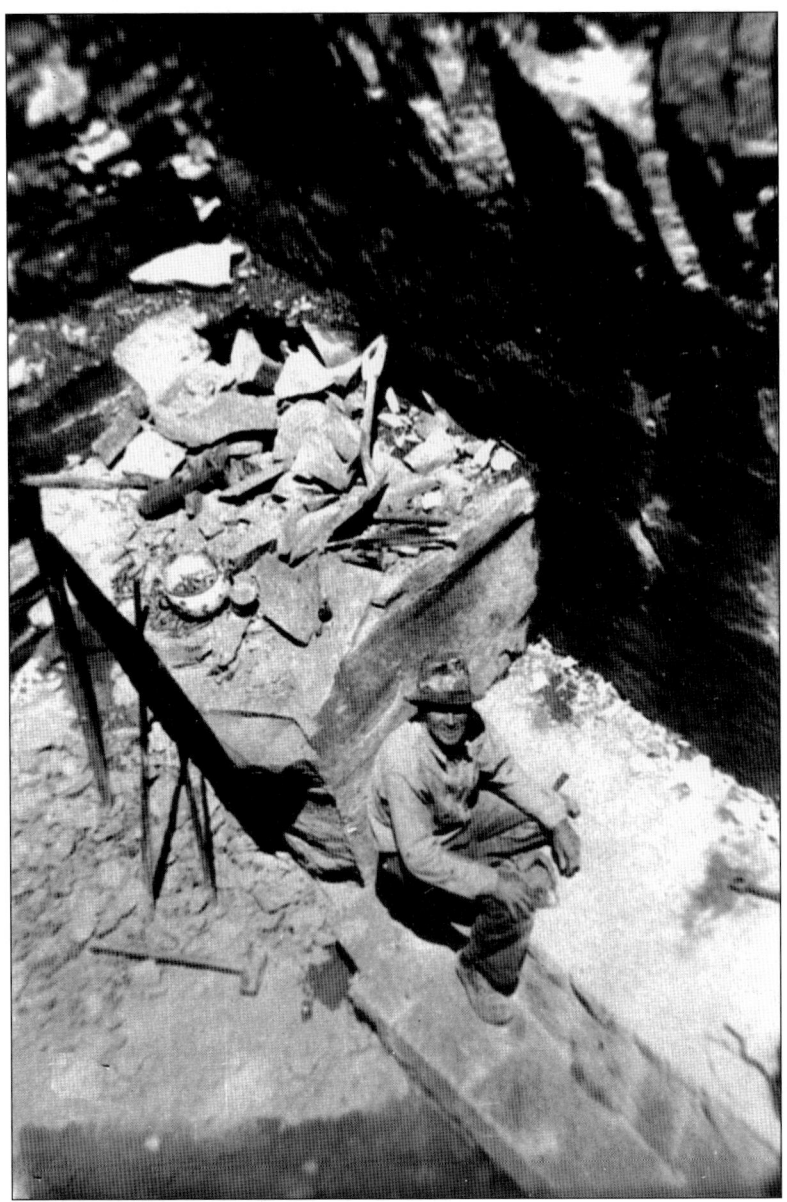

The bluestone industry began in 1832 and peaked in 1905. Although it had greatly dwindled by 1947, it still flourished in scattered quarries to meet the needs of road builders and landscaping contractors. Terence McDonald ran Terry's quarries near the Sawkill Creek and adjacent to John McCaffery and Company (see page 24). McDonald shipped rough-cut edging stone to Hewitt Boice at Rondout. In many cases, the larger quarries were owned by riverfront stone dealers. This allowed them to control the quantity of stone on the market. The dealers only occasionally actually operated the quarries. They preferred to rent them out for a percentage of the profits. McDonald employed 17 men throughout the year and had the luxury of a hand derrick to load the wagons. The tight grain of the vein they worked required the regular services of a blaster. This was an extremely well-paying job with a high turnover rate due to the unstable nature of the blasting powder of the times. Sitting on the block is Harry Hulsair, one of the survivors. (Town of Kingston.)

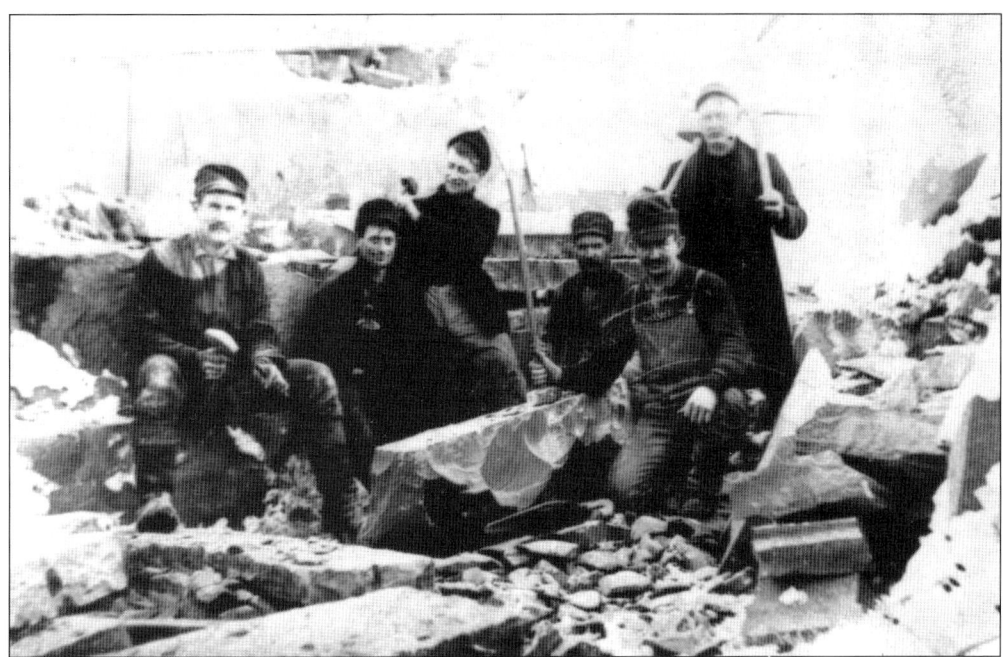

Seen here from left to right, Edward McCaffrey, two unidentified men, John Burns, William Clearly, and William Bonesteel are taking a break from their stone jockey duties at the Ledge in 1904. Longest lived of the quarry sites, the Ledge sits on Jockey Hill. Located in lots No. 65 and No. 66 of the Binnewater class in Kingston Commons, Samuel Coykendall was the owner and employer at the time. (Town of Kingston.)

For centuries, hand crafted millstones from the Blue Hills have made their way around the world. In this 1940s photograph, a Jockey Hill millwright pecks the face of a millstone. Milling stones are not just for gristing grains. They are also used to grind cement, mustard seeds, and cosmetic ingredients. Each purpose has a uniquely etched pattern that must be exactly followed to produce a perfect product. (Bob Haines.)

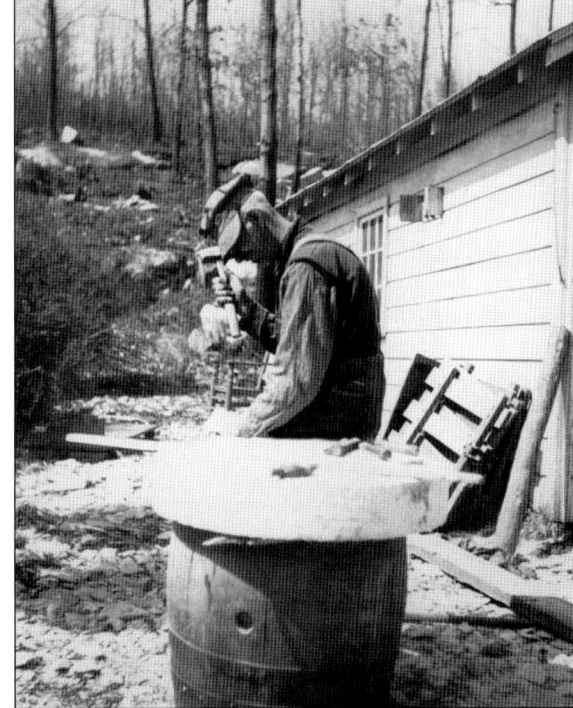

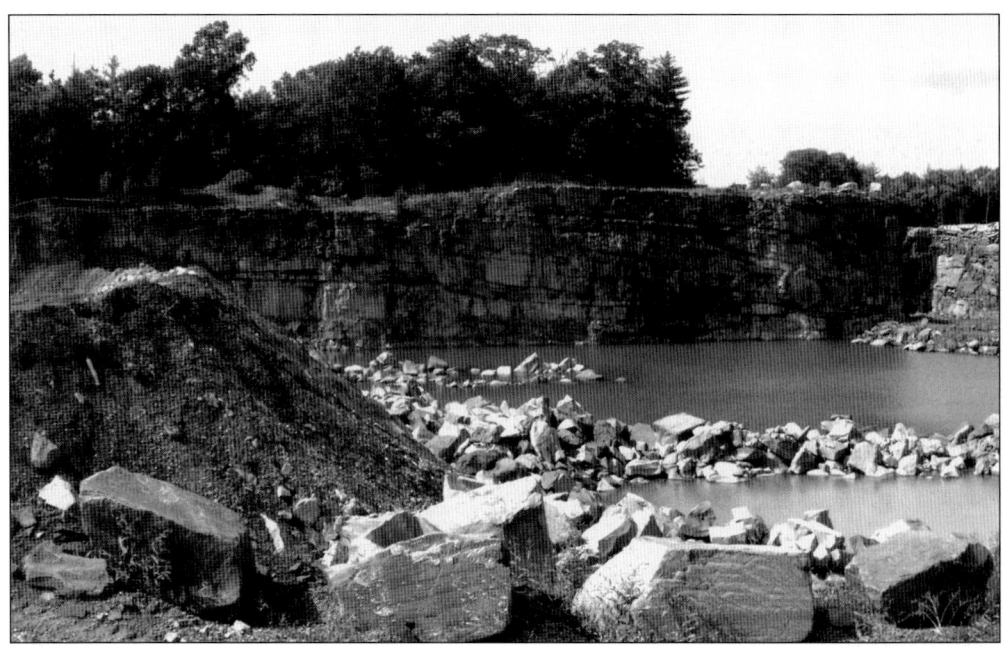

A century and a half ago, Irish quarrymen scrambled about these rocks, pecking and blasting, setting free large blocks of stone destined to build impressive town and city edifices and pave the ways beside them. When the quarrymen were done they packed their bags and moved on as truckloads of portland cement moved in and took over the road building. (Atkarton History Project.)

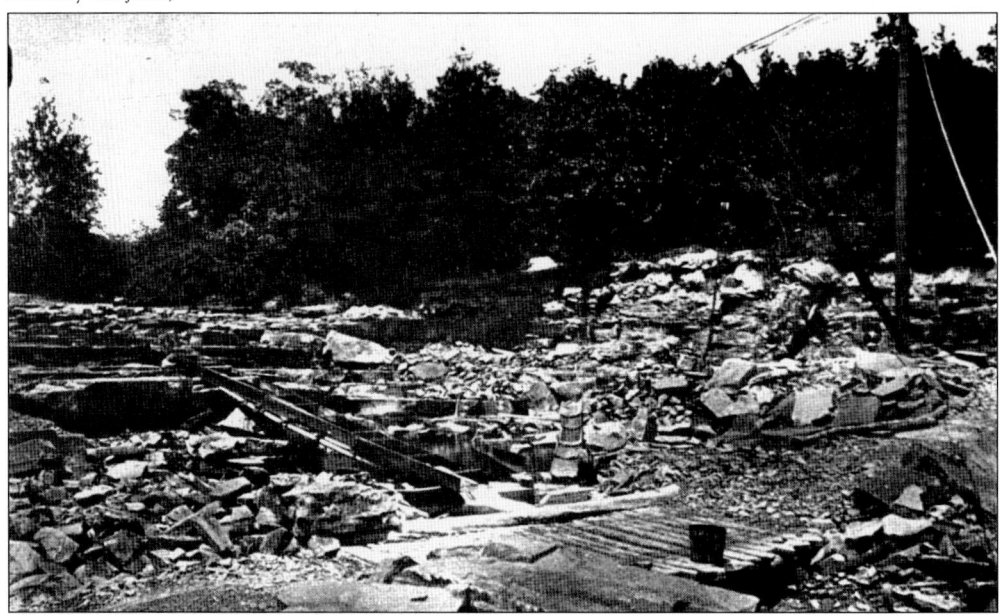

Four to five men were employed throughout the year by John McCaffery and Company to work this 10-foot-thick stone bed situated well below the bottom of the Sawkill Creek. A flume was installed to divert the creek away from the quarrying. All varieties of a good blue color, medium grain, commercial stone were produced and sold to the Bluestone King at Rondout. A horse-powered derrick was used for lifting. (Atkarton History Project.)

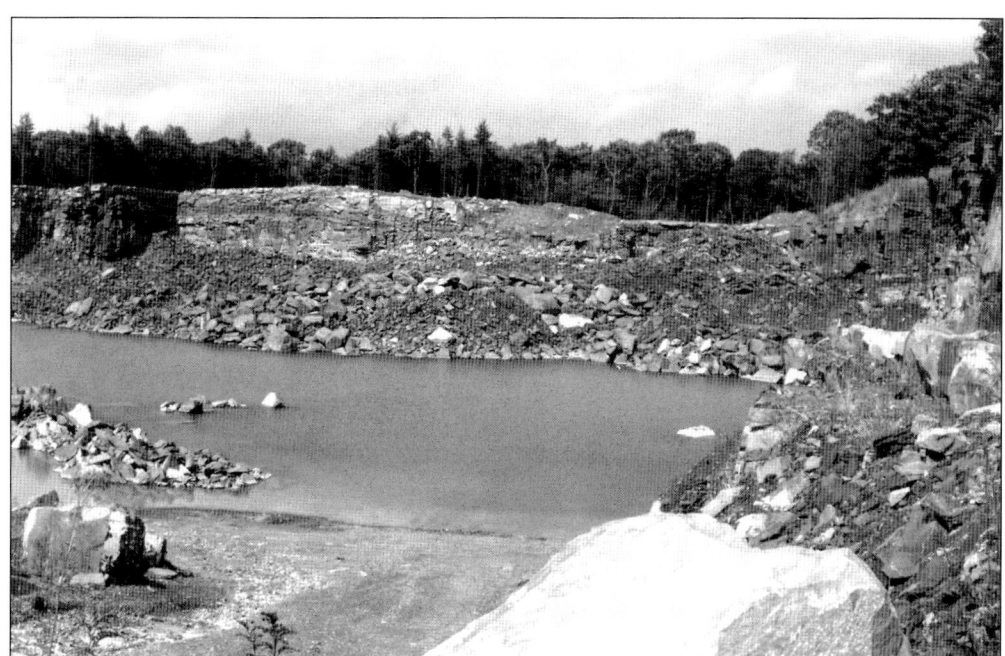

There at the Ledge they left a mess of rubble and rubbish stone. It was garbage, useless tailings worth nothing. That rubble is worth something now. Advancing technology has found a use for the quarrymen's leavings. The waste stone of the Ledge is gathered and sold as aggregate for concrete and asphalt. It seems these days bluestone is viewed as a higher quality material for paving roads than limestone. (Atkarton History Project.)

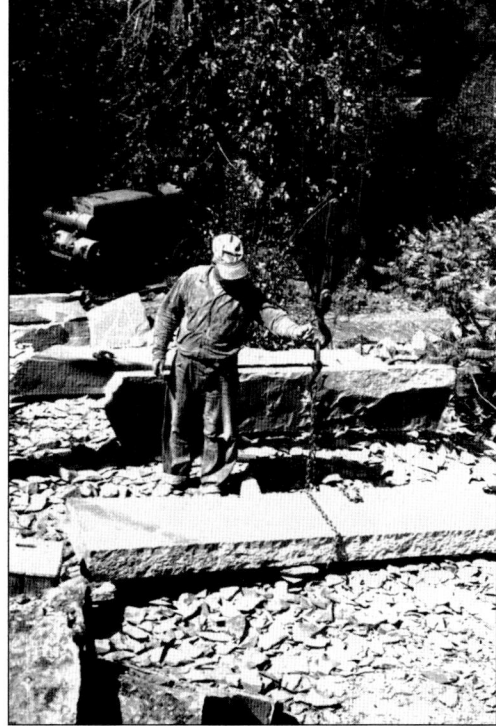

William "Stony Hollow Willie" Dunn lifts a just-completed slab of bluestone in the Ledges quarry. The year is 1952 and Dunn uses a pneumatic compressor to drill the splitting holes in the stone ledge. Otherwise he still employs the old and best method of splitting—wedges, feathers, and lots of moving iron at the end of a hammer. A 1,000-pound stone was easily shaped using simple physics. (Town of Kingston.)

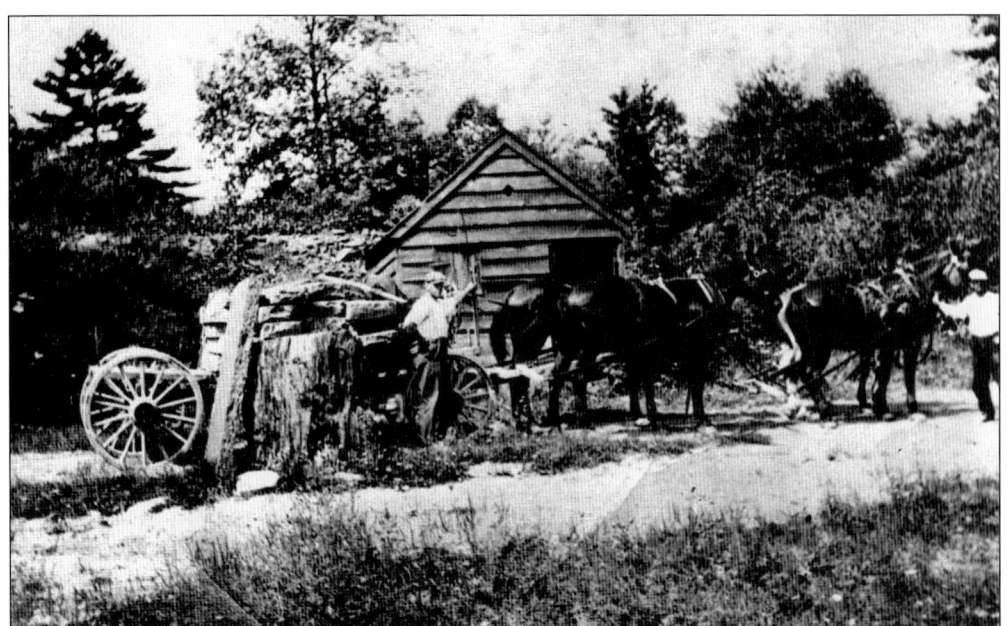

If an axle is going to break, what better place than in front of the blacksmith's shop? Most quarries had an on-site smith. Often a quarryman with a knack for forging would sideline in this regard. The shop itself was a gathering spot for the men to exchange the latest news over their dinner pails. The warmth of its forge was especially welcome in the cold weather. (Town of Kingston.)

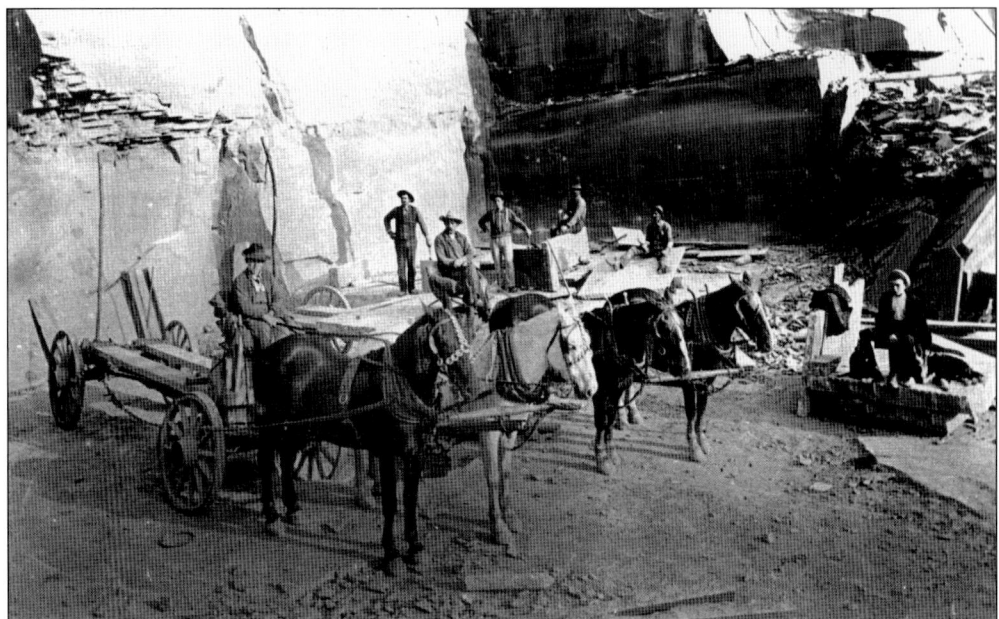

Teamsters are ready to have their wagons loaded at one of the Booth Brothers quarries. Since there are no hand or steam derricks available, they are awaiting the gangs from other quarries to come lend a hand in lifting the stone slabs that weigh upwards of 300 pounds. Wholesale dealers in bluestone, the Booth Brothers contracted out the quarry and teamster work on a percentage basis. (Town of Kingston.)

Blacksmith William Hulsair is reshaping, retempering, and sharpening a quarryman's bar. This bar is used to pry apart slabs of bluestone. Sharp tools make the job of working stone go smoother and faster. Many blacksmiths have a creative eye and are experts in recycling, turning worn out axles into pry bars, and wheel rims into feathers that work in conjunction with wedges to split the stone. (Town of Kingston.)

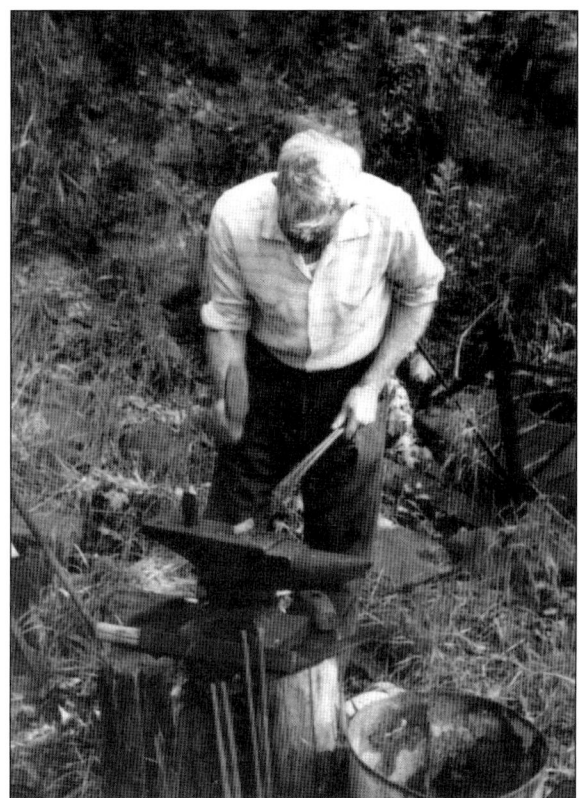

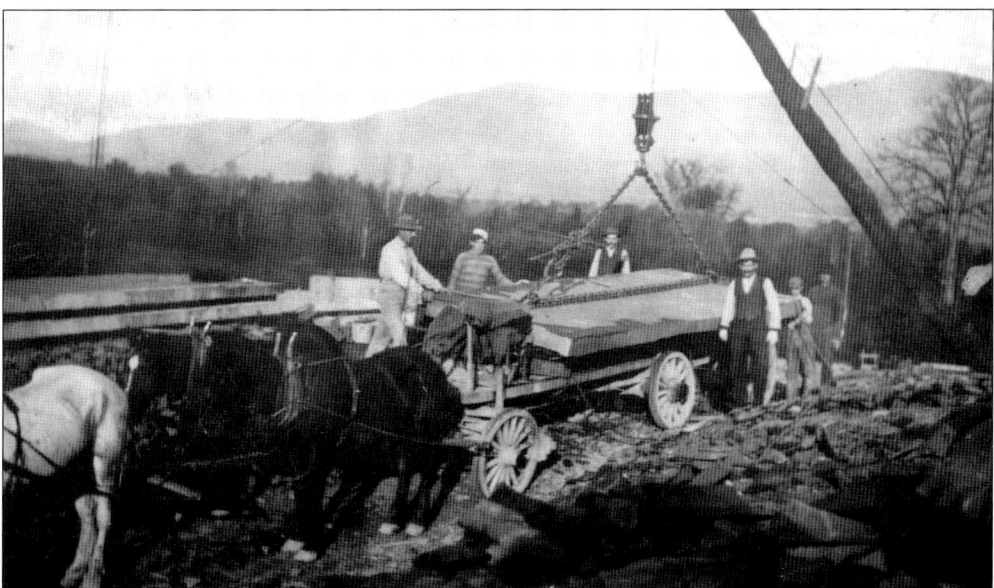

Carle and York's was an operation of unique features, its quarry was a pit sited in an open field. The company used up-to-date equipment including a steam-driven rotary sump pump and a horse derrick for lifting and loading stone. Fifteen men worked the quarry 10 months a year. The fine grained bluestone was covered with hardpan that was blasted and then removed by shovel and barrow. (Town of Kingston.)

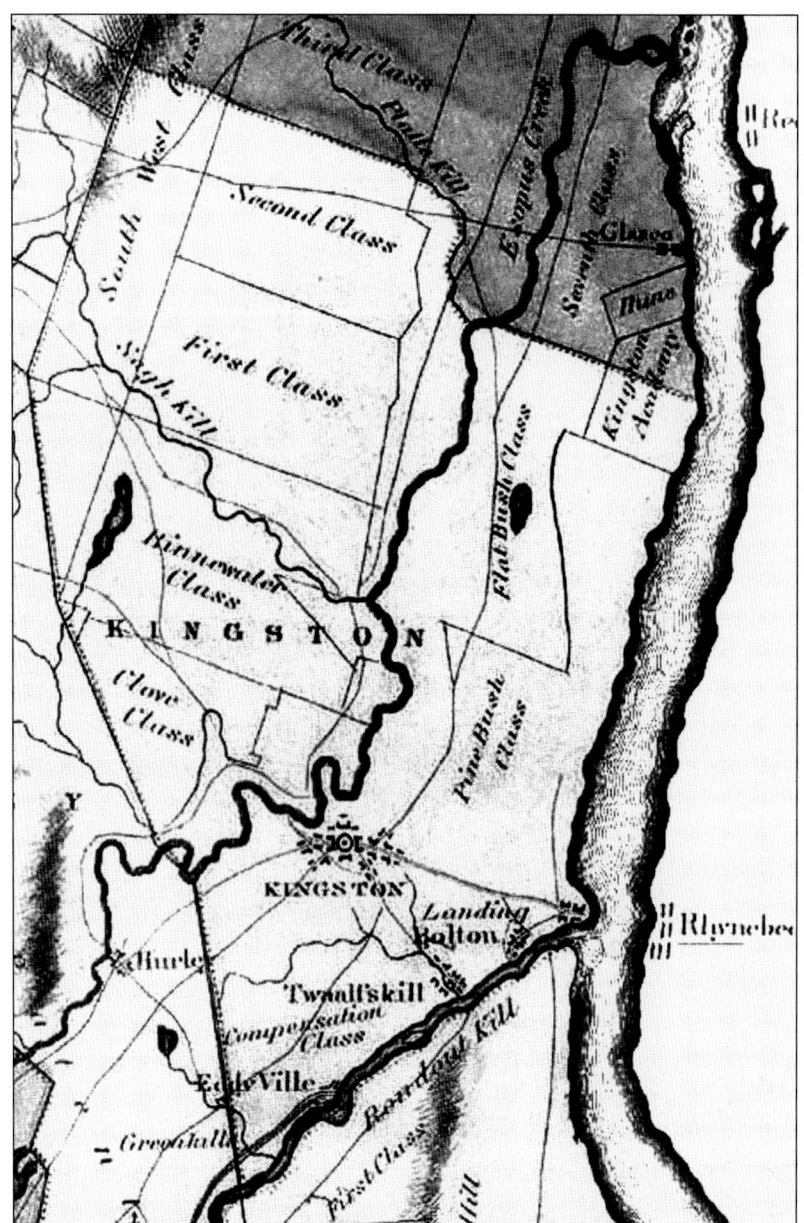

The localities for this chapter range along the western side of the Esopus Creek from the Ulster and Delaware plank road on the south to the Kingston patent line on the north. Ruby has a section on the hill above the Esopus valley as well as one within it. The upper area was originally named Dutch Settlement. This map dates from 1829 and the Esopus Creek is the dark line winding through its center. The various classes refer to an 1804 division of lands for the Kingston Commons. With the exception of Dutch Settlement, all of the area along the creek was primarily the home to large family farms. The land was fertile lowland, and a number of ancient stone homes and Colonial barns dotted the landscape. Dutch Settlement, in the far corner of the original Kingston patent was a well settled hamlet, as evidenced by the map on the facing page. It hosted a pair of modest stone quarries, two churches, a hotel, and several small shops. It also had its share of small farms and small businesses. (Atkarton History Project.)

Three
THE BRABANT AND DUTCH SETTLEMENT

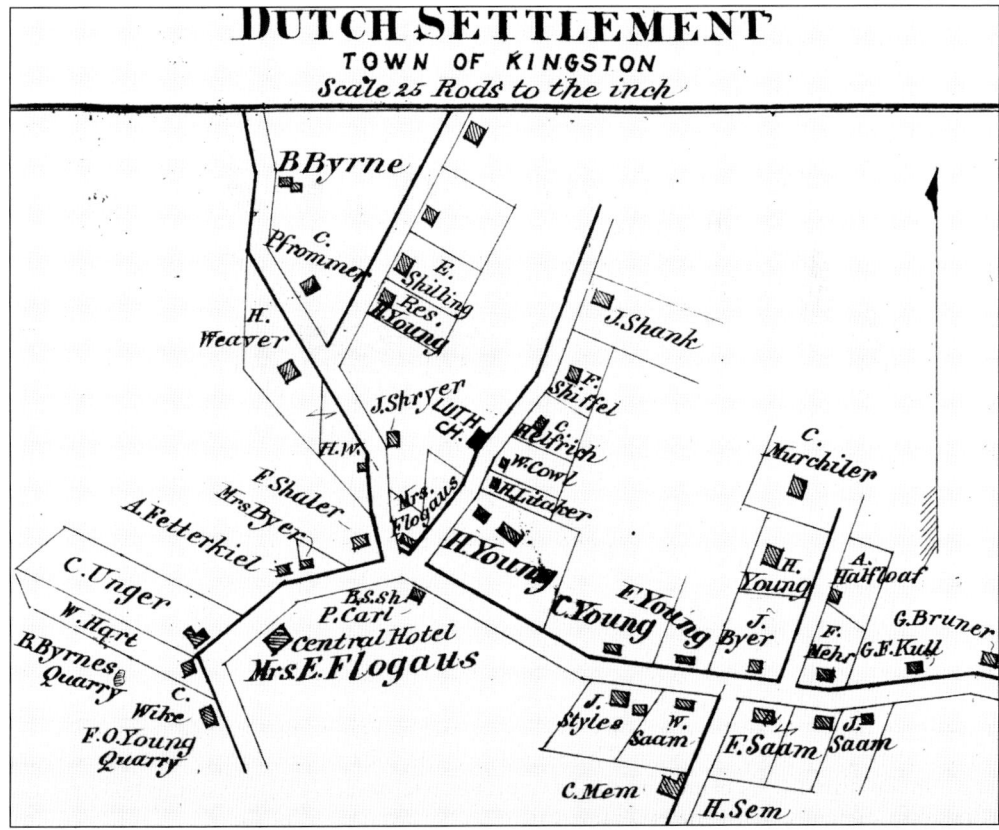

By June 1896, Dutch Settlement even boasted of having its own post office. With that post office came a change of name to Ruby, New York. Contrary to rumors, Ruby was not named after a barmaid. The oldest resident, Thelma Felton wrote that the hamlet was named for Rube Quick. Albert Felton attended the meeting where the name change was ratified. (Atkarton History Project.)

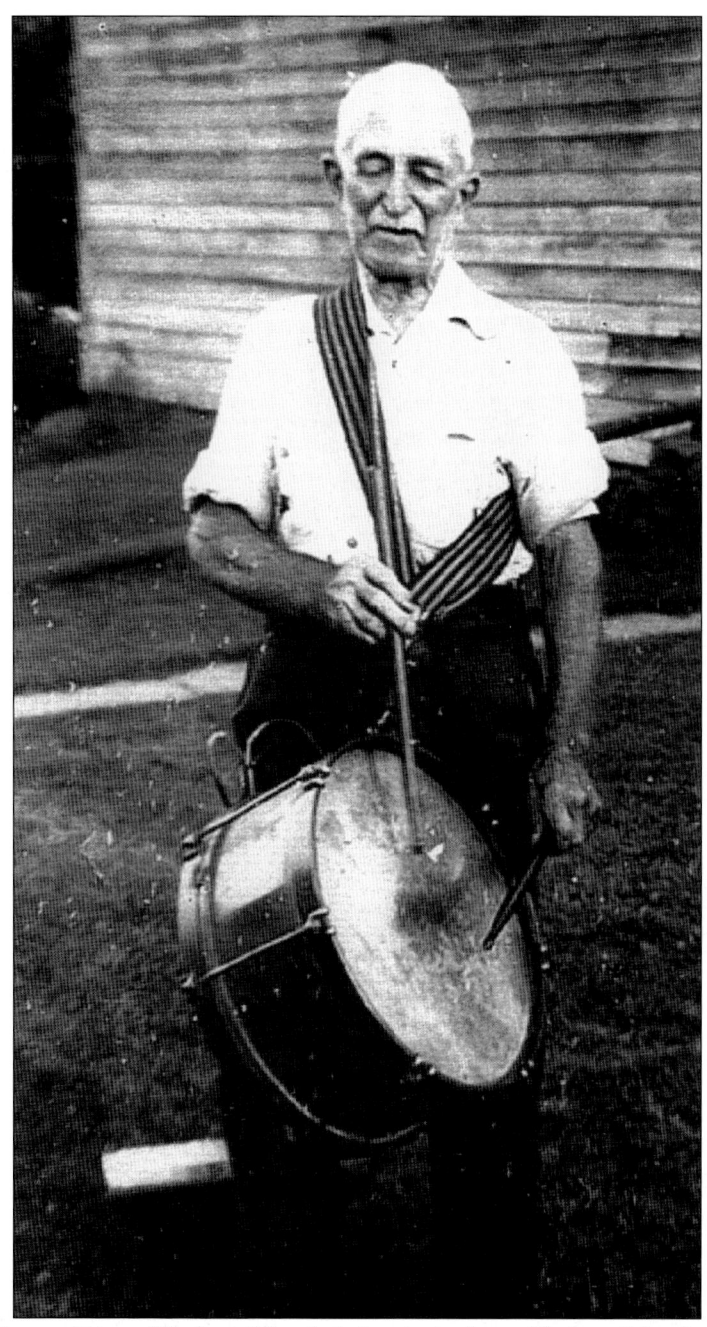

Albert and Vernon Felton (Thelma Felton's father in law) are Thelma Felton's source for the information about the moniker Ruby. Albert was somewhat of a local legend. Born on August 23, 1862, in Ruby, he lived there all his life except for five years in Tuxedo, New York. A 1946 newspaper article credits him with being the oldest man in Ruby and welcomes him to the Fourscore Club. Up until the age of 25, he farmed, but in 1887, the quarry business struck his fancy and therein he worked until 1940. His sideline specialty was sharpening tools in his blacksmith shop. Albert lived on South Road, over a mile from the town center, but made the trip on foot twice daily even at the age of 84. This photograph was taken in 1947. (Thelma Felton and Sean O'Connor.)

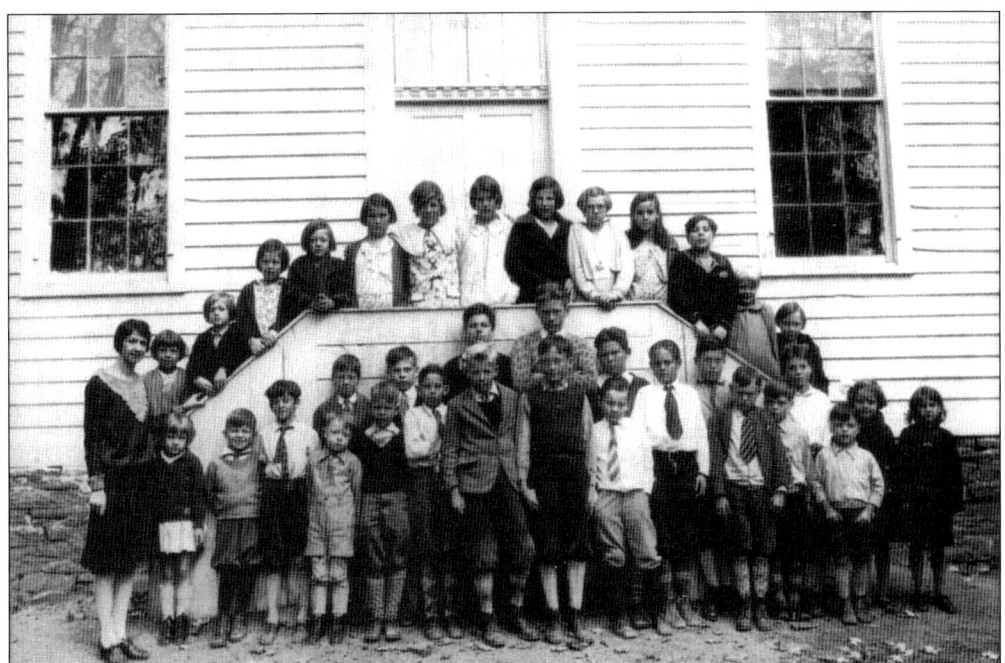

The Ruby School was situated at the edge of the lowlands on the old road leading from Mount Marion in the township of Saugerties to Dutch Settlement. This class photograph was taken in the late 1920s, and the schoolhouse is still standing today at the junction of Sheehan Lane and Schoolhouse Road. The schoolhouse is currently being renovated as a private residence. (Town of Kingston.)

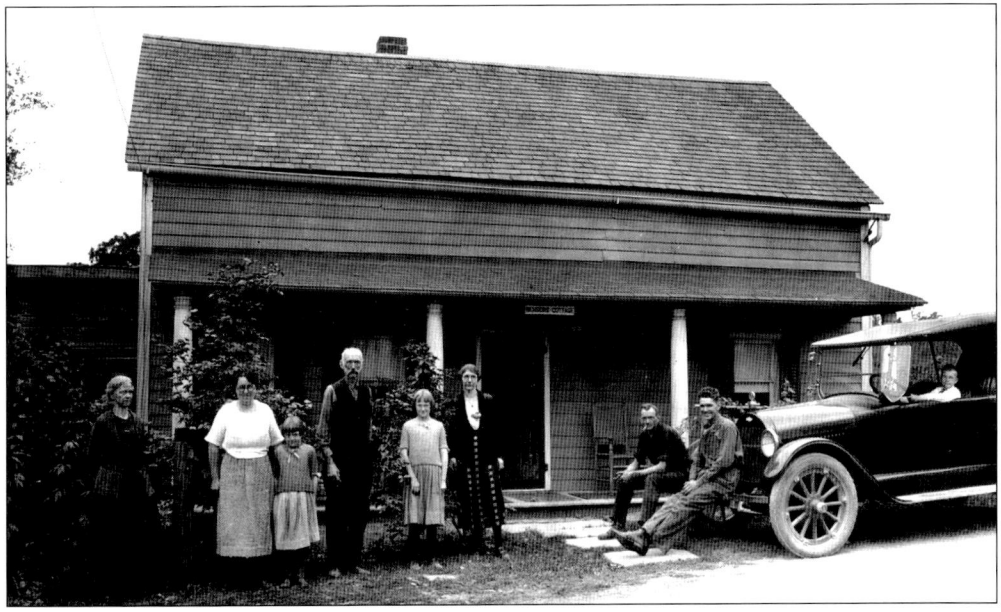

The Longyear family poses in front of Bensons Cottage. The year is 1922. The names on the back of the photograph are out of order: Kenneth Longyear, Louise Longyear, Mary Benson, Ray Scheffel, Francis Longyear, Rebecca Longyear, Eddie Longyear, Grandpa Benson, and Mrs. Longyear. (Sean O'Connor.)

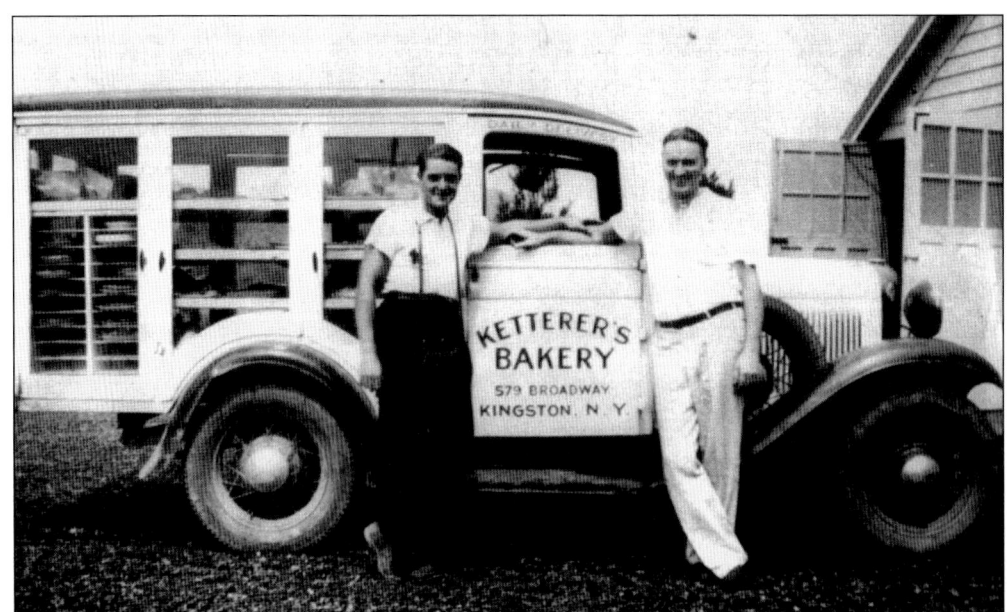

Charley Malony (left) and Bill Miggins (right) ran a delivery route for Ketterer's Bakery. The route covered the Sawkill–Ruby area in the 1930s. This 1937 photograph shows the boys pausing for a short break while the smell of fresh pies permeates the air. The truck appears to be a c. 1932 Ford delivery truck. Ketterer's Bakery is still in business under new owners in the city of Kingston. (Sean O'Connor.)

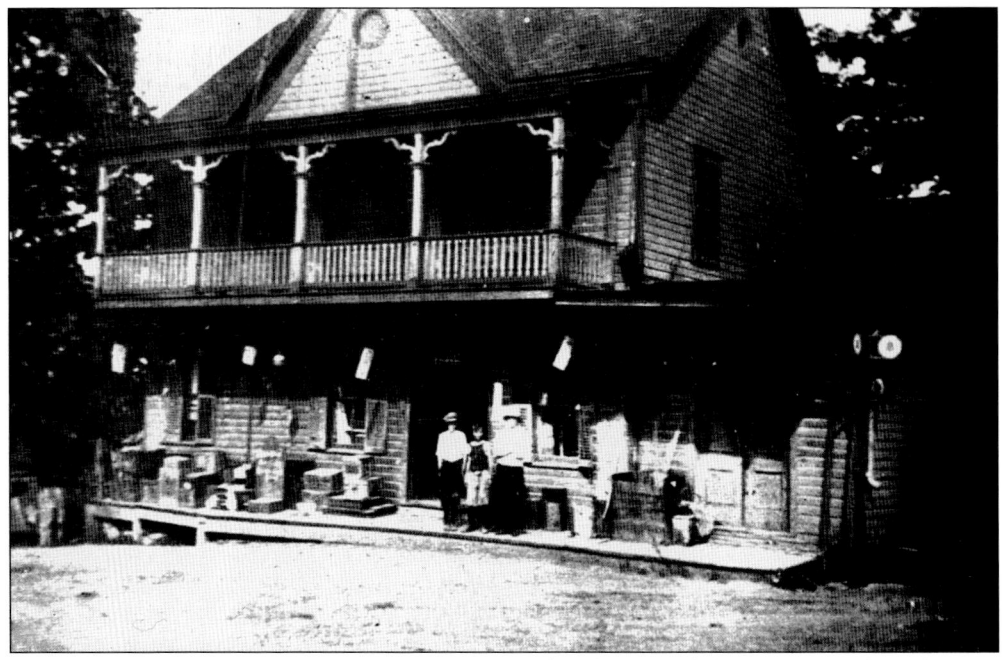

This is Snyder's store, one of several general merchandise establishments in Ruby. The year is 1920. Like many of these family stores, Snyder's occupies the bottom floor of a converted residence. This one, built around 1880, is in the carpenter Gothic style. The device at the right may be an old railroad signal. (Town of Kingston.)

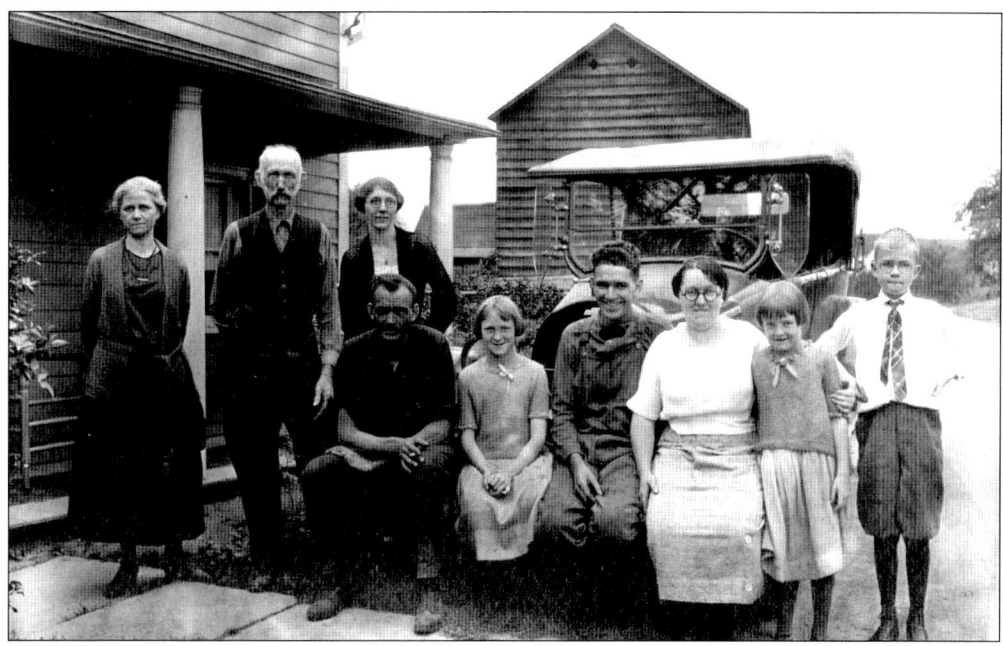

This image shows the Longyear family in 1922. The house and barn were located at the intersection of South Road and Main Street in Ruby and the car is a Chevrolet touring car, possibly a series 490 of 1922 vintage. Identified here, in no particular order, are Grandpa and Mary Benson, Ray Scheffel, Louise, Frances, Rebecca, Eddie, and Mrs. Longyear. (Sean O'Connor.)

Carrie Gaddis sweeps the stoop of the original Ruby Post Office located on the long hill. The building was one of the oldest in the hamlet. Carrie Gaddis was the wife of Clyde I. Gaddis who was postmaster of Ruby from January 7, 1914, until his death in January 1942. Clyde replaced the first postmaster, James E. Snyder, who helped name Ruby in June 1896 and was succeeded by James M. Young. (Town of Kingston.)

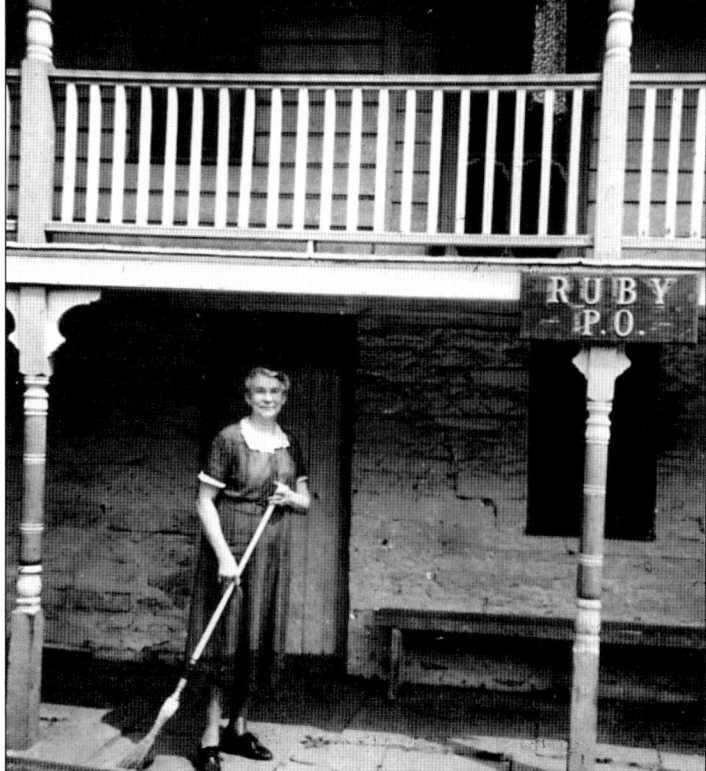

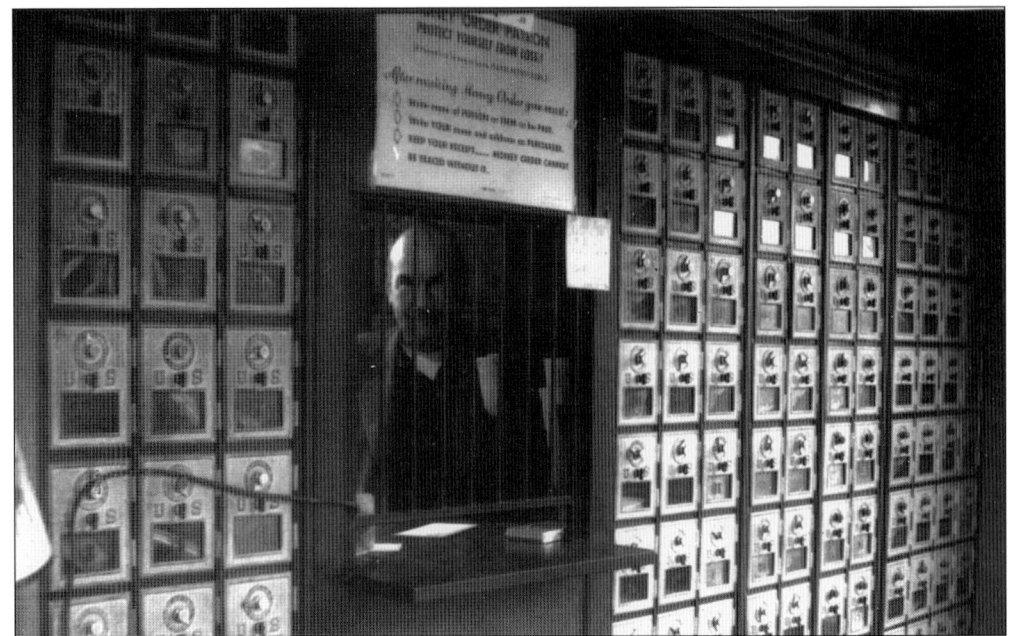

James M. Young became the acting postmaster of Ruby on January 31, 1942, and was appointed full postmaster on February 27 of that year. This photograph was taken on December 16, 1965. Young served until October 1977, when he was succeeded by officer in charge Eileen Reilly. Subsequently in 1978, Gloria A. Mason became postmaster and remained in the position for the next 14 years. (Town of Kingston.)

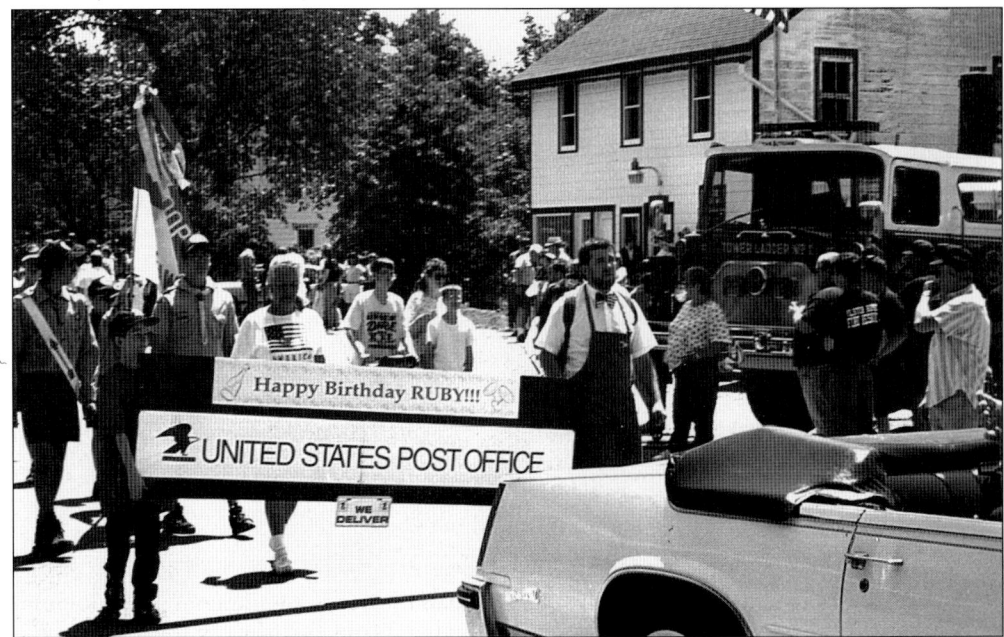

Carrying the banner at Ruby's 100th anniversary parade is current postmaster Sean O'Connor, who generously spent time with the authors and loaned numerous images. O'Connor has been postmaster since March 6, 1993, following five months of service as clerk in charge. (Sean O'Connor.)

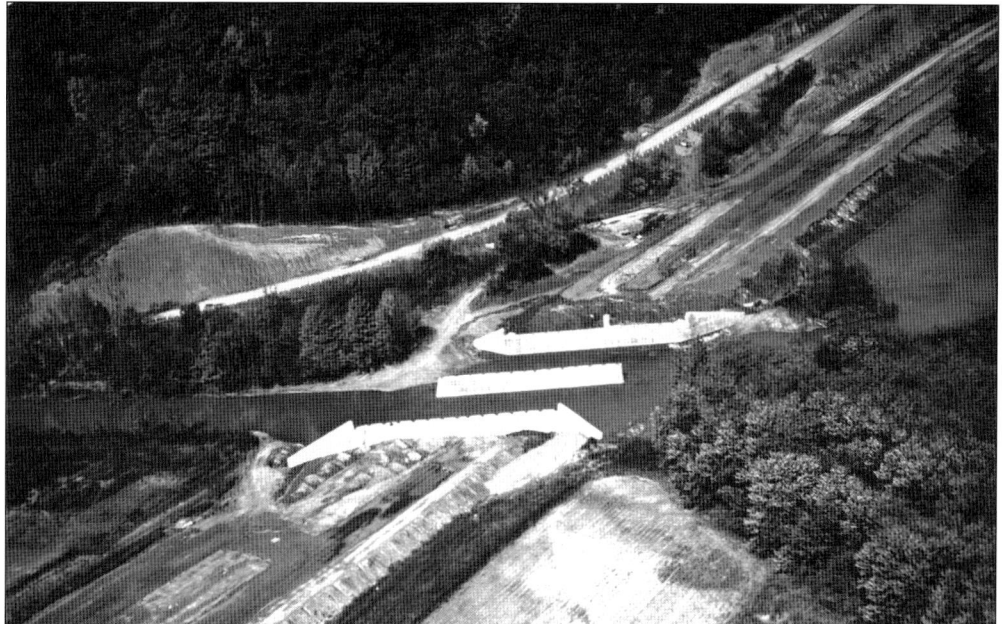

And then along came the largest public works project to ever hit Ulster County, the construction of the New York State Thruway, crossing Ulster through the fertile heart of the Esopus valley. The process was far from painless. The chosen route clove asunder many large family farms dating from pre-Revolutionary times. These are the abutments at the Sawkill Creek near its confluence with the Esopus Creek during construction in 1952. (Bob Haines.)

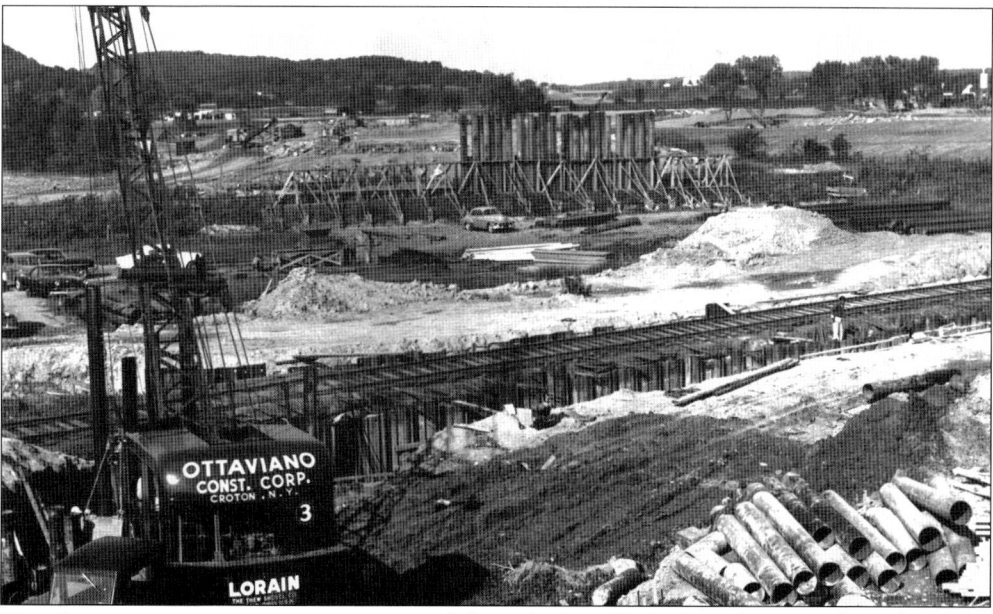

The thruway was a necessary project, and Sen. Arthur Wicks brought it to this side of the Hudson River. It was a farsighted project designed to speed travel across the state while taking the burden off of two-lane rural highways. In Mutton Hollow, two railroads had to be reworked. In the foreground is the Ontario and Western Railway with the Catskill Mountain branch of the New York Central Railroad near the rear. (Bob Haines.)

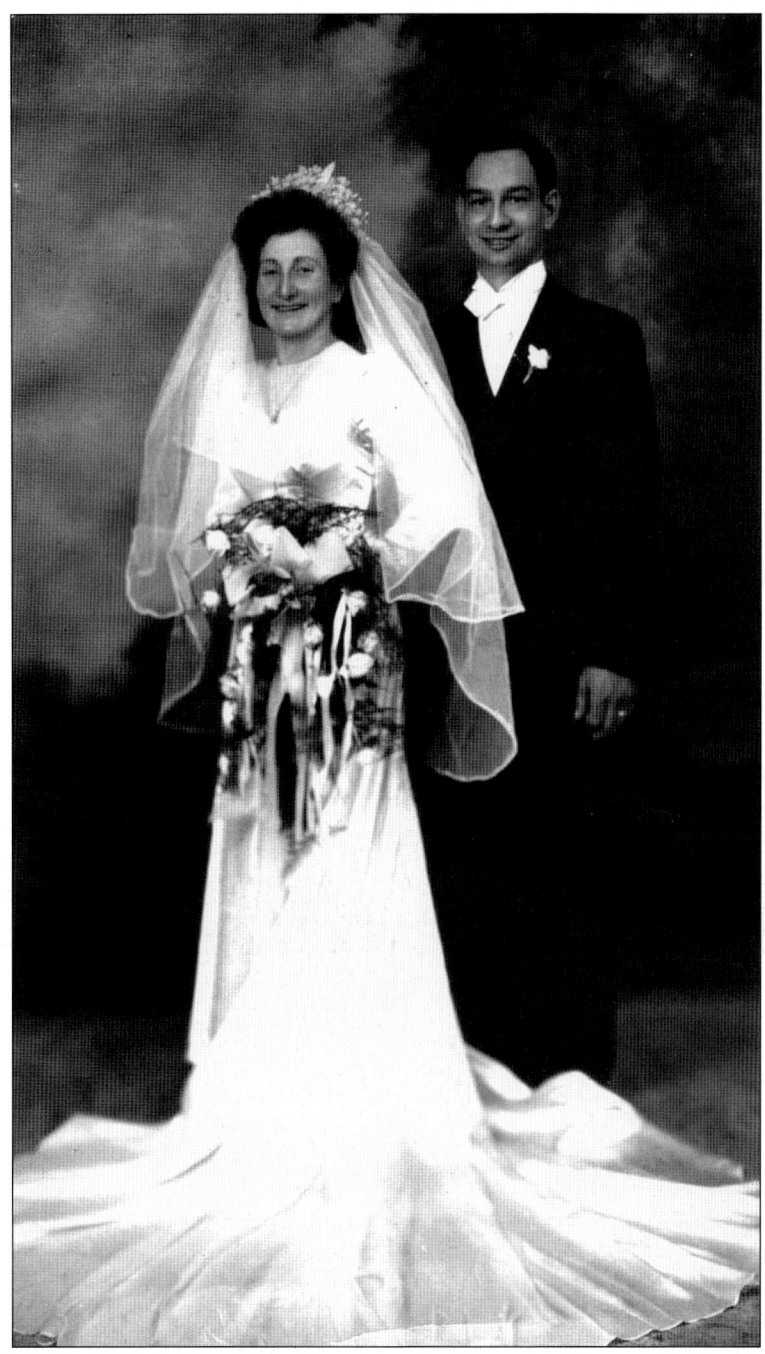

On December 29, 1946, clad in pure silk and barely 5 feet tall, 22-year-old Angelina Sorbello took Joseph Buzzanco to be her husband. Wanting to stand tall beside him, Angelina tucked several catalogs beneath her feet for this formal portrait. Side by side for decades, the Buzzanco's built greenhouses, planted seeds and made their gardens on the Ruby–Sawkill Road grow lush and luxurious. They passed their love of the land to daughter Angie, who has managed the farm since 2005. After years of green-thumbing, she is still thrilled by the annual miracle that occurs when a dusting of seeds comes in contact with her special growing methods. (Angie Buzzanco.)

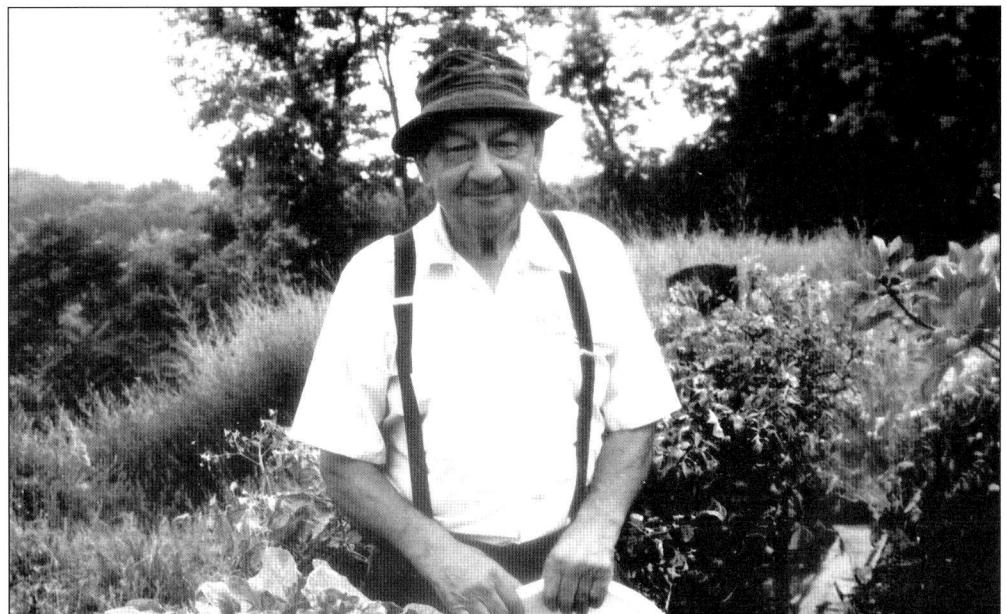

In 1962, Joe Buzzanco farmed as his father before him; about 120 acres with a strip down the middle removed for the thruway in 1950. Fields burst at the seams with glorious mums and fresh tasty vegetables. Joe sold vegetables all around town in his Model T truck. Tomatoes, strawberries, raspberries, and "aspara-grass" were all three pounds for 25¢. Up in the back woodlot they ran free-range pigs for meat. (Angie Buzzanco.)

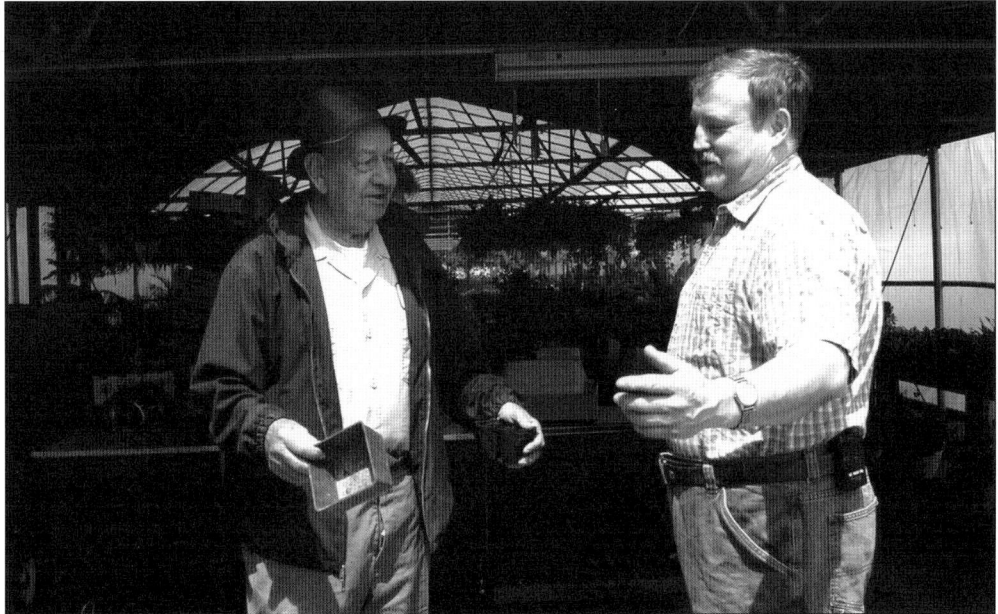

Joe Buzzanco explains to author Karl Wick some of the techniques he uses in producing his superior plants. Buzzanco's Farms was purchased with house, barn, and cows in 1901 by Joe's father Salvatore. After construction of the New York State Thruway split the farm in two, the Buzzanco's switched to truck farming. These days, daughter Angie oversees the operation of the 14 greenhouses that Joe and Angelina built. (Susan Wick.)

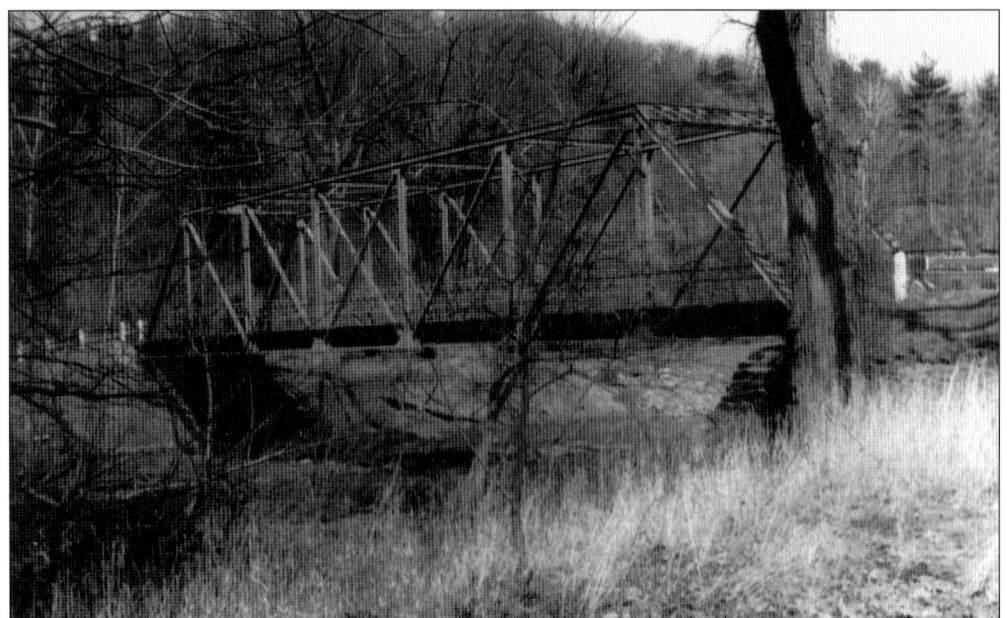

The first crossing of the Sawkill Creek was by a ford laid out by the county road commissioners in 1789. A covered bridge built in the mid-part of the century was repaired in 1899 by the Brabant Plank Road Company. Sylvester Myers said, "I was sitting on a fence when I heard a cracking noise and saw the old bridge tip over and go down in the creek." The bridge fell in 1904. (Town of Kingston.)

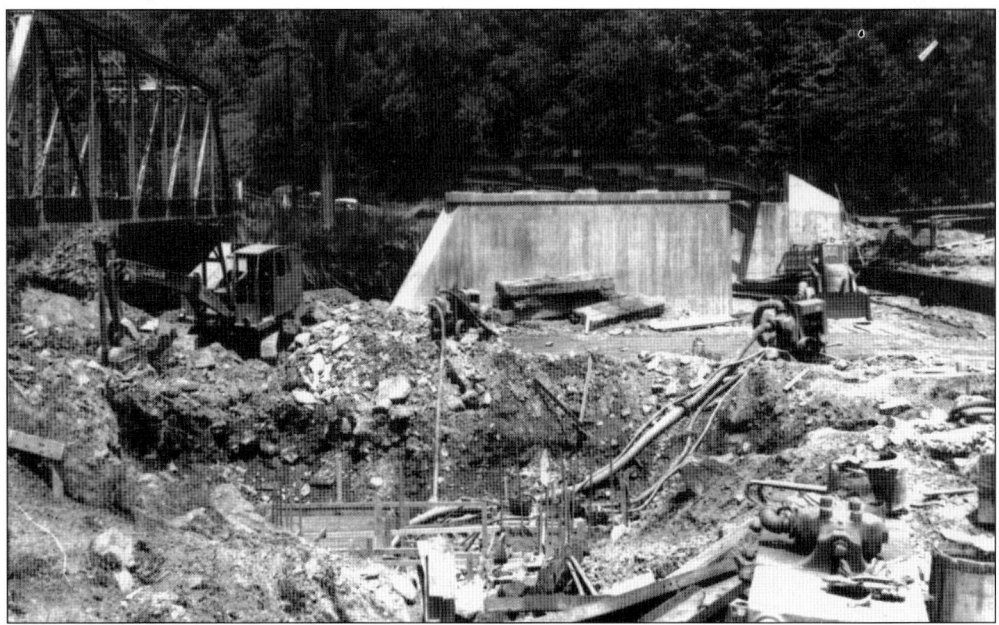

This iron version (top) replaced the covered bridge in 1905. By March 1957, the iron bridge had become too narrow and weak. Construction of a new span was begun. This photograph was taken on July 18, 1957. The wild creek kept filling foundation holes with water and once even threatened to wash away the equipment. Nevertheless, the new bridge opened on December 22, 1958. (Town of Kingston.)

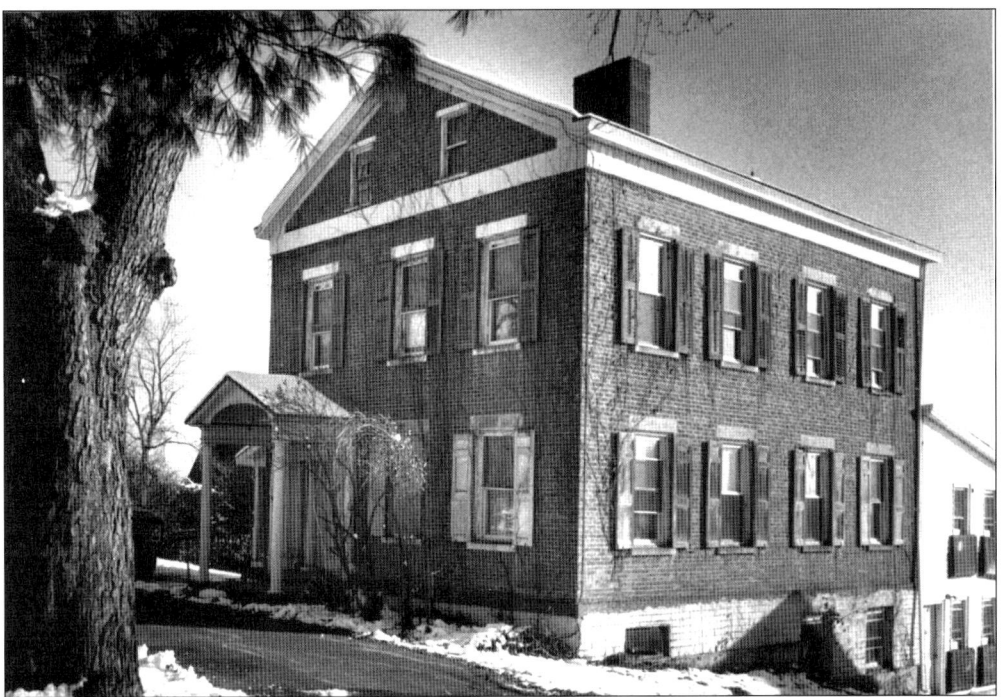

Prior to the 1804 division of the Kingston Commons, James Cockburn owned one of two stone houses within the Edward Whittaker patent in Brabant. By about 1840, a descendant (possibly William Cockburn Jr.) had constructed this brick house. The rear section was an early addition. In a 1967 survey, the house is described as having 15 rooms and five fireplaces. It has been the center of the Boice farm since then.

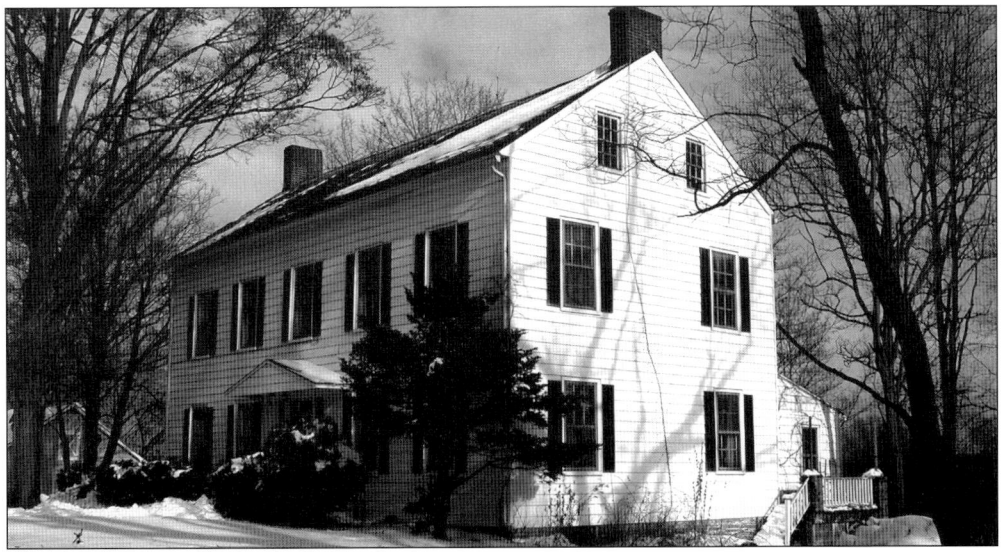

The next farm along the Brabant (Sawkill) Road was also built by a Cockburn on the same 135-acre parcel, probably before 1850. In 1867, the farm was sold by Edwin Cockburn to Thomas Cornell of Rondout for $15,500. It passed next to Cornelius Dumond of Hurley in 1896, then through various deeds, eventually to Carolyn Kirchner. Carolyn's brother Richard and his wife Elsie became the inhabitants.

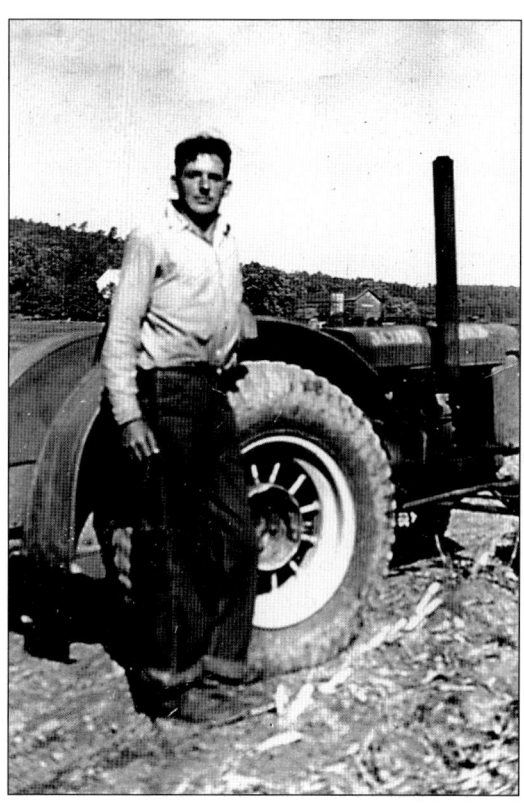

Elmer Kirchner, along with his siblings Anna, Ernst, and Inice, grew up on the farm. Anna died from tetanus at the age of 16. This is Elmer in 1944 working the fields with the family's 1929 John Deere model GP tractor. This was the year that rubber tires replaced full metal wheels. In the far center background are the barns and silo still in use at the Boice farm. (Martha Nickerson Cummins.)

In 1956, after the division by the thruway, Elmer Kirchner built a small brick house across the highway and sold the large house and the remaining eight-acre western part of the property to Floyd and Polly Nickerson. Floyd Nickerson was a plant engineer for the IBM Corporation, with farming and restoring old houses as his sidelines. The image shows Mary Nickerson and her calf Iris in the fall of 1960. (Martha Nickerson Cummins.)

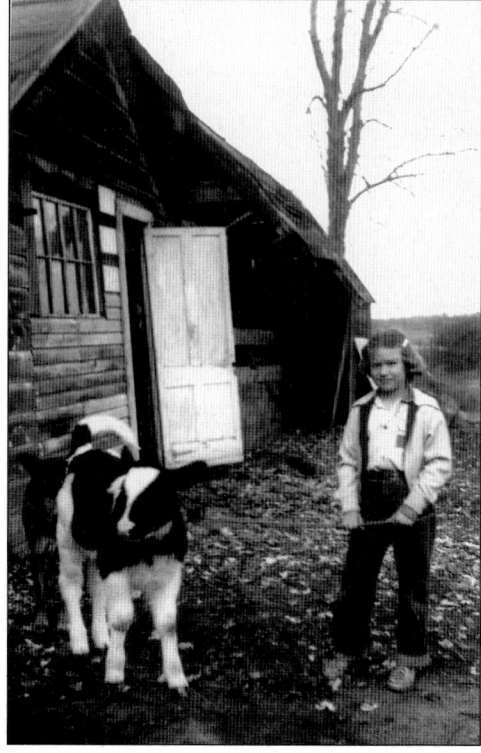

As a teenager, Floyd Nickerson worked on the Kirchner farm and his family became friends of the Kirchners. Floyd often brought the family to enjoy the land. This is Martha Nickerson and her faithful sidekick Spud in 1949. In the background are part of the fields of the 143-acre farm plus those of the original land patent to Edward Whittaker. The Esopus Creek is just behind the far tree line. (Martha Nickerson Cummins.)

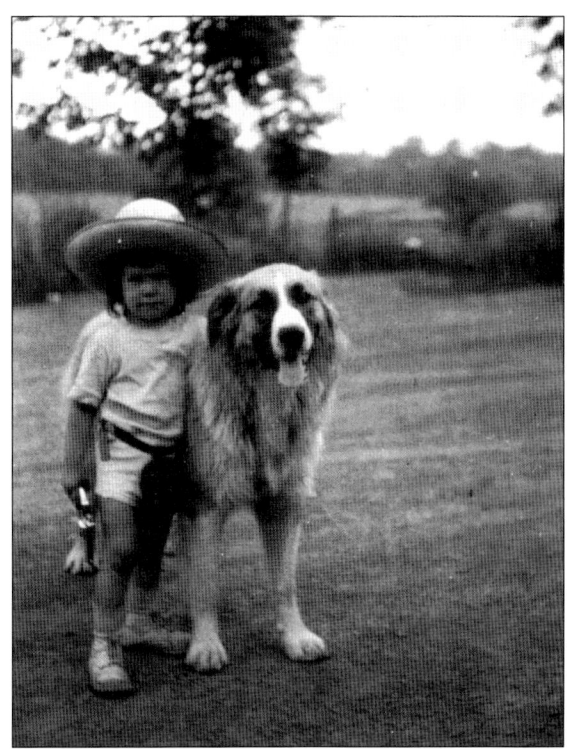

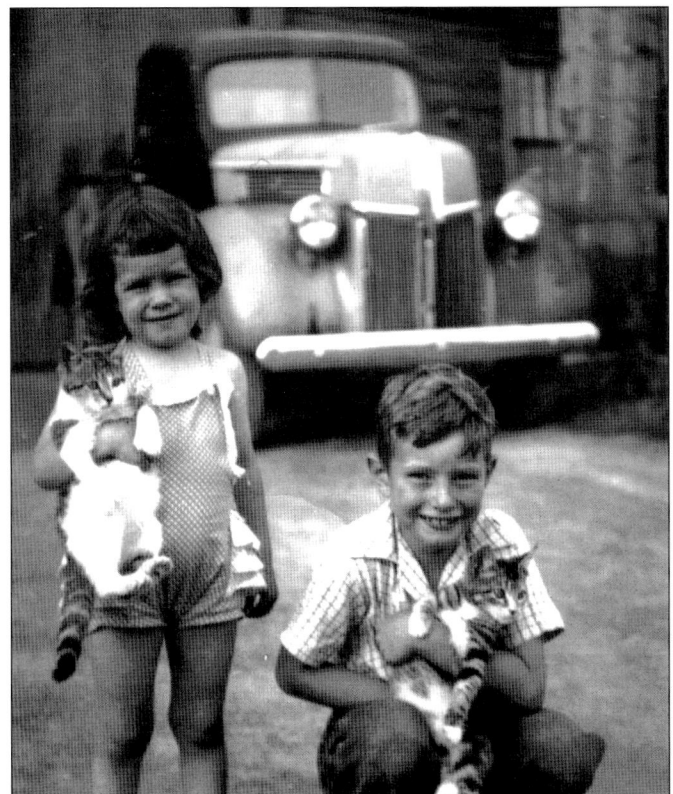

Mary and Gary Nickerson play in front of the barn in 1950. They had no inkling that in just six years an opportunity would arise and their family would call these grounds their own. The pickup truck is a 1941 Ford. The history of the farm would be incomplete without noting that on April 28, 1988, the eight acres and homestead were purchased by the Ulster County Unitarian Fellowship. (Martha Nickerson Cummins.)

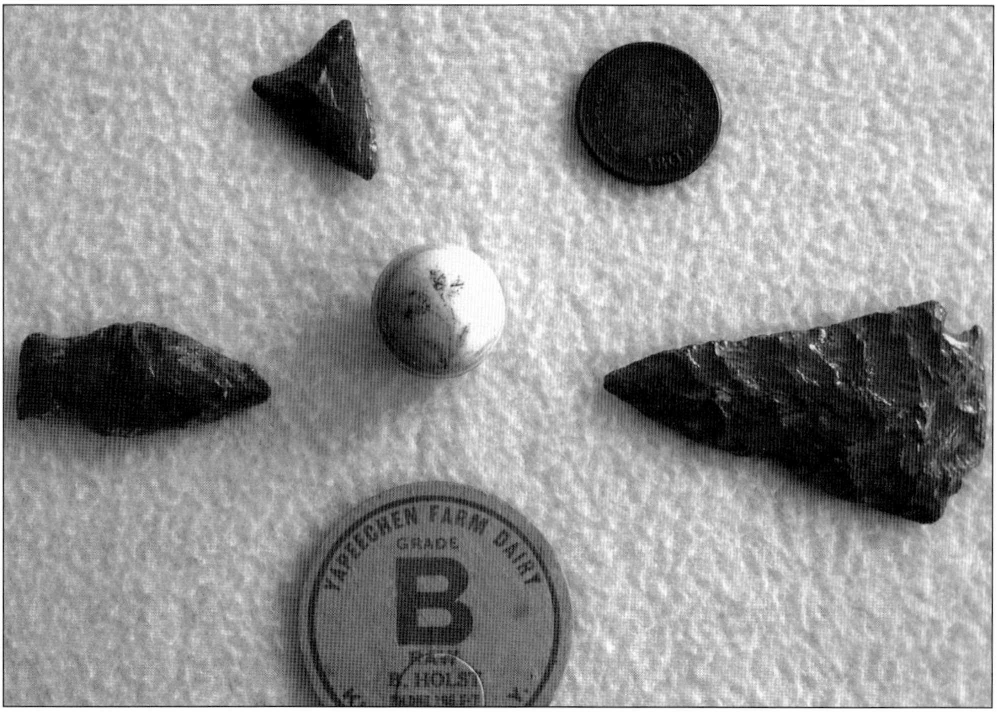

These are artifacts found on the Cockburn farms. The fertile valley of the Esopus Creek was used by the Lenape Indians for millennia before the coming of white settlers. Three styles of points are samples of the styles and eras found here. The button is post-Colonial era while the coin is an 1809 half cent in remarkably good condition after having been buried for a century and a half. (Martha Nickerson Cummins.)

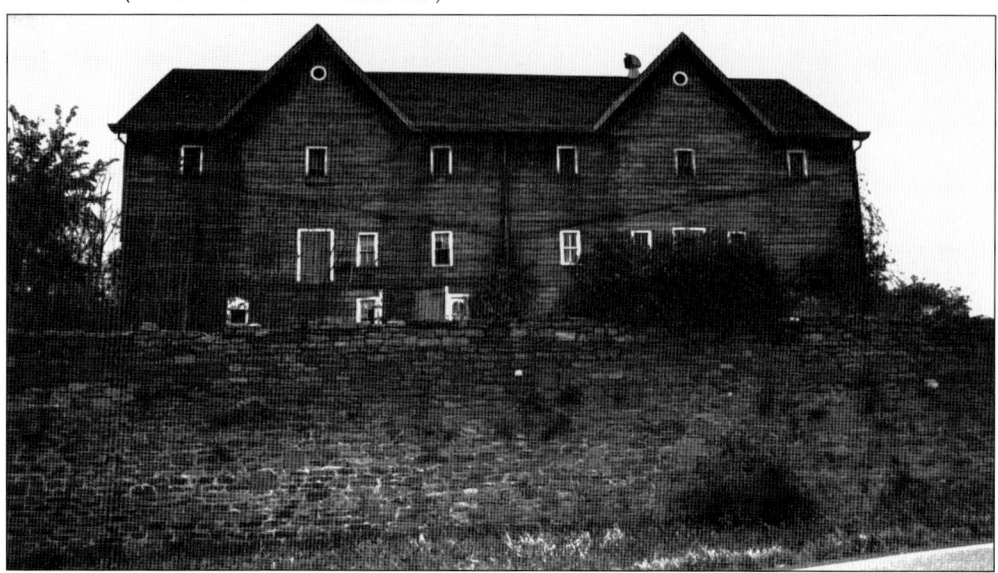

This rare double-gabled Victorian barn graces the turn on Sawkill Road just before the thruway overpass. It was constructed around 1879 and is commonly known as the McSpirit barn. The retaining wall is as massive as those found at European castles. The barn survives well and is currently undergoing restoration. (Town of Ulster historian.)

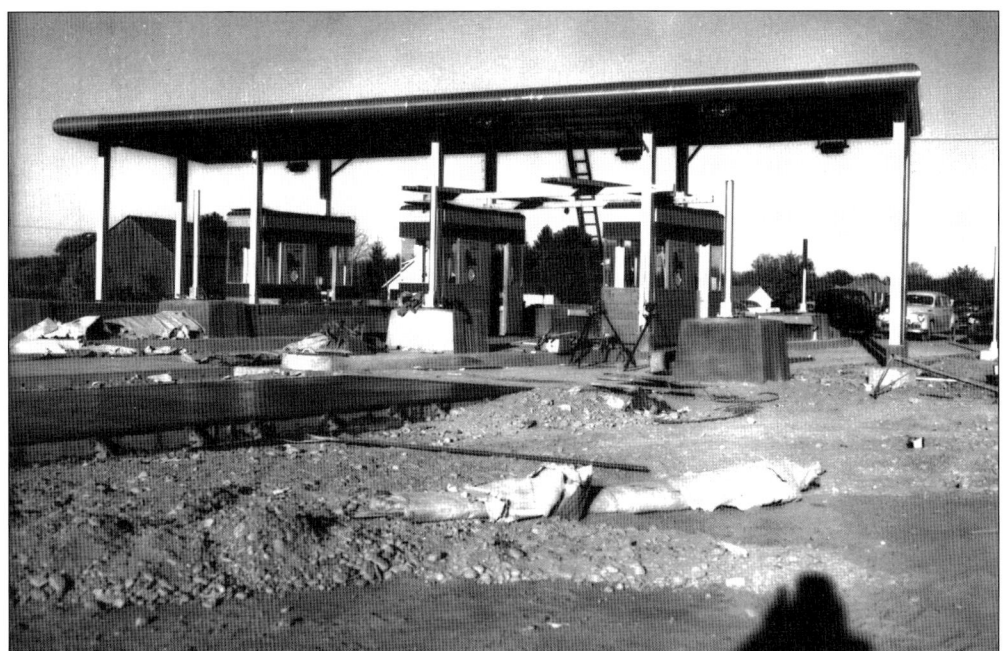

From the Colonial era to the modern, time marches on. With the arrival of the New York State Thruway, it has come full circle. In early days, the Ulster and Delaware Turnpike and Brabant Plank Road each had tollbooths near the current roundabout. This must have been a natural center of travel, because the tollbooths of the thruway were also placed here more than a century and a half later. (Bob Haines.)

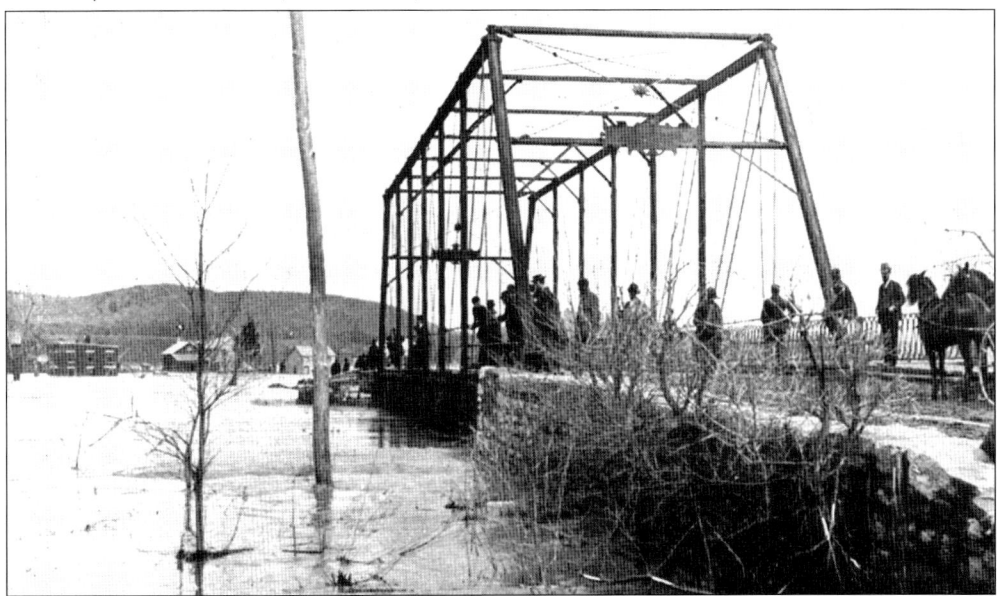

Mutton Hollow was the gateway for stone wagons to the village of Kingston and beyond. It was also an area prone to floods. DeLisser said the area was "more or less half the time under water after each fall of rain." Perhaps he exaggerated, but as this pre-1896 westward-looking photograph attests, flooding was certainly not unknown either. The bridge was relatively new and survived the slow-moving inundation. (Atkarton History Project.)

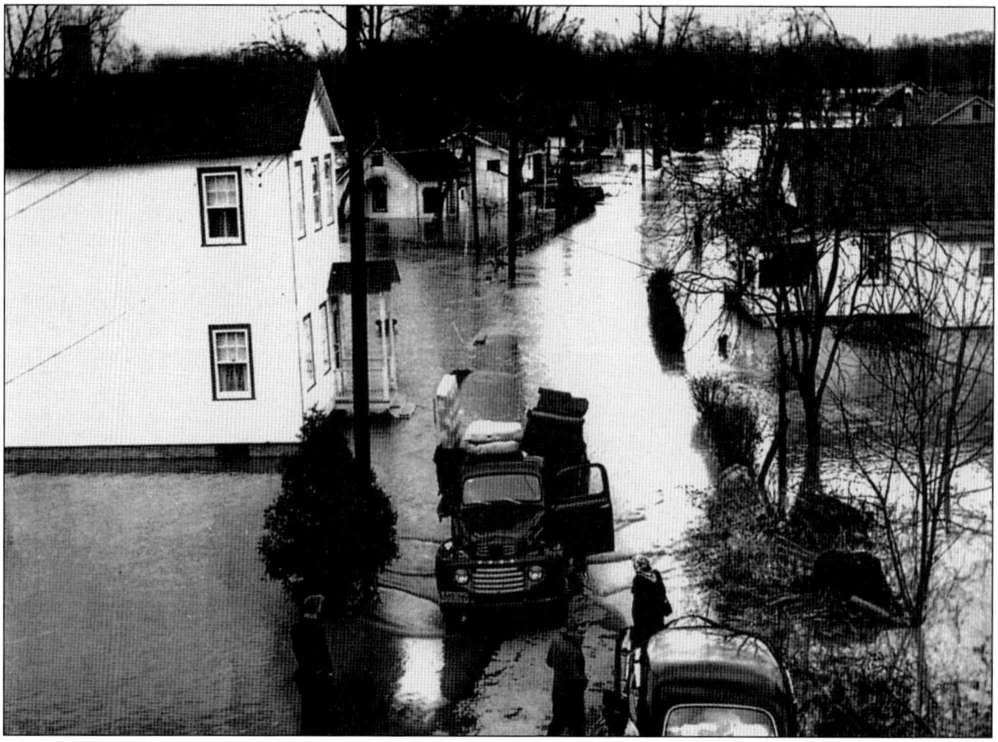

The spring of 1955 brought "fifty year floods" to much of Ulster County. Here the residents of Murphy Street are taking no chances as the waters rise in their neighborhood. Basements are already full and the waters lap at many front doors. This area is now occupied by the Dutch Village Apartments and is protected by a dyke built in the 1970s by the Army Corps of Engineers. (Bob Haines.)

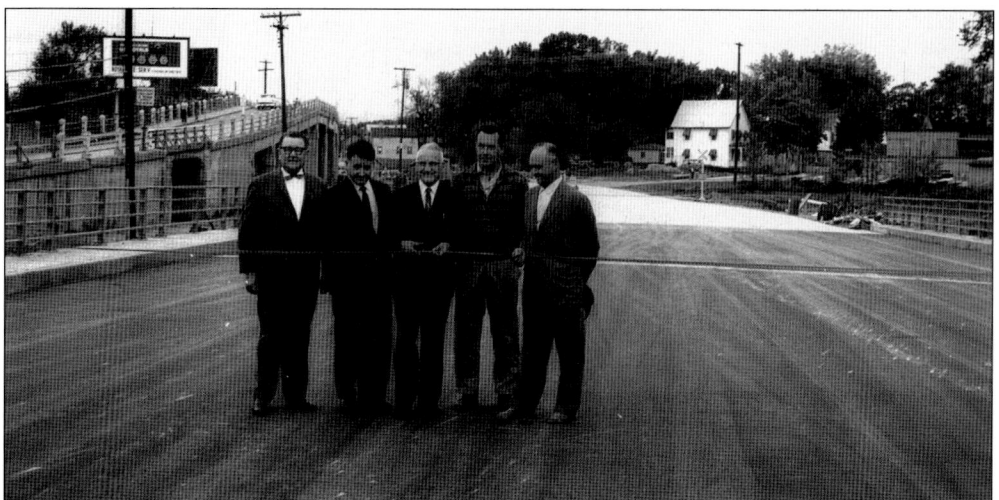

What a change from the original Revolutionary-period covered bridge from Frog Alley to the lowlands. These are the dignitaries cutting the ribbon for the "new" bridge across the Esopus Creek almost two centuries later. With this bridge and some massive land reshaping, flooding of Mutton Hollow became an unusual occurrence. See page 46 for the removal of the old viaduct. (Bob Haines.)

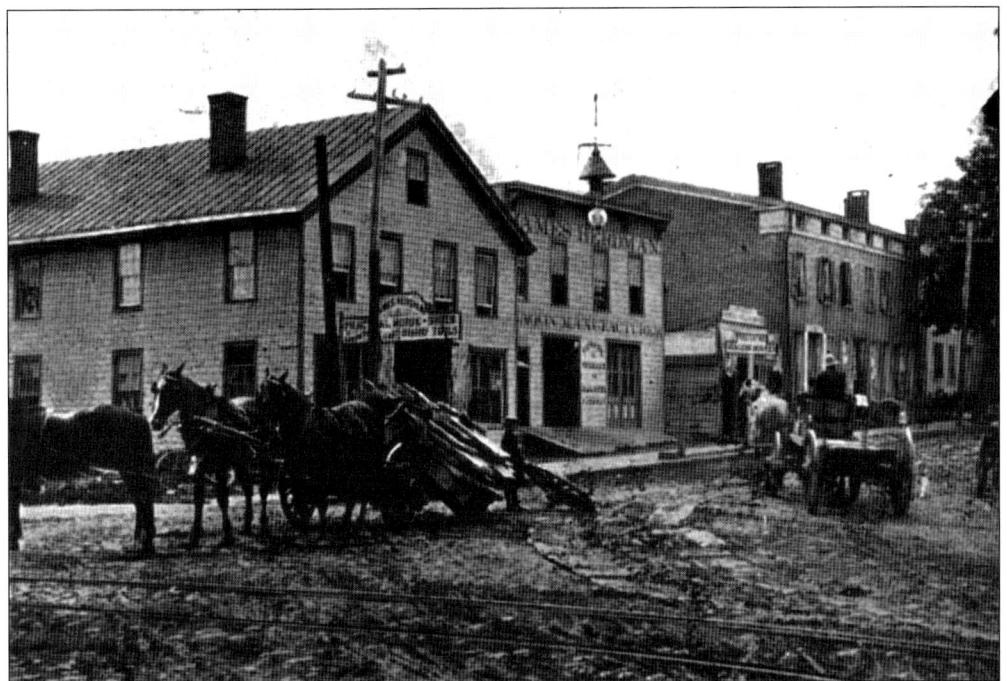

Higginsville is pictured here in 1896. As the western gateway to the village of Kingston, Higginsville was at the south end of the Mutton Hollow bridges. The three-horse team (a common arrangement) is getting a rest due to a broken rear axle. Fortunately, there is a wagon shop next to the general store. The rails are for a horse-drawn streetcar.

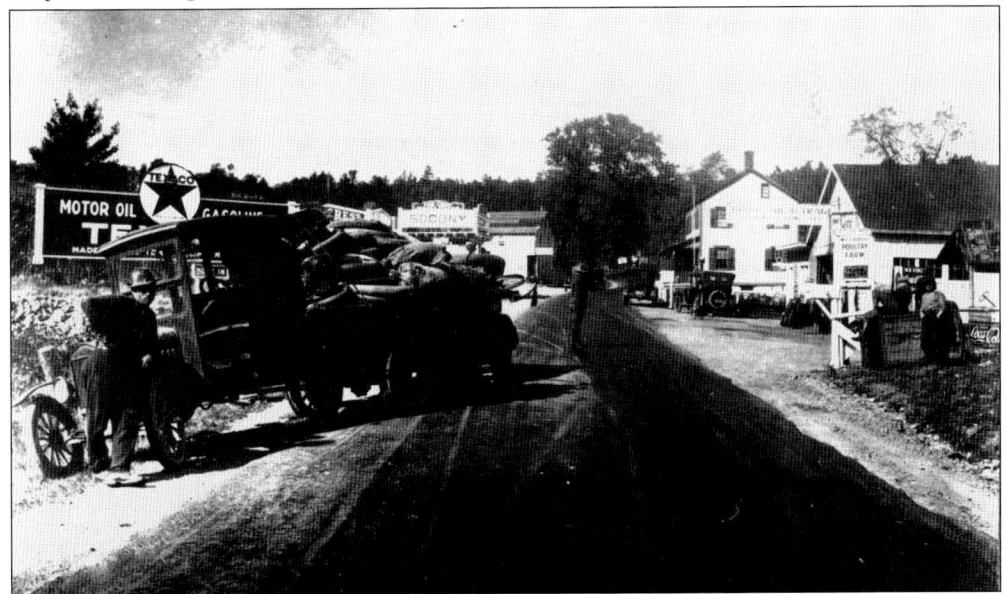

Oscar Beesmer, looking rather displeased, leans on the front fender of his 1920 Model T delivery truck. A c. 1928 Chevrolet touring car is implanted firmly under its bed. To the right, Oscar's brothers Burton, Henry, and Charles look on as a New York state trooper directs traffic. Behind the car stand a wealthy-appearing couple—she in a full-length mink coat. They are obviously not locals. (Rob Sweeny.)

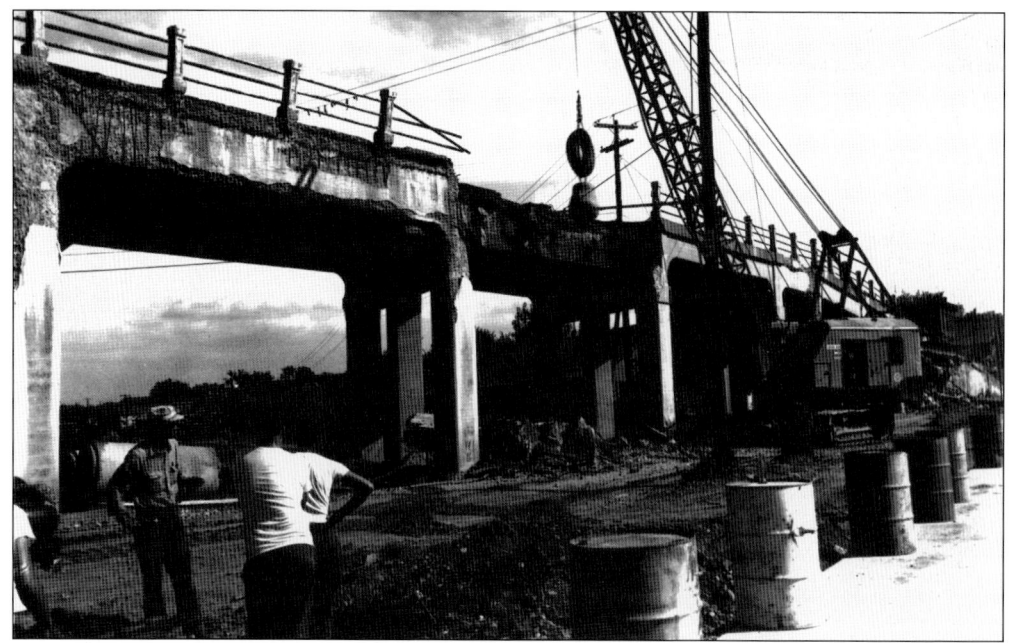

In the mid-1960s, the Washington Avenue viaduct was replaced by a modern concrete span that was wider and offered better visibility. For a short time both spans carried traffic, and then the wrecking ball and bulldozers appeared to remove the outdated structure. The "sidewalk superintendents" watch from a distance that would likely be considered unsafe by today's regulations. (Bob Haines.)

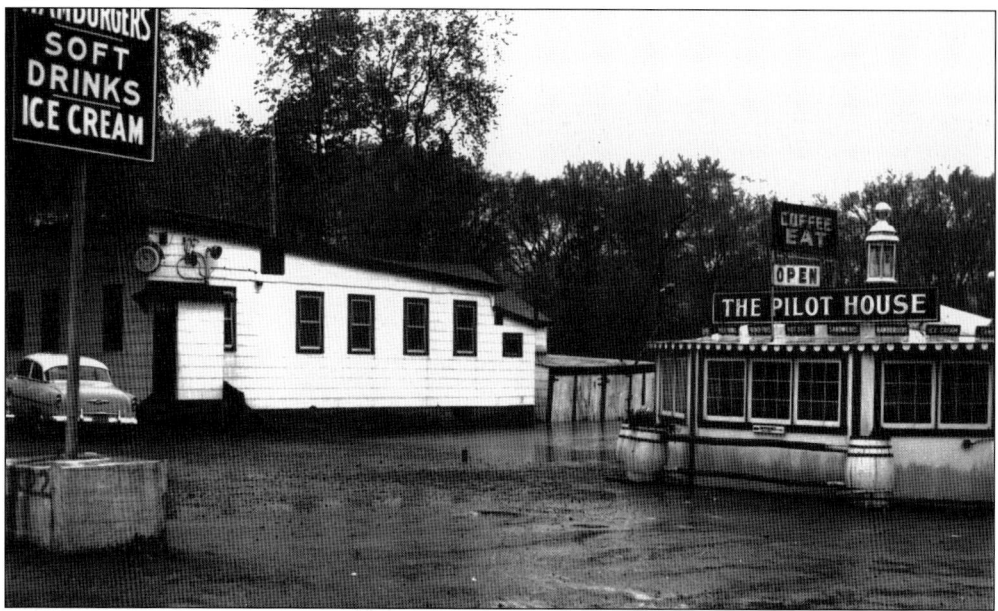

Mutton Hollow was home to a thriving business community during the 1950s and beyond. There were service stations, restaurants, taverns, a discount beverage store, and all of the other expected offerings of a small commercial center. The Pilot House Restaurant was constructed from that part of a Hudson River steamboat. Some say it is the pilothouse of the *Mary Powell*, but a quick study of contemporary photographs puts that legend to rest. (Bob Haines.)

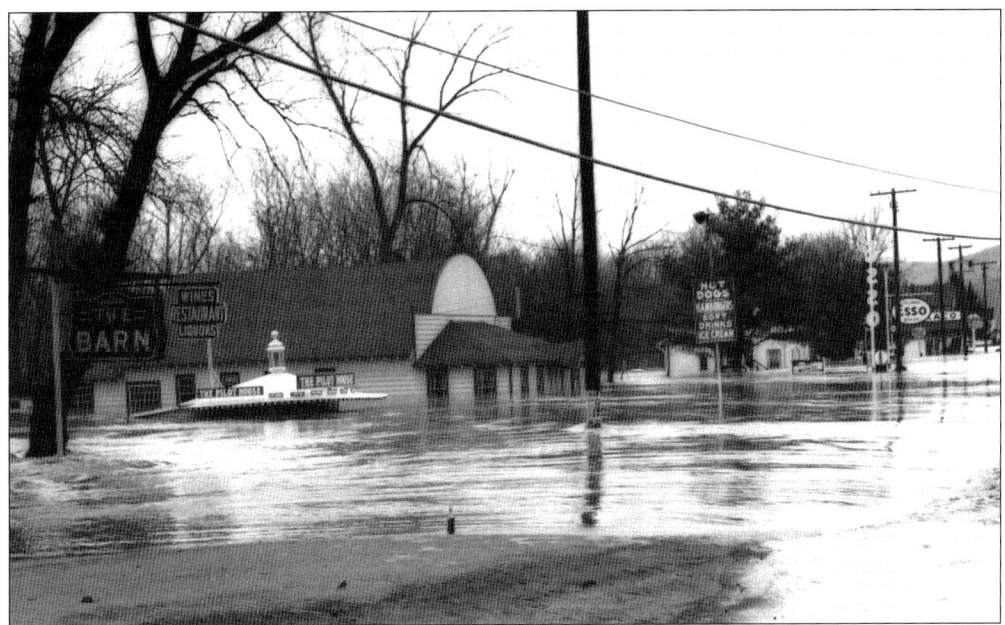

Mutton Hollow was also home to a seal college (the domed structure). Ray and Jane Huling owned the college from the 1930s through the 1950s. There Ray and Bill Rowe trained performing seals, the most famous of which was Sharkie. Sharkie appeared on a number of television variety shows and was given a funeral at the Waldorf-Astoria hotel in New York City. Ray's favorite seal, Charlie, is buried under a stone bearing his name behind the family home on Green Street in Kingston. According to the *New Yorker*, Charlie was the only seal in captivity able to sing as well as dance. In closing this chapter, do not look to man-made edifices, but rather to those who grew up along the Esopus. Seen below are the students of a local school, possibly No. 14, in the Township of Kingston. (Above, Bob Haines; below, Town of Kingston.)

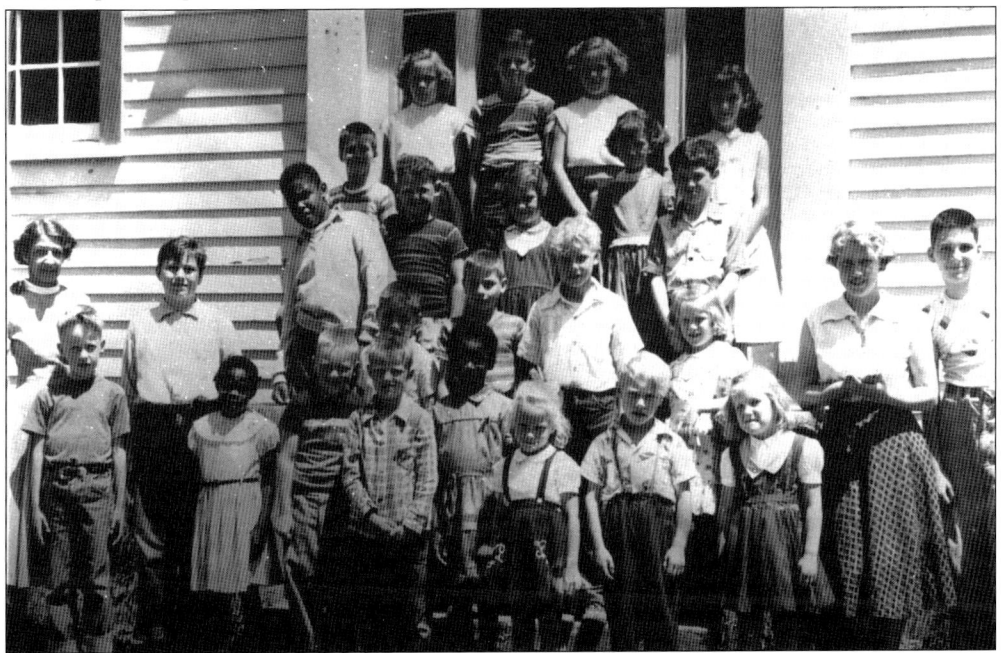

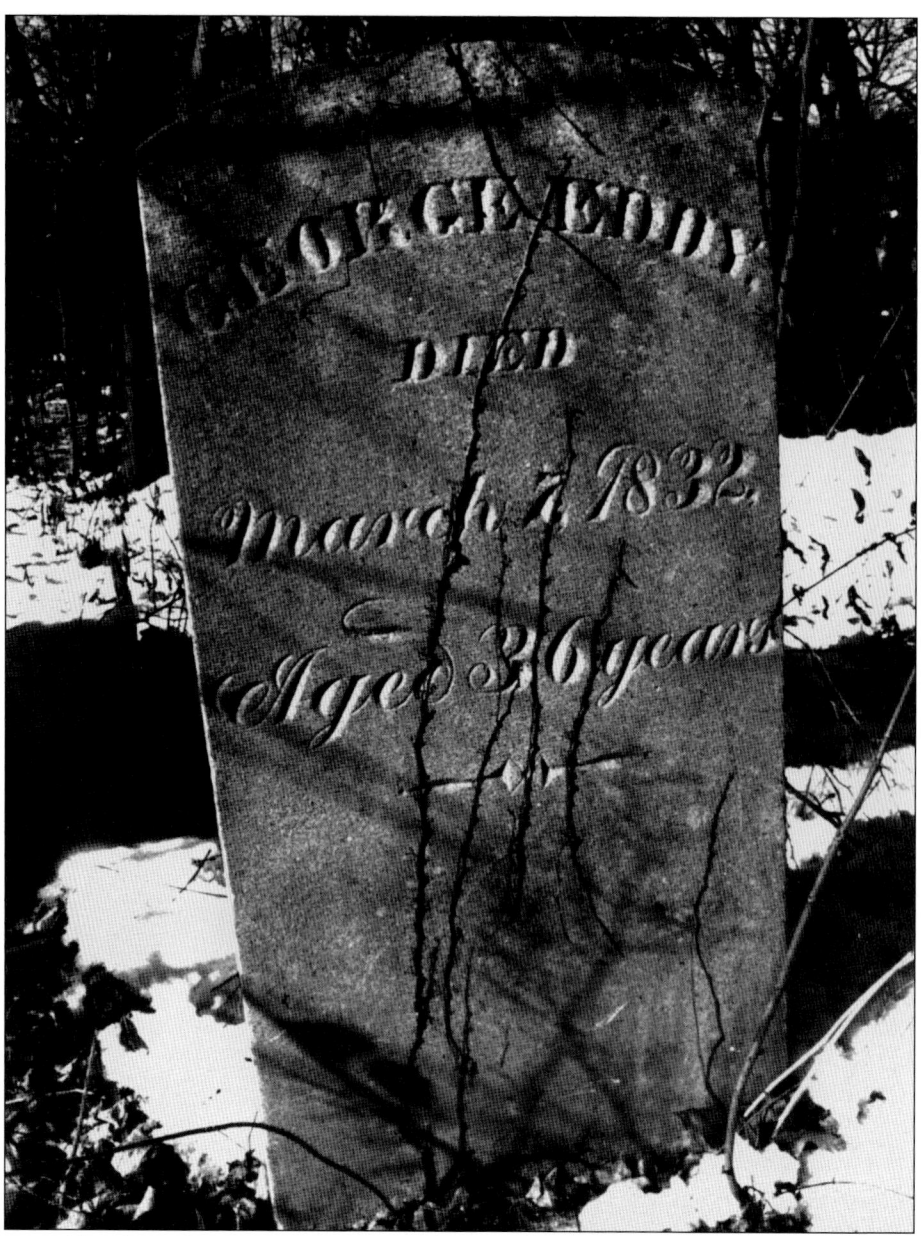

George Eddy is buried atop Church Hill overlooking the Rondout River. His mills were already a going concern when the Delaware and Hudson Canal came through. The canal's grand opening spanned several weeks and 216 miles as a flotilla of 11 boats carried dignitaries up the canal and back again. When the finale came on December 5, 1828, Eddyville and Rondout saw a glimpse of things to come. Bands and cheers, the boom of musket and fireworks, toots of whiskey, and river craft saluted the arrival of this new venture. The rowdy riverfront days lasted nearly 60 years, with robber barons making money hand over fist. Even the little guys survived in style, as attested to by the goods available in the many local mercantiles. Winters were usually more sedate, as the canal was closed due to ice. When roads of rail with year-round schedules were laid through the town, the writing was on the wall. The season's last boat in November 1898 was also the last to make the full run, and so ended an era. (Bruce Berger.)

Four
ON THE RONDOUT RIVER IN EDDYVILLE

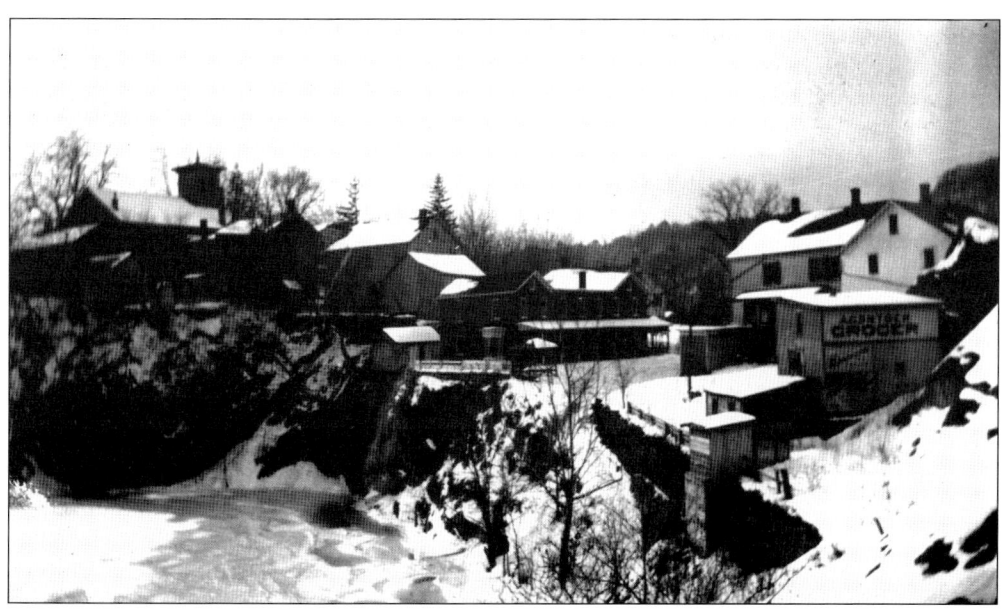

At 2:30 a.m. on Tuesday, December 10, 1878, the guard lock of the Delaware and Hudson Canal burst. The resulting deluge swept through the whole of the lower village, taking several dwelling houses with it and rendering about 20 families homeless. It took nearly all of the canal barns, drowning approximately 25 horses, and destroyed vast amounts of other property. Wreckage was found the next day strewn on the Hudson River's far shore near Staatsburg. (Martin Jordan.)

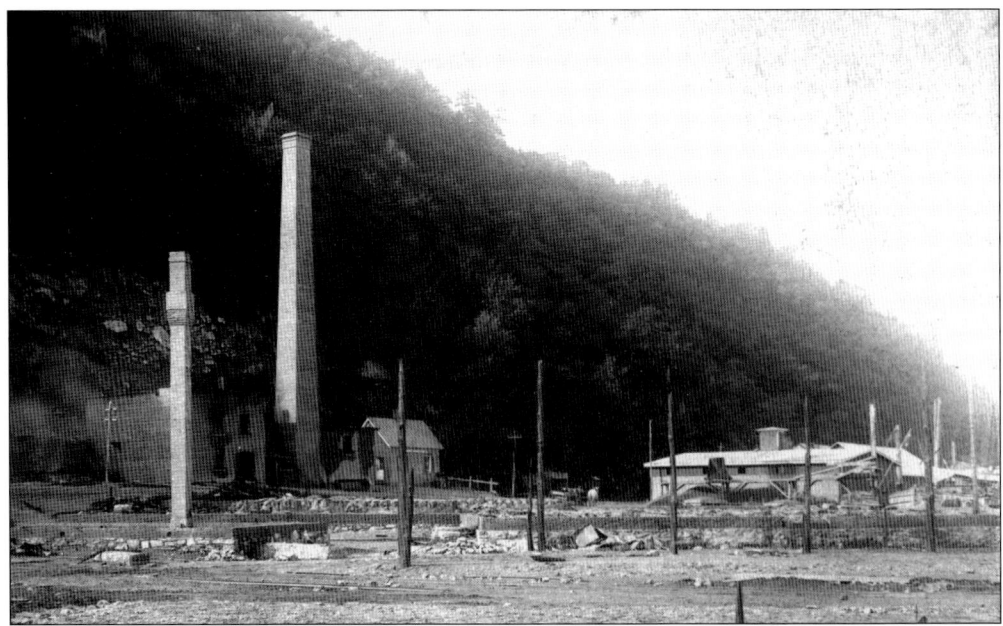

Lawrence Cement Company had its mills in Eddyville with its quarries adjacent to Newark and Rosendale Lime and Cement Company. In 1850, the companies partnered to build a plank road from their quarries to tidewater. They abandoned the road in 1869 and a horse railroad was laid on its bed. Even with the addition of seven miles of spurs and sidings, the companies realized a 60 percent savings due to the upgrade. (Martin Jordan.)

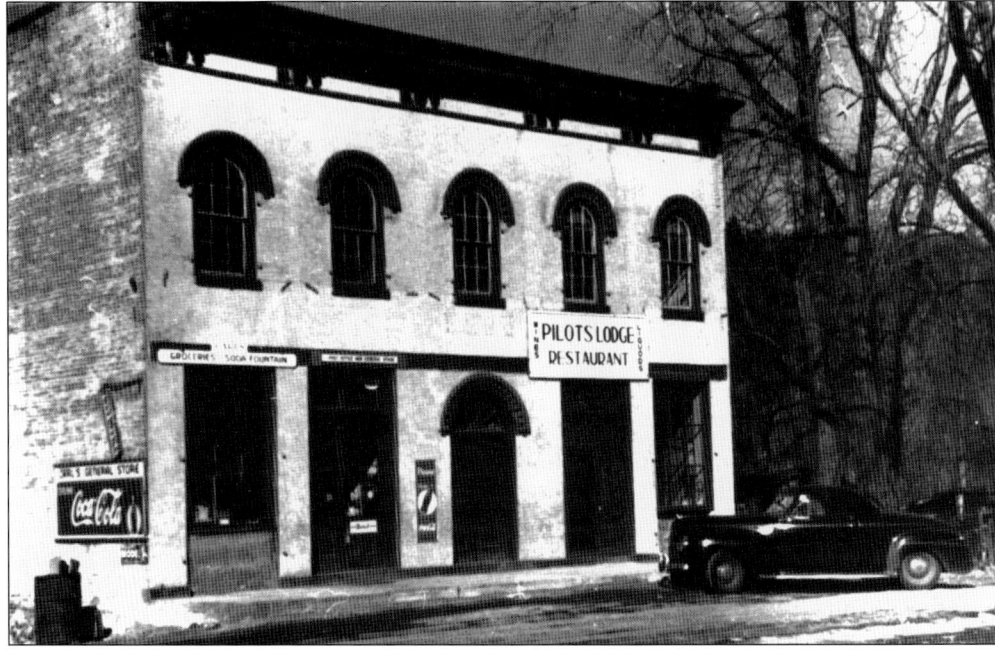

One of the older restaurants in Eddyville is still in use today as the Anchorage. In fact, it is also the oldest surviving structure within the hamlet proper, having been originally named McNamee's Hall. In the 1940s, it was home to Carl's general store, the Pilot Lodge Restaurant, and the post office. (Town of Ulster historian.)

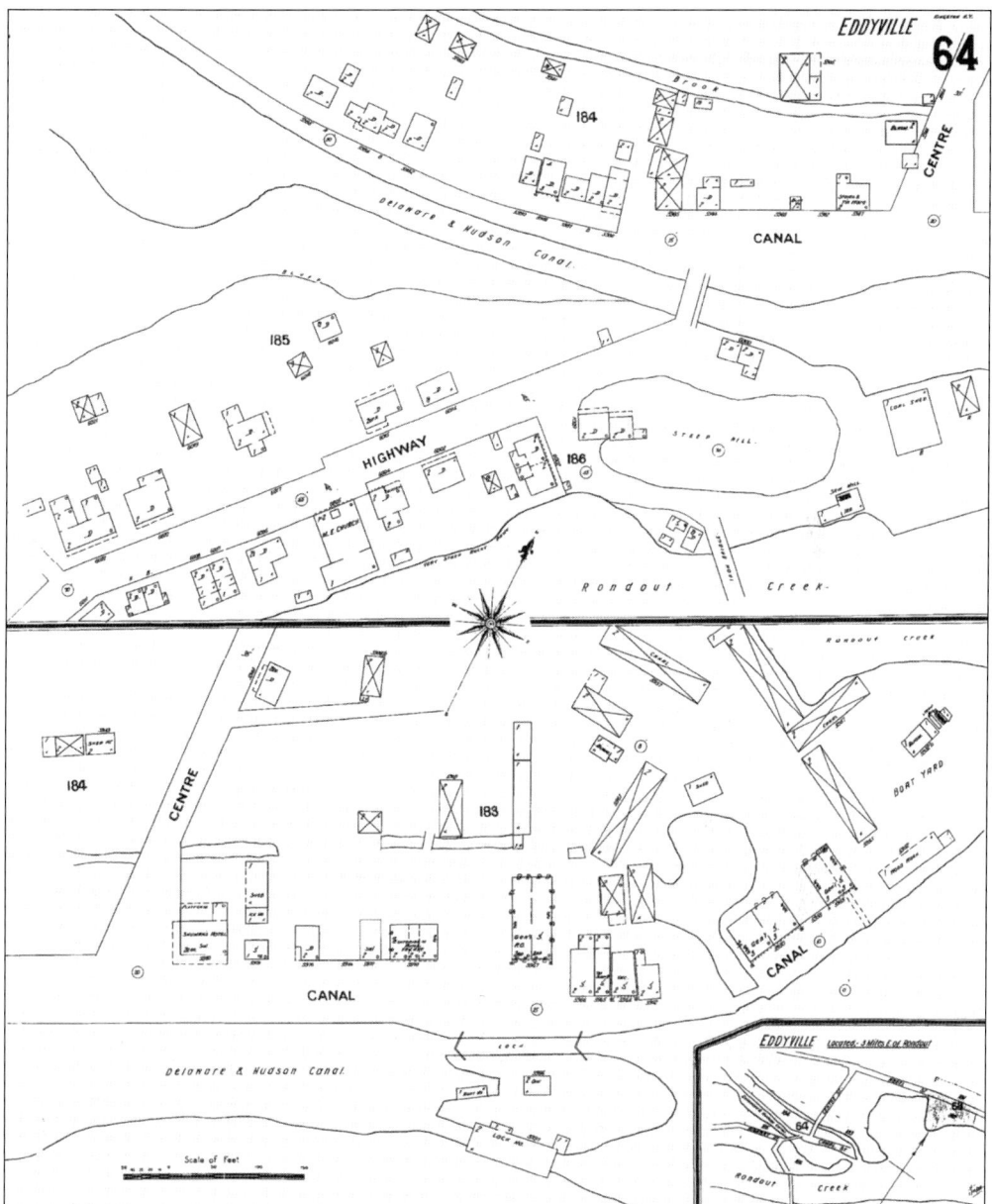

The Sanborn Insurance underwriters carefully mapped many communities from the 1880s until 1950. The maps were of areas that they insured and were mainly concerned with fire hazards and protective measures. This is the 1899 Sanborn map for the riverfront of Eddyville. This part of the hamlet contained most of the holdings of the Delaware and Hudson Canal Company. The map shows the locations of ancillary buildings like the sawmill, blacksmith shops, church, powerhouses, and businesses as well as canal-owned structures. The authors plan to include a large version of this map on their Web site at www.stremy.net. (Atkarton History Project.)

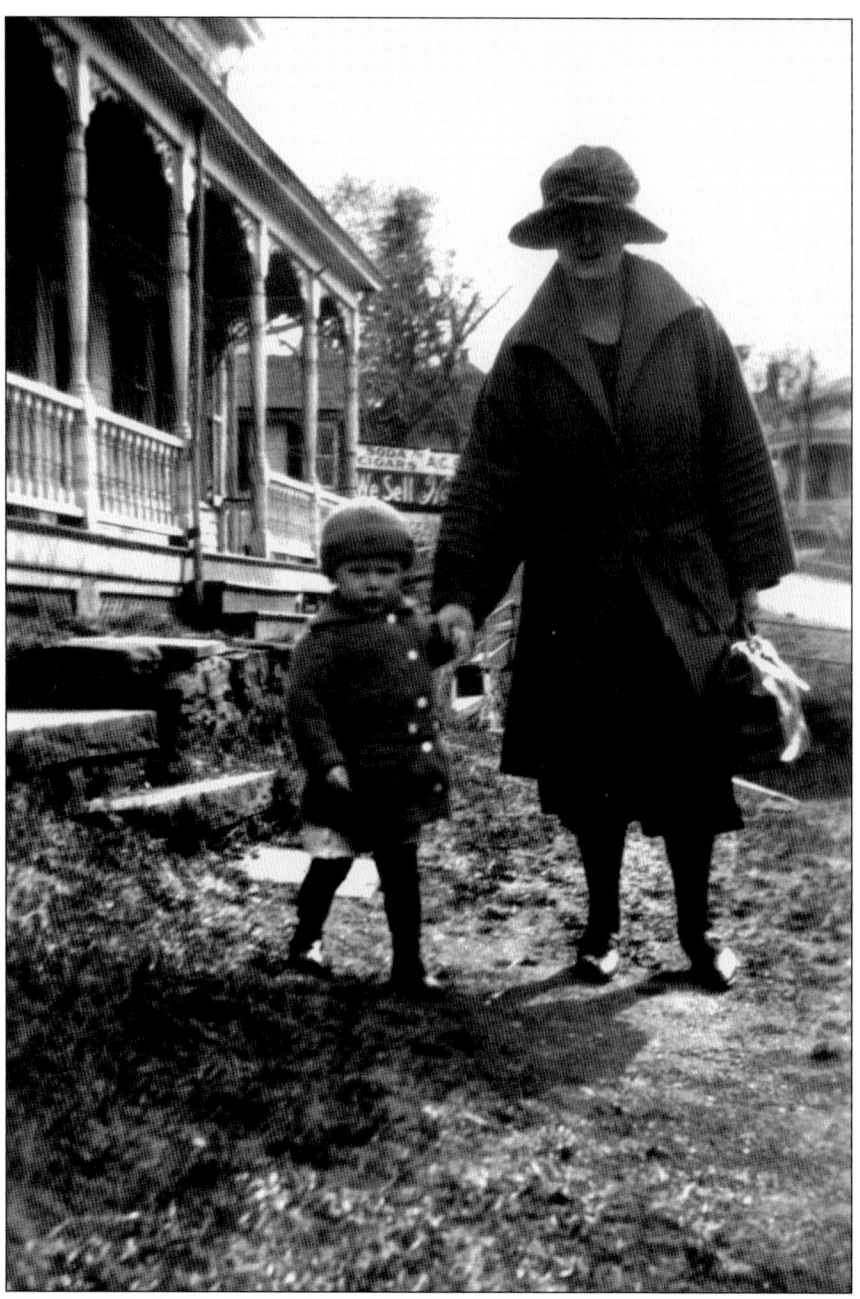

Martin Jordan Jr. and his mother, Catherine Meyers Jordan, pose for the camera on April 25, 1924. The Jordans lived on Cutler Hill near the Methodist church in what one might call the Siamese twin houses (Snyder/Meyers house). Martin "Duksey" Jordan Sr. drove a Pierce Arrow bus along the route from Kingston to New Paltz via Eddyville, New Salem, and St. Remy. He eventually lost the route because he was too good-hearted and let many people ride for free. The Eddyville Methodist Episcopal Church built in 1872 offered the community at large generosity and salvation of another sort after the flood of 1878. By some miracle, no human lives were lost and the church lecture hall and the schoolhouse were warmed and lighted to afford temporary accommodations to those who had lost their homes. (Martin Jordan.)

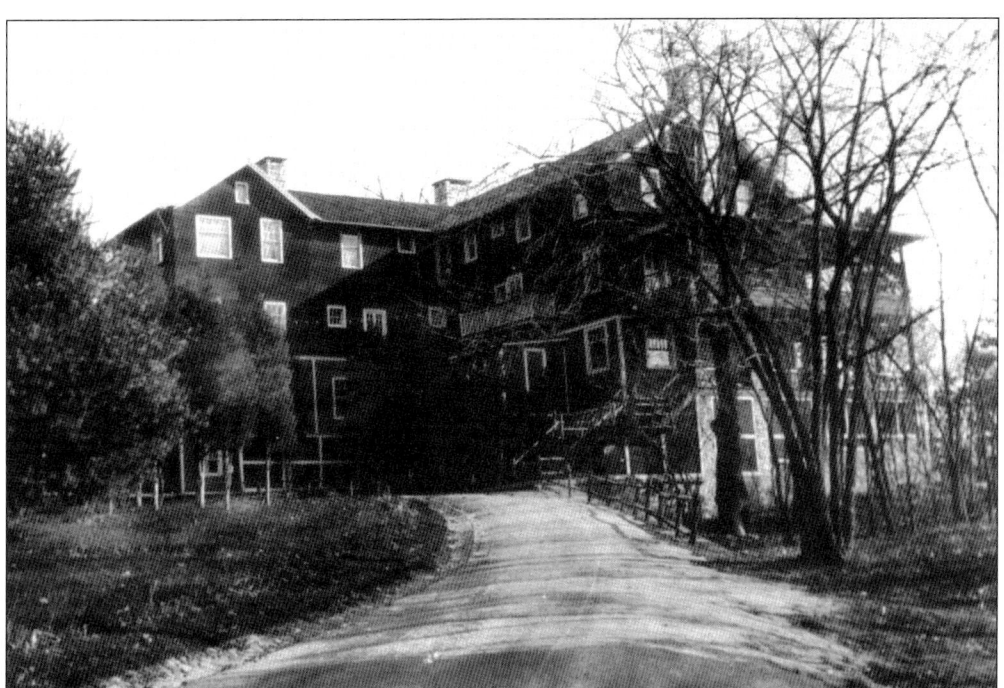

Greenkill Park was a large resort situated at the southernmost part of Ulster Township, near Eddyville. This large four-story edifice was the centerpiece of the complex, with medium sized structures and collections of cabins making up the rest. This photograph of the front of the building was taken on November 4, 1923. Shortly after this time, the park became a Father Divine peace mission. Father Divine was a charismatic preacher. (Martin Jordan.)

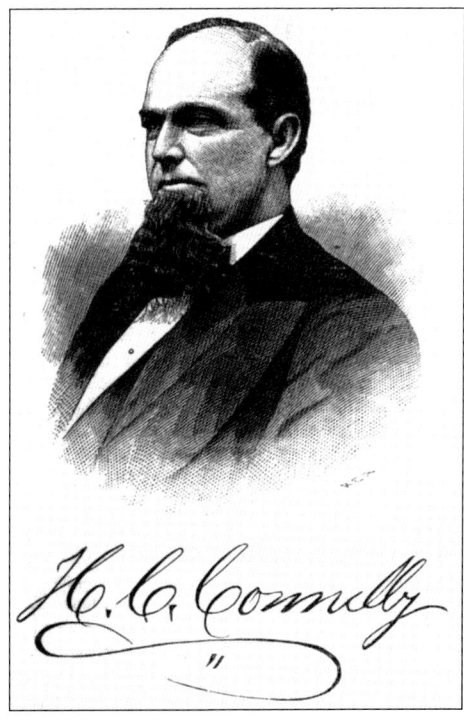

In 1852, Henry Connelly arrived in Eddyville to run a general store. By 1856, he was running the show. He served four consecutive terms in the New York State Senate. He helped to charter the Kingston Savings Bank in 1875. Brother Connelly was a pillar of the Eddyville Methodist Church. Sunday School superintendent and church treasurer for 20 years, he often reached deep into his own pocket to help keep things afloat. (Atkarton History Project.)

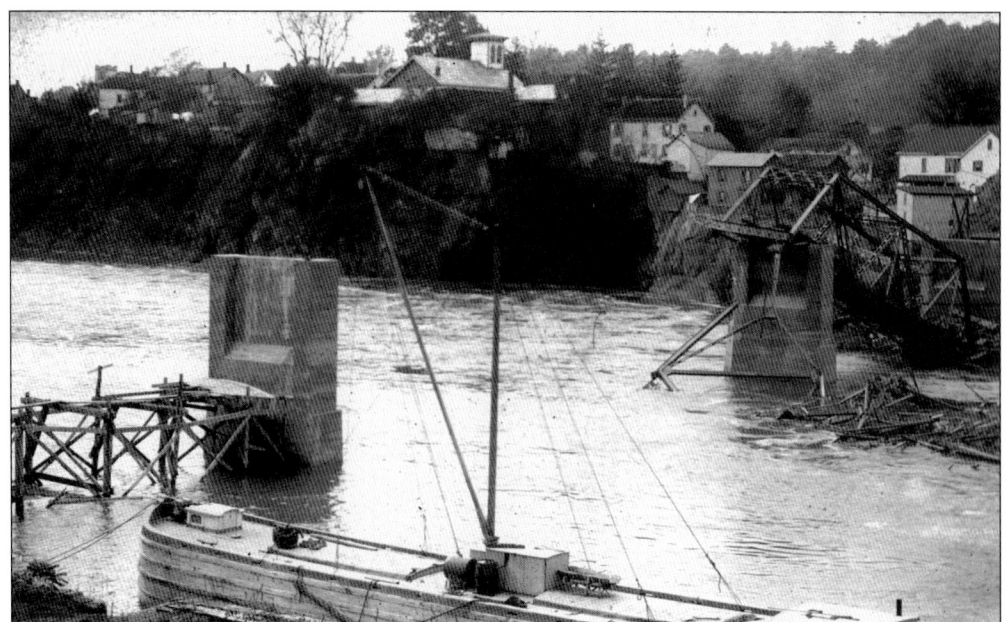

This photograph shows the fate of the 1912 bridge. The best workmanship of that time could not stand forever. By 1954, the center supporting pier under the now old bridge was severely undermined. Fishermen reported seeing the entire pier rattle and shake when heavy trucks crossed the bridge. Finally on June 8, 1959, at a cost of $736,000, a new single-span bridge was opened. (Martin Jordan.)

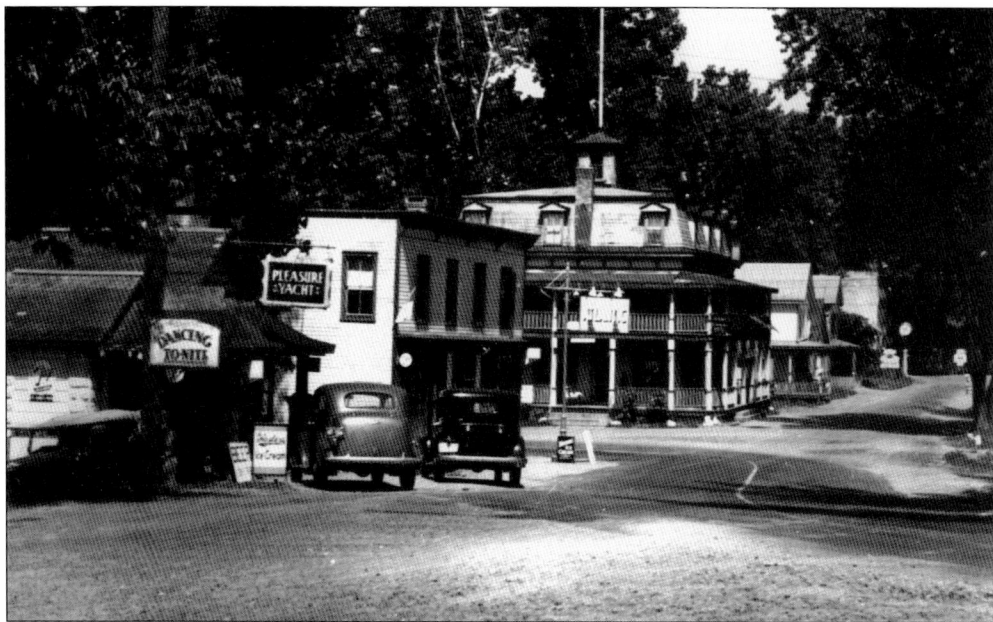

In the depression years of the 1930s, with the canal and cement industries closed down, Eddyville became a far more sedate hamlet than in its heyday. Baldwin's ice-cream parlor had been turned into a bar, the David Building and Schuman's Hotel were still in use (the Twin Motels and the Ulster were others). A detailed chapter about Eddyville can be found in the authors' sister Arcadia publication, *Esopus*. (Bob Haines.)

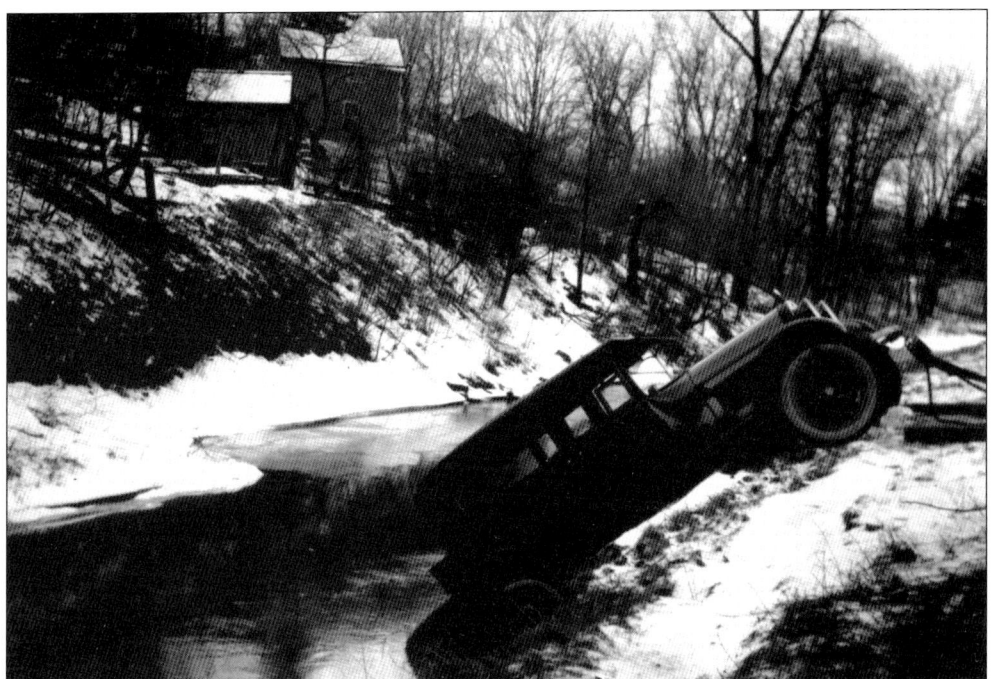

In January 1924, the Chrysler Corporation unveiled its first entry into the midscale market—the B-70 touring car. It boasted a newly engineered engine and a top speed of 70 miles per hour. Voted best in class, it competed with much more expensive models. Unfortunately even four-wheel hydraulic brakes could not stand up to winter weather on March 24. It is being towed out of the former Delaware and Hudson Canal. (Martin Jordan.)

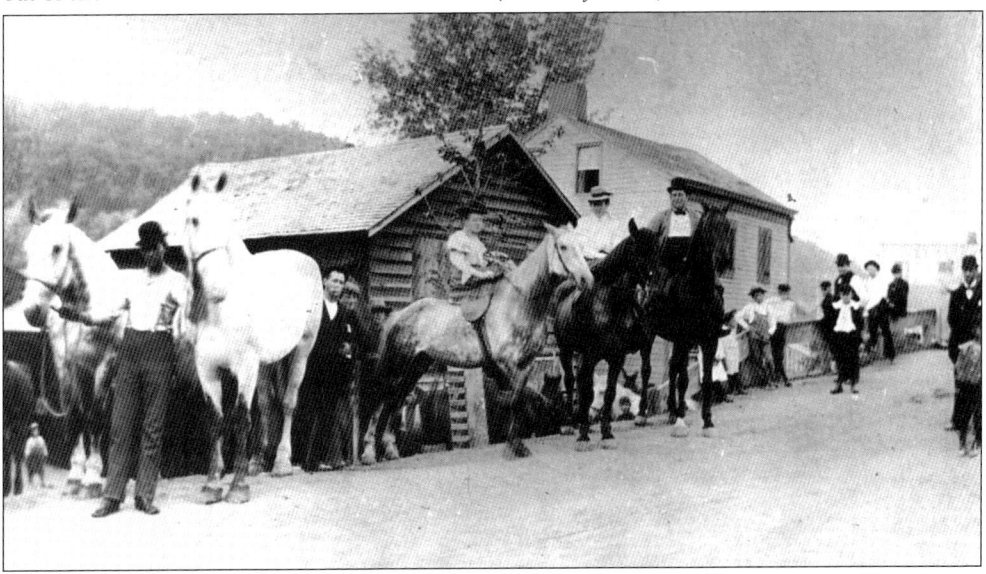

Back in the mid-1880s, one did not have to worry about rubber tires slipping on ice. Here during nicer weather, a selection of canal men and their teams pose for the camera along Canal Street in the eastern half of town. Canal men were a proud, hardworking, and hard-drinking sort of people. The latter is evidenced by 23 taverns making their home in Eddyville during canal days. (Town of Ulster historian.)

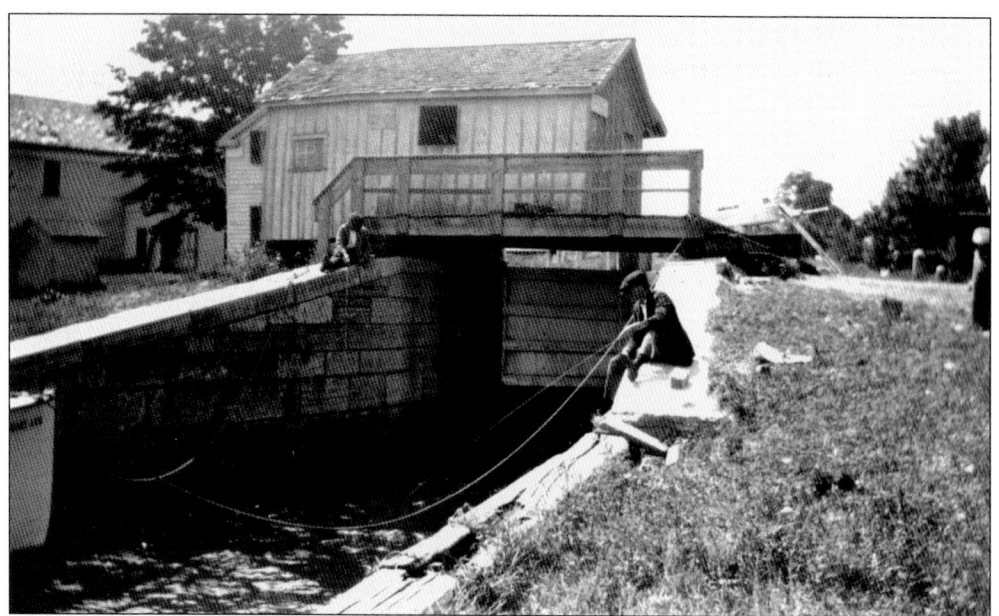

Summertime is a time to relax and catch a few fish. It is August 22, 1922. The canal is no longer in operation, but the locks are still intact, and it appears that the fish are biting. This is the former tidewater lock where canal boats once left the canal for the open water of the Rondout River on their way to Island Dock. Contrast this view with the image below. (Martin Jordan.)

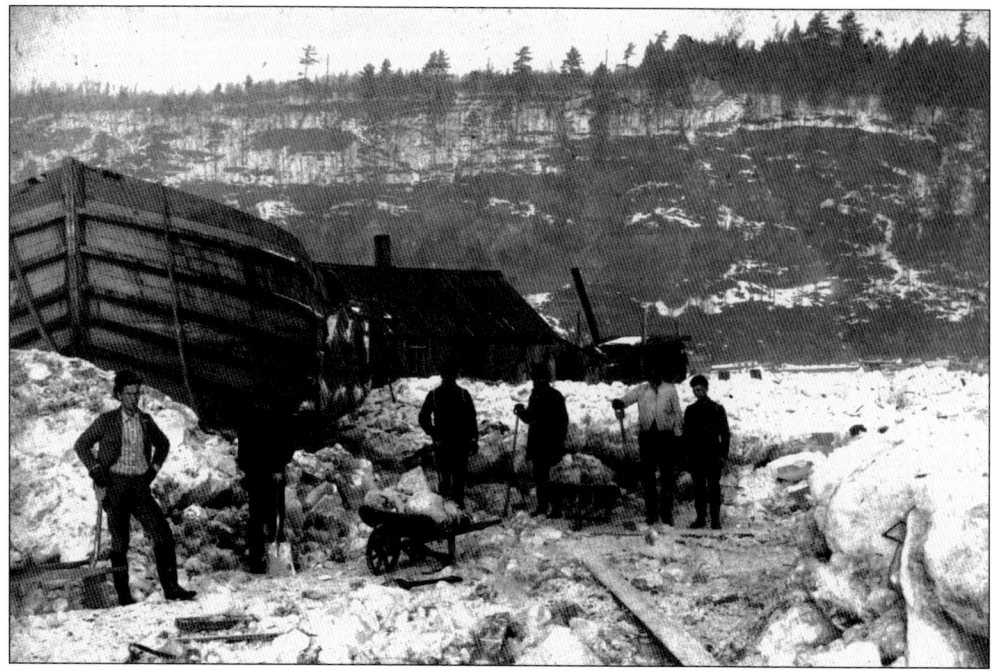

The great blizzard of March 1888 hit the waterfront community particularly hard. Residents and workers had to contend with 20-foot drifts of wind-blown snow, ice jams, and excavating homes and businesses. This is a view from Canal Street toward Haber's Hill. The men are attempting to clear a work area around the boat so that they can move it back to its dock. (Town of Ulster historian.)

Incorporated in 1886, the Haber Steamboat Company of Freerville (New Salem) owned three steam yachts that plied the river from Freerville and Eddyville to Rondout. The company and their boats ferried both passengers and freight for the three-mile distance. The boat shown is the *Charles A. Shultz*, the pride of the fleet around 1910. The Habers also owned Fly Mountain Park on Haber's Hill overlooking the river.

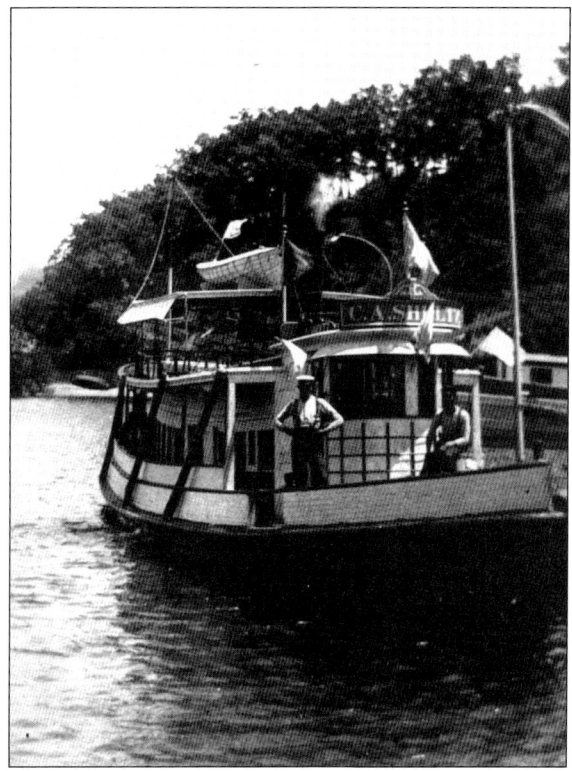

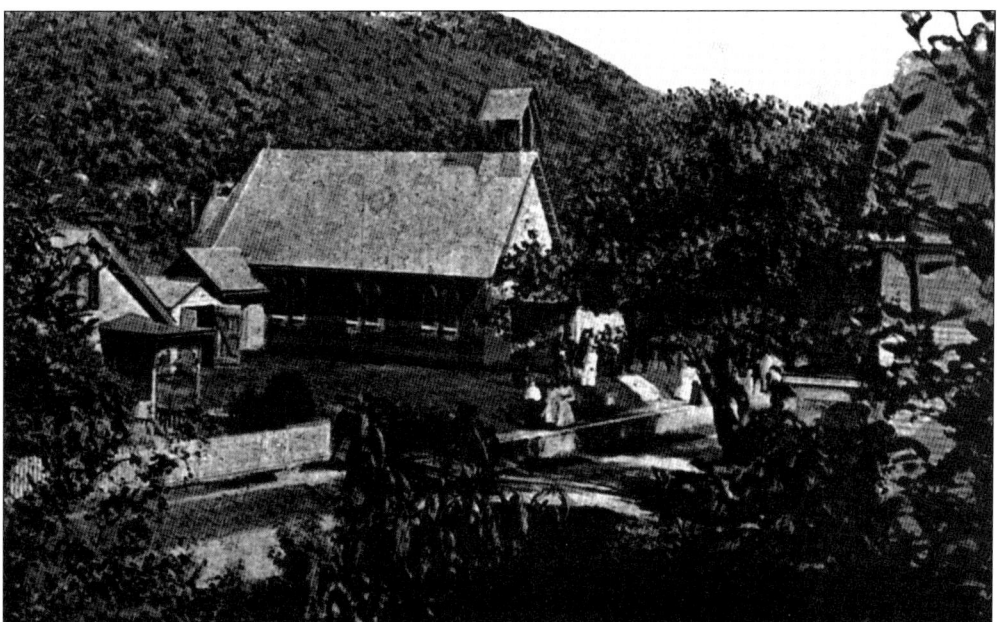

The Eddyville Methodist church and parsonage on Church Hill is no longer standing, but can be seen in the opening photograph. This edifice is the Sacred Heart Roman Catholic Church built in 1874 and located on Cutler Hill. It is a more modest structure but outlasted its sibling, now being a private residence. The owner donated its nicest stained-glass window to Sacred Heart Church in Esopus during the 1990s. (Century House Historical Society.)

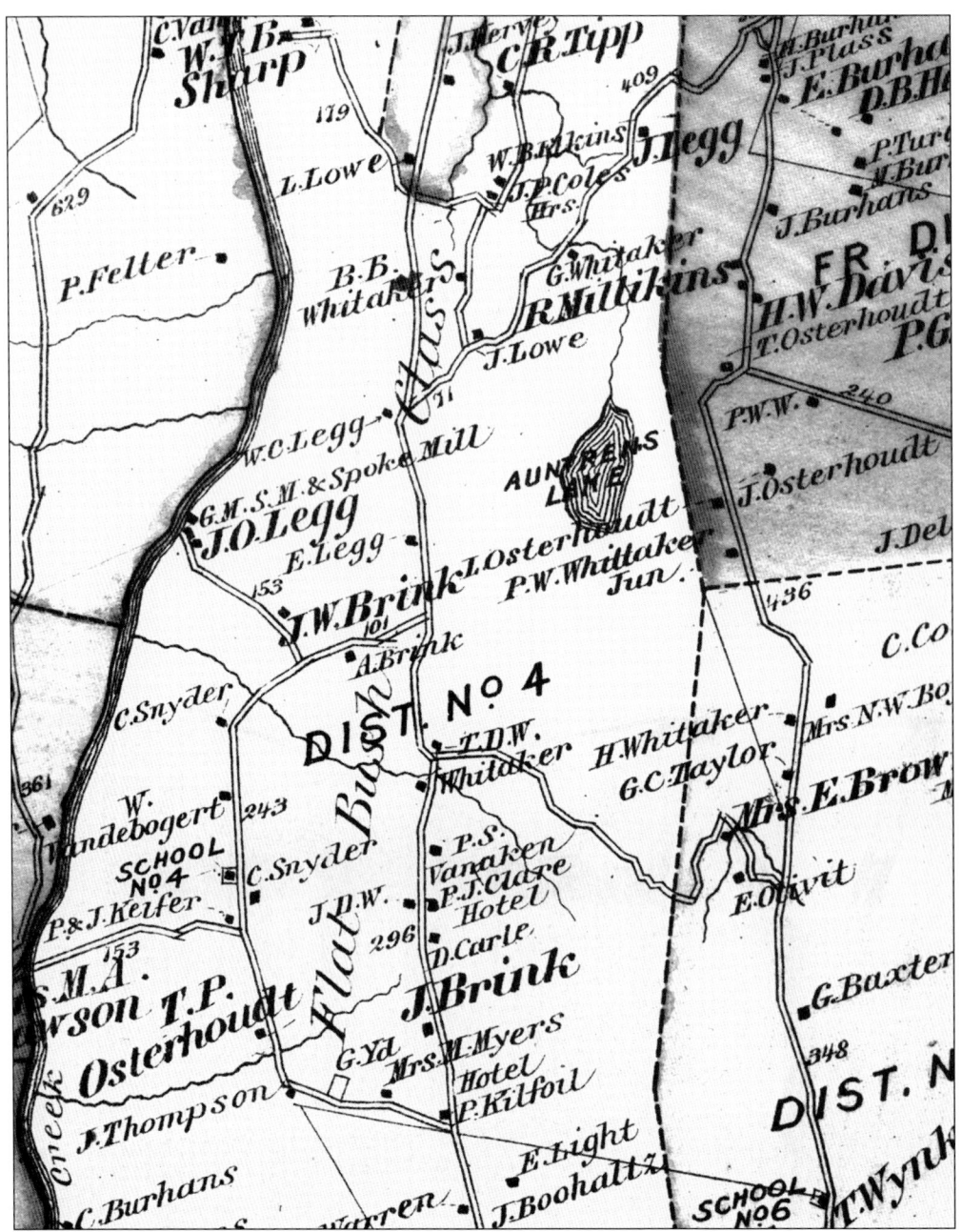

Slightly north of the center of Lake Katrine lies a sizable lake that eventually feeds into the Esopus Creek near Glasco. Bounded by the old Flatbush Road to the east and the Saugerties Road to the west, this was a well-known vacation spot with several resorts and large boardinghouses, including the Pinewood Lodge. The lake was guarded by a tollgate and a woman by the name of Katrina or "Aunt Ren." Dr. Jacob Brink (page 62) was named after his paternal grandfather who was also a doctor. He was born on September 29, 1808, and although blessed with little formal education, he did inherit his grandfather's healing talents and used them to alleviate physical ailments of many friends and neighbors. The Brink progenitor came to America in 1659, and the family also farmed for many generations. (Don and Shirley Briggs.)

Five
LAKE KATRINE

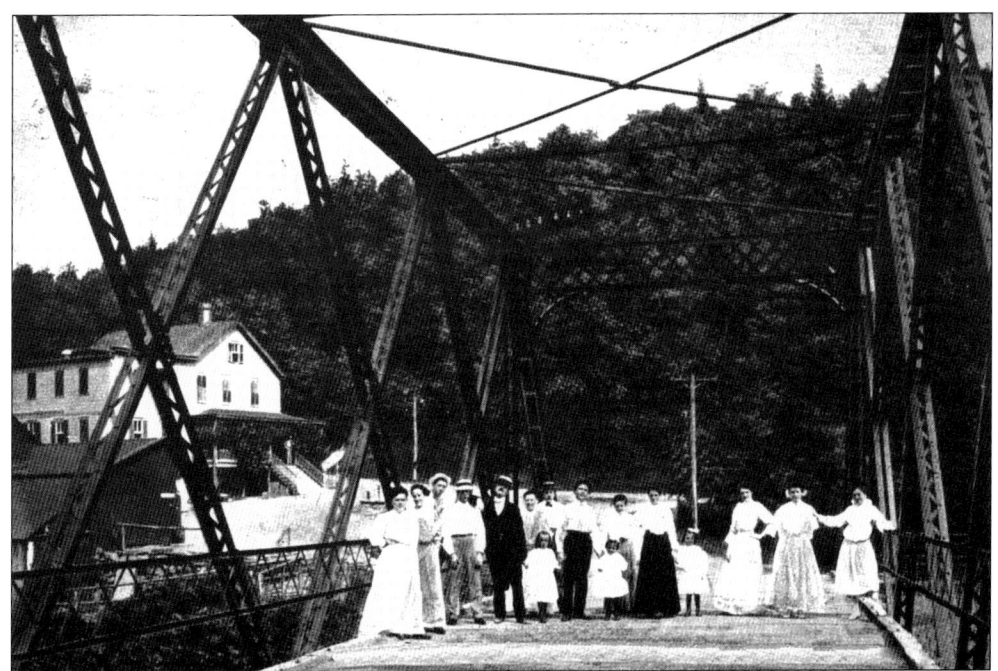

She was affectionately known as Aunt Katrina which was shortened to Aunt Ren or Auntren. The lake took on this name by the mid-19th century. The town center took on the name of Katrine Station when the West Shore Railroad established a station there. Eventually both hamlet and lake came to be known by the moniker Lake Katrine. This is the Pleasant Valley Hotel and Glenerie Bridge in 1917.

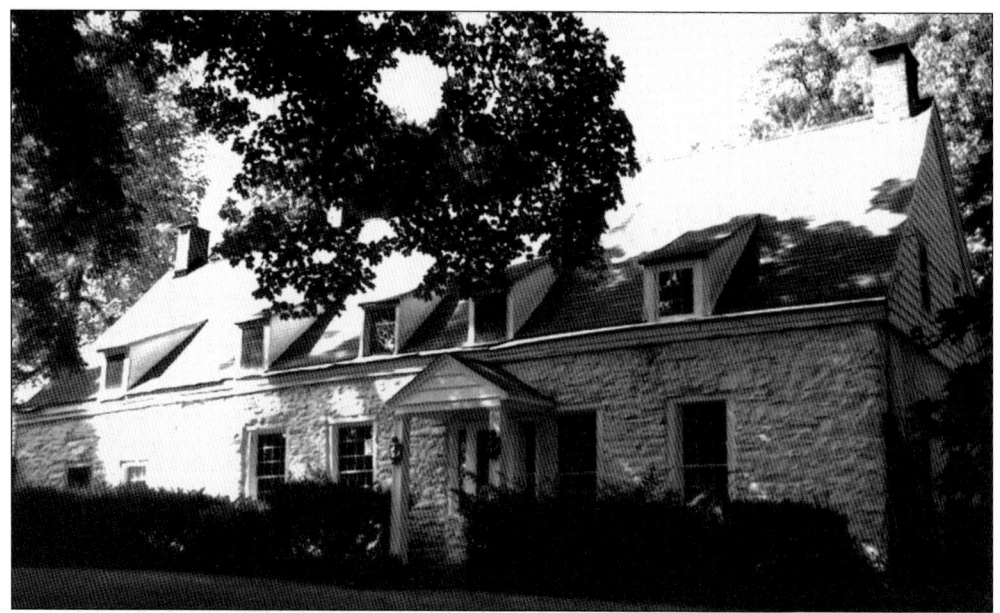

Reputed to be the oldest house in Lake Katrine, the Jan Janszen Osterhoudt house is believed to have been begun between 1688 and 1691. The eastern portion was added in 1740 by William Osterhoudt and Sarah Hasbrouck. The dormers date from that era. The original farm was extensive and partly bordered the north line of Fox Hall Manor. In 1821, the property was divided among family members.

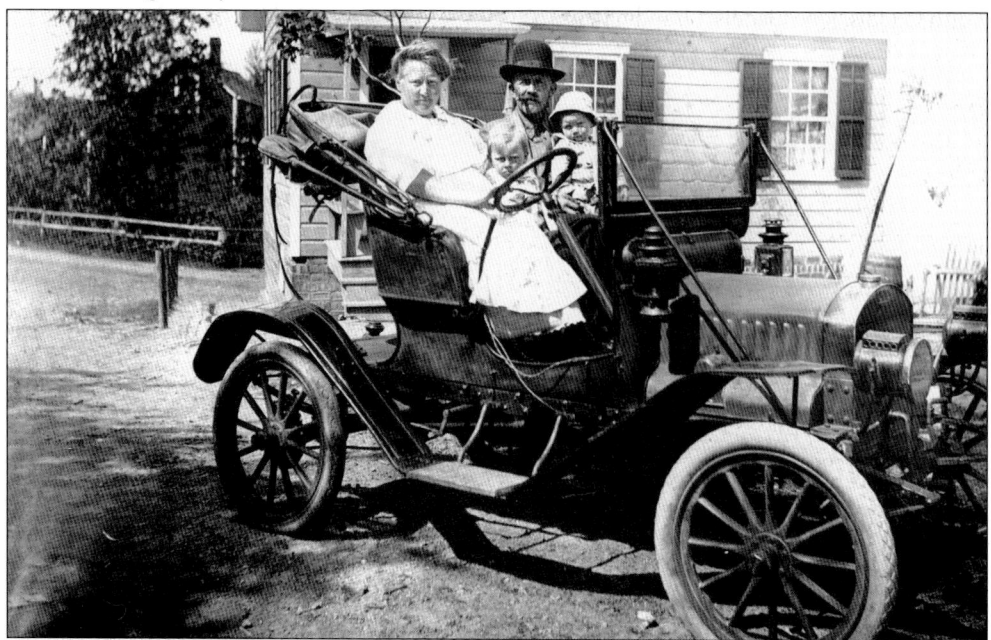

Mr. and Mrs. Sparling pose with their sons for a photograph at a turn in the road in front of a friend's house. The automobile appears to be a 1909 Maxwell Motorcar. The deep headlights are carbon arc lamps—bright but potentially dangerous. Electric headlights were not yet commonly available. Note the right-hand drive and which half of the couple is in the driver's seat. (Pat Clausi.)

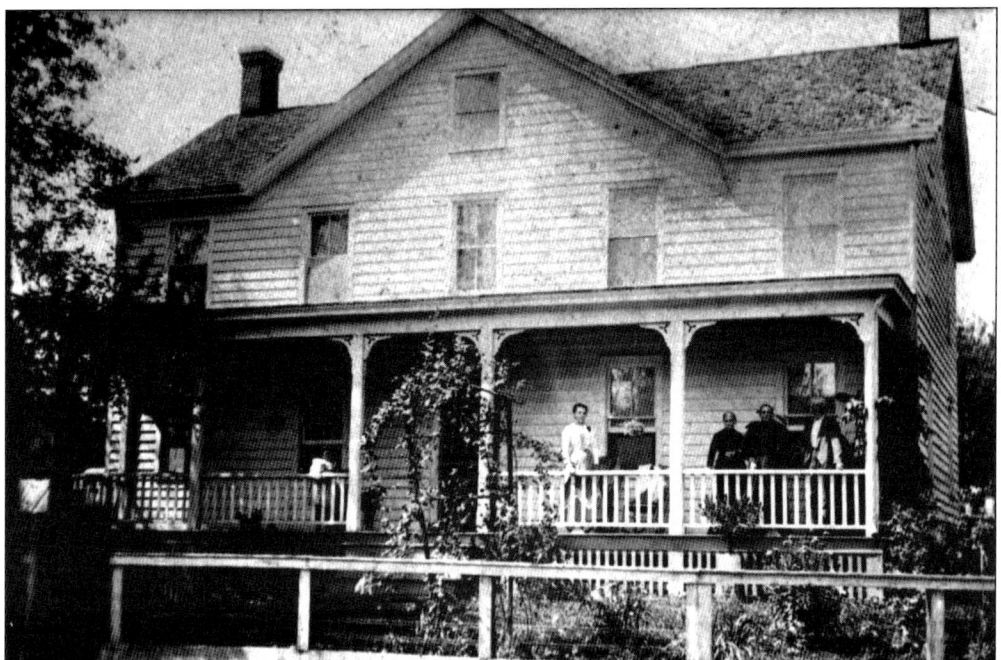

This is the Valentine Gaddis house. Occupying the site of a c. 1700 stone house built by William Legg that burned in the 1880s, this house used the original cellars. The photograph was donated to the Town of Kingston by Edith Gaddis Legg. From left to right are Mary Morton Gaddis, Edith Gaddis, Jane Gaddis, Grandma Eliza Quick, and Valentine Gaddis. According to the back there is also a dog, Rover, and "kitty cat." (Town of Kingston.)

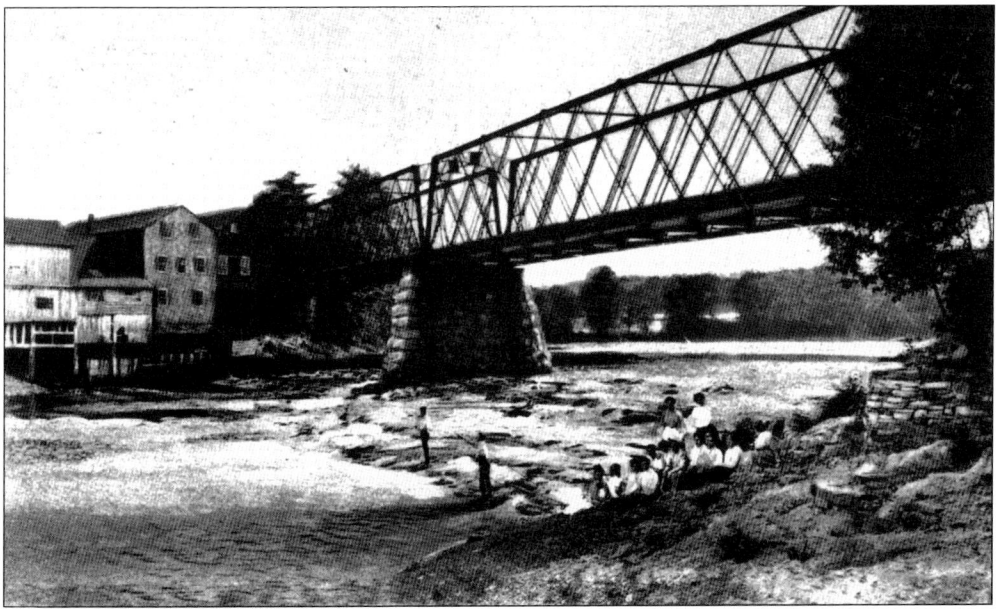

This 1907 image shows the Leggs' gristmill, sawmill, and spoke mill on the left and the bridge along the Post Road on the right. J. Legg had the largest mills in the towns and one of the best sites for waterpower along the Esopus Creek. Lightweight iron-truss bridges like this one were designed for horse-and-buggy traffic and served until the early part of the 20th century.

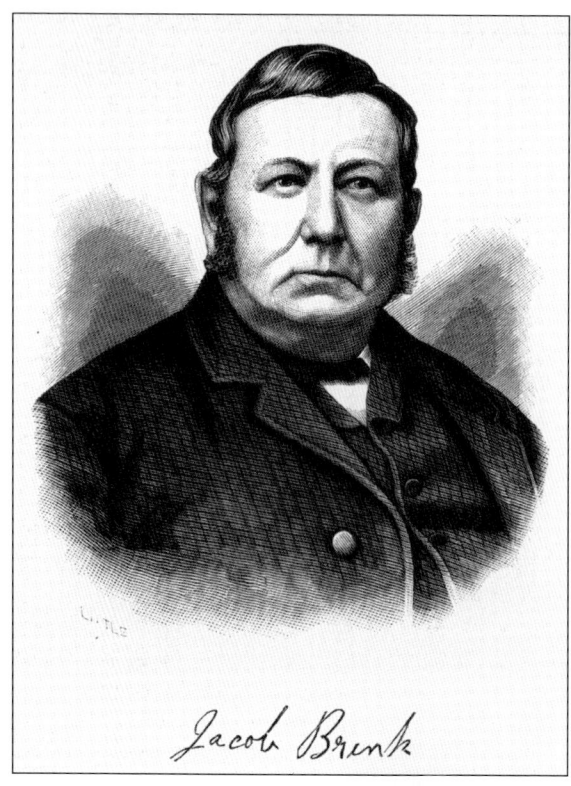

Some affectionately called Dr. Jacob Brink "witch doctor" because of his strong innate abilities and psychological insight. In addition to farming, he held the position of assessor for the town of Kingston from 1858 until 1872 and that of supervisor for two years. At the time of his death on March 8, 1879, he was president of the Pine Bush Rural Cemetery Association and active in the Flatbush Reformed Church. (Atkarton History Project.)

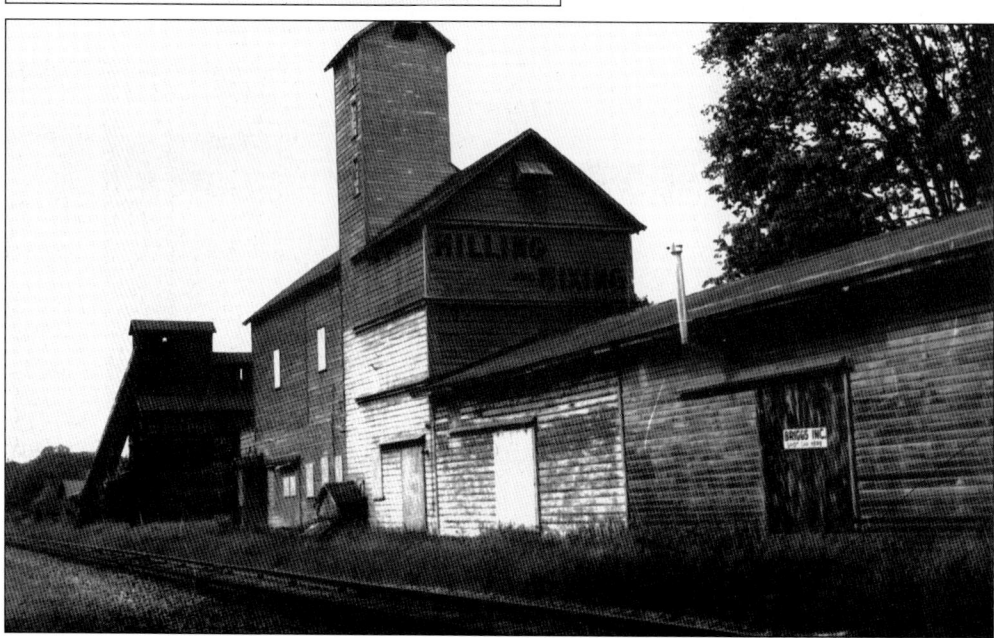

Both Drs. Jacob Brink practiced psychology and herbal medicine. Early on, this care included removing hexes of witches. Frances Wolven recalled that there was a fair amount of money to be made in that field. Dr. Brink was well to do. His progeny used this nest egg and business acumen to do well for themselves. They had a coaling facility, lumberyard, and feed mill on the West Shore Railroad. (Town of Kingston.)

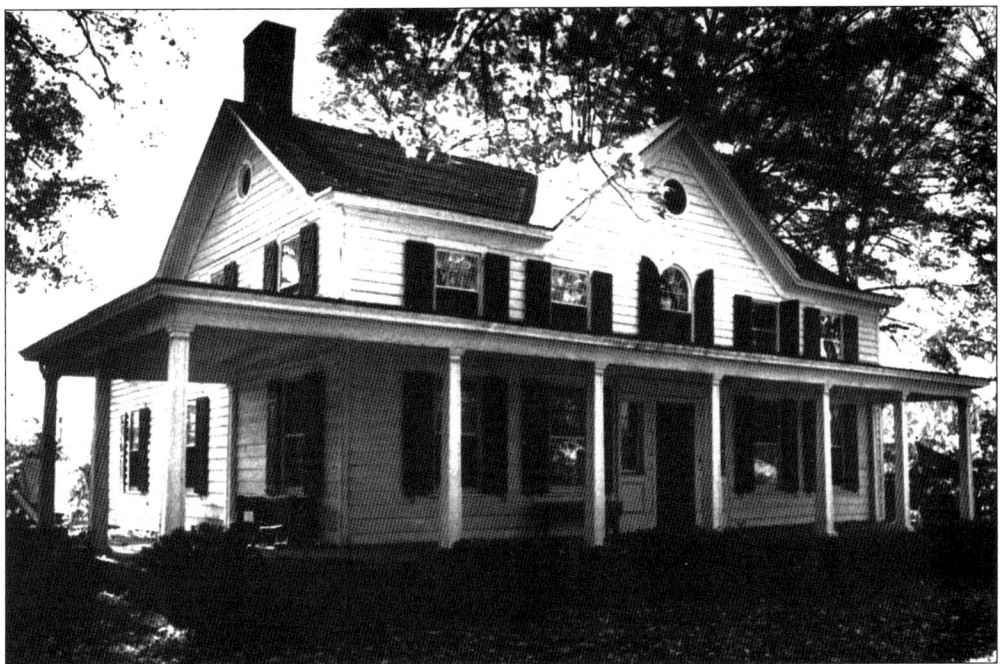

One of two Brink homes on Legg's Mill Road, this one was constructed by Willem Brink and his father Jacob between 1820 and 1830. A Victorian home stands across the street. The oldest part of Jacob's house is of post and beam construction. This led to speculation that an older house once stood on the site. It also features a hand-cranked two-story elevator installed around 1920. (Town of Ulster historian.)

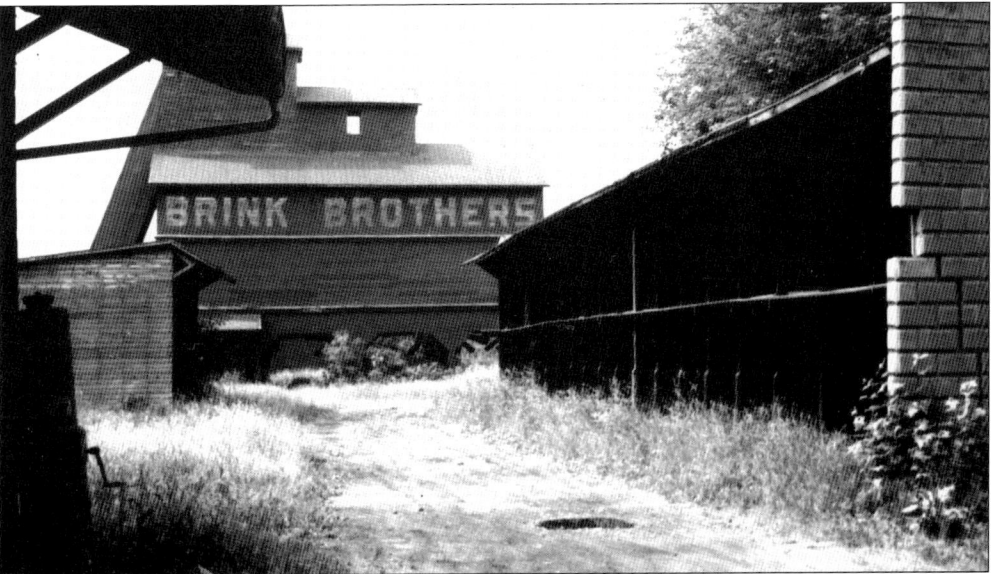

Andrew, born in 1835, was the grandson of Jacob. By around 1890, he had entered the mercantile business with his sons Theodore and Joel. First they kept a general store and took part in bringing both a railroad station and post office to the community. Eventually the Brinks dealt in coal, feed, and lumber from a complex of structures with their own spur track off of the West Shore Railroad. (Town of Kingston.)

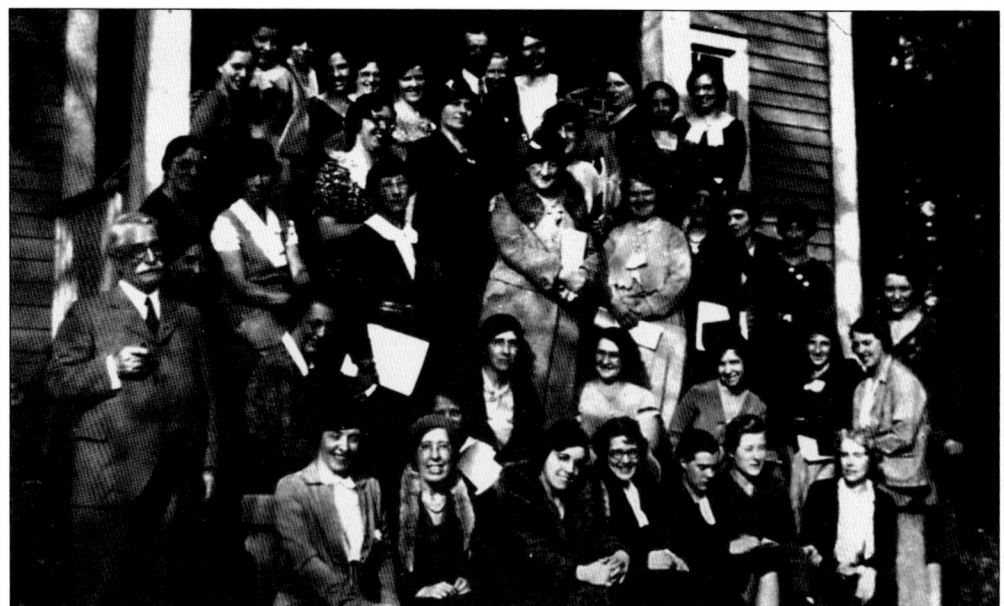

These are the women of the town of Ulster Grange Hall around the 1930s. Unfortunately a full listing of names is not available. However, a few are known, Mrs. Frank Ford—teacher at the Lake Katrine School, Mrs. Myron Boice, Catherine Burhans, Edith Legg, Mrs. William Hookey, Mrs. Anvin Kiefer, and Nettie Auchmoody. The Grange hall was located near the Lake Katrine station. (Town of Ulster historian.)

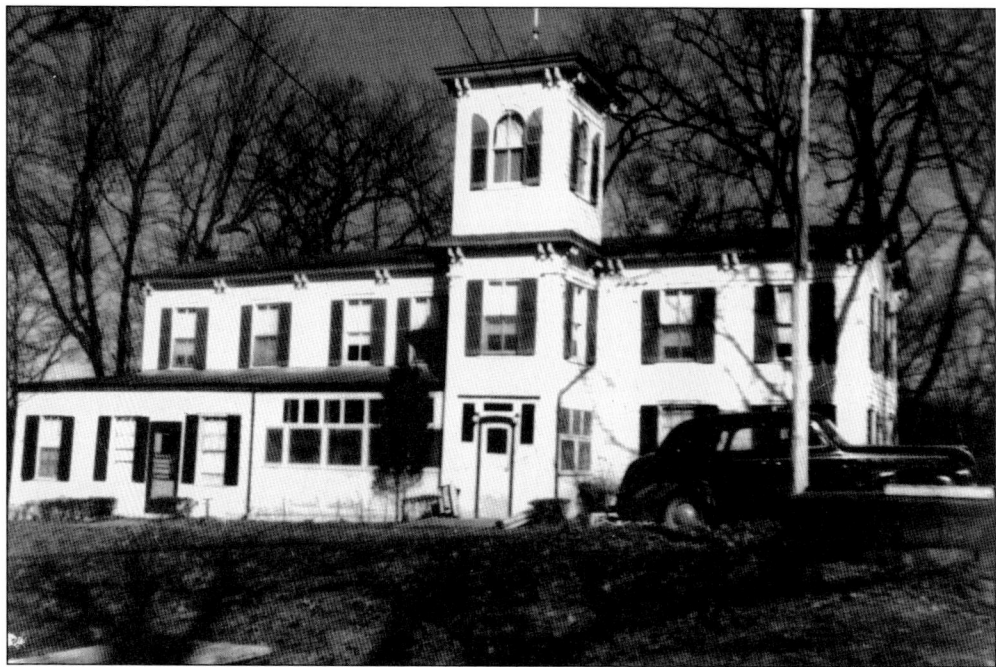

Rose Cliff Villa has long been a Legg family homestead. It is an early home not far from the Legg mills. A window frame in the cupola bears the date October 9, 1814. This cupola is the home's signature feature. The home had been extensively remodeled and contained 14 rooms in 1967. The photograph dates from the early spring of 1952. (Town of Kingston.)

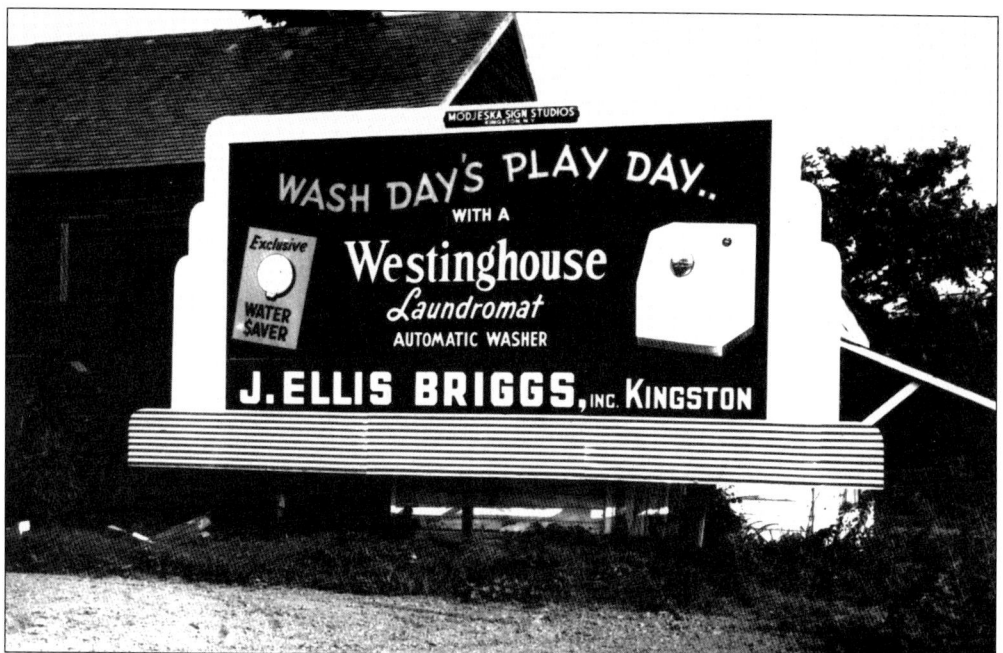

The coal, feed, and lumber businesses were closed. Because of their size and proximity to the railroad, entrepreneur J. Ellis Briggs purchased the complex from the Brinks. Briggs took advantage of the billboard already on the property to advertise his appliance business. (Donald Briggs I.)

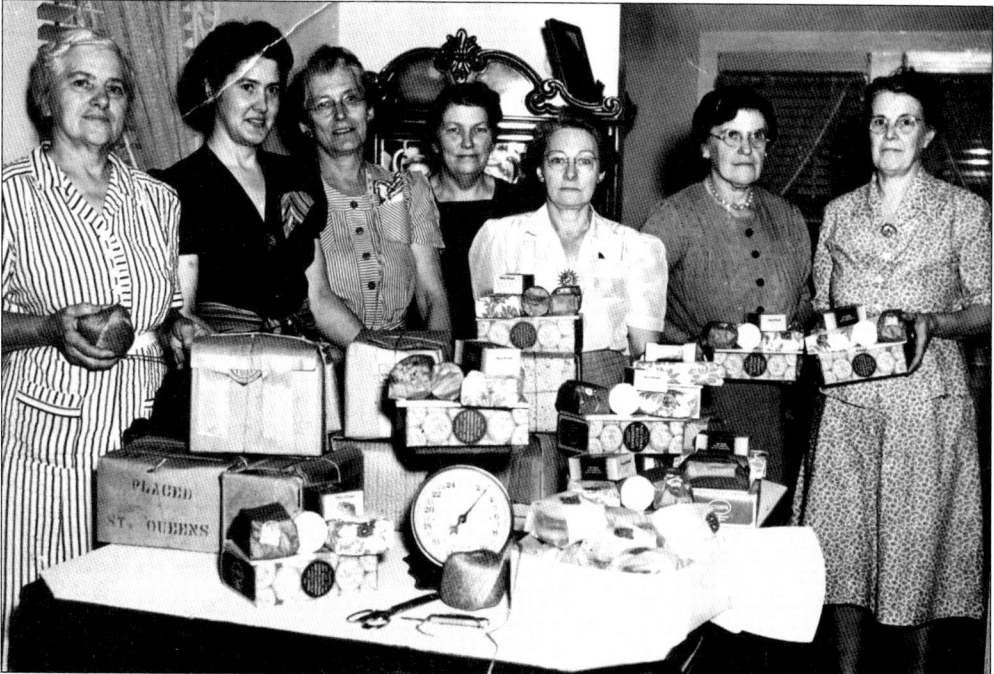

The Lake Katrine Home Department is preparing packages for servicemen during World War II. From left to right are Mrs. William Legg, Nettie Auchmoody, Margaret Gaddis, Mrs. Minner, Bessie Nichols, unidentified, and Mrs. Churchill. (Town of Ulster historian.)

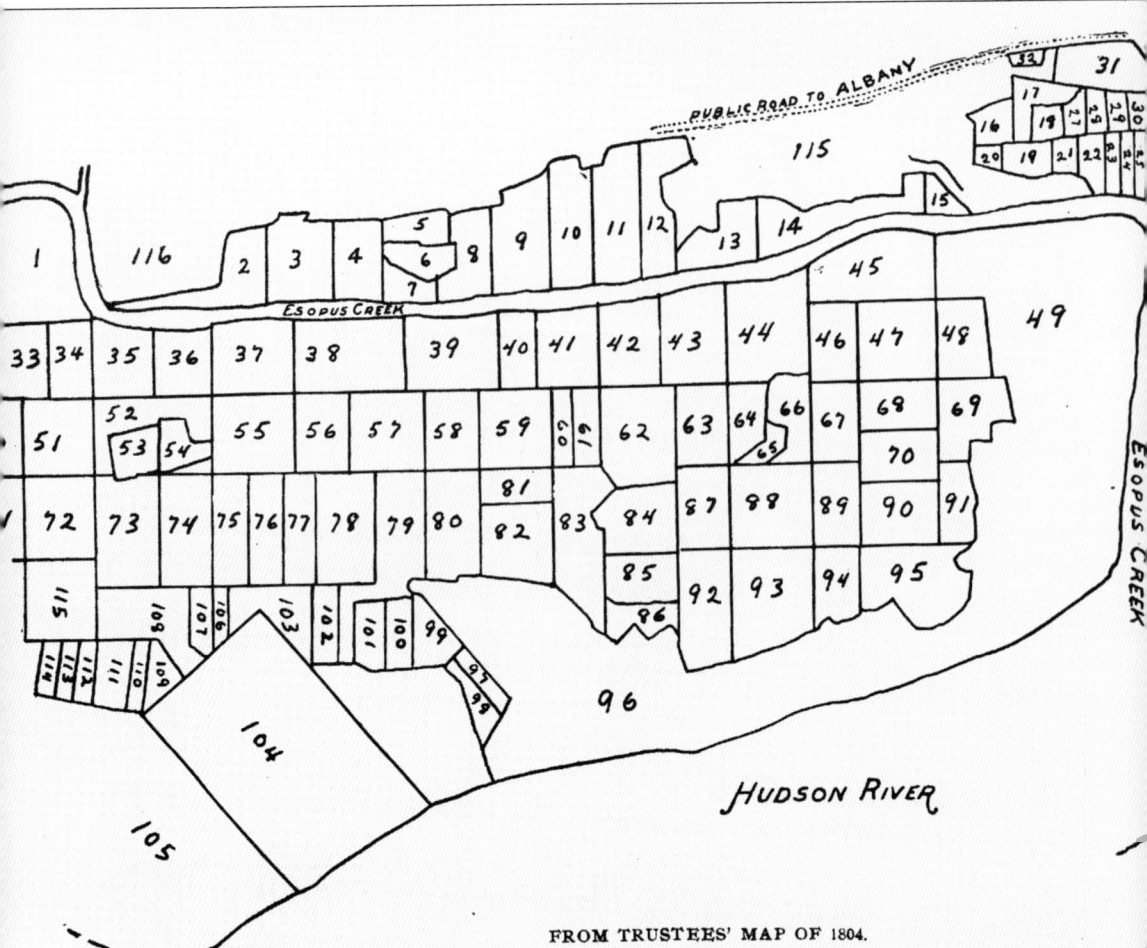

FROM TRUSTEES' MAP OF 1804.

Flatbush came early. Laid out parallel to the Hudson's River (as it was originally called), it skirted prior grants that hugged the river shore. Its name came from the early Dutch, who adopted it from the "native savages." In 1677, Kaelcop, speaker for the Lenape, had pointed out Fen-dey-ack-a-meck "the place of low bushes" encompassing hundreds of acres loosely bounded by the Groote Revier, Ka-hak-as-nik (the Sawkill), and Ma-go-was-ing-inck (Plattekill Creek), which was ceded to the inhabitants of Kingstowne for the lordly sum of a blanket, a shirt, and a loaf of bread. The Dutch rendered it Vlakke Bosch meaning "flat woods" and the English twisted it to its present form. In 1804 came the mapping and parceling out of the commons lots to the freeholders and inhabitants of Kingston. The map, seen here, is laid on its side, with north appearing to the right. With deeds in hand, the Burhans, Osterhoudts, Swarts, Leggs, and VanLeuvens settled in. The year 1808 brought the Flatbush Reform Church, erected with funds and sweat equity contributed by the community on land from the farm of Hendrick E. Schoonmaker. Built in a location central to the congregation, the church still stands on the Het Kalkoen Pot, the road to Turkey Point. (Flatbush Reformed Church.)

Six
ON THE HUDSON RIVER IN FLATBUSH AND EAST KINGSTON

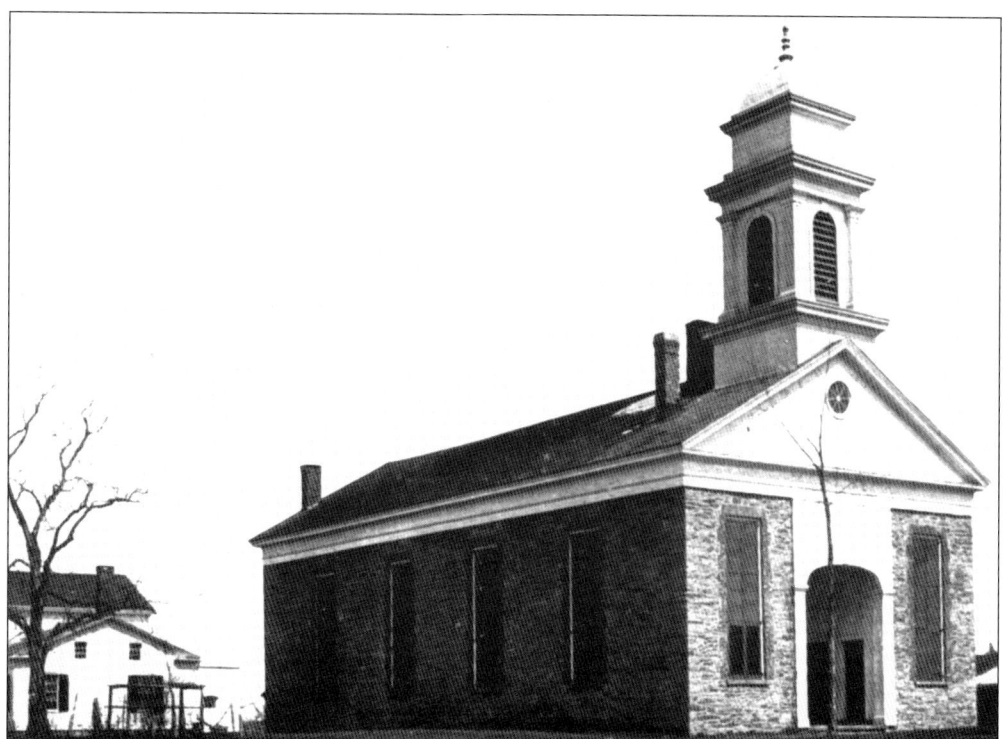

In 1907, the Reformed Protestant Dutch Church of Flatbush had already been enlarged twice and received the addition of a bell tower and a parsonage. Initially the settlers of Vlakke Bosch made the long and sometimes difficult journey to Kingston or Katsbann "for the enjoyment of their religious privileges." As the community grew, visiting domines arrived to administer the sacraments in schoolhouses, homes, or even the convenient barn of Peter Osterhoudt. (Flatbush Reformed Church.)

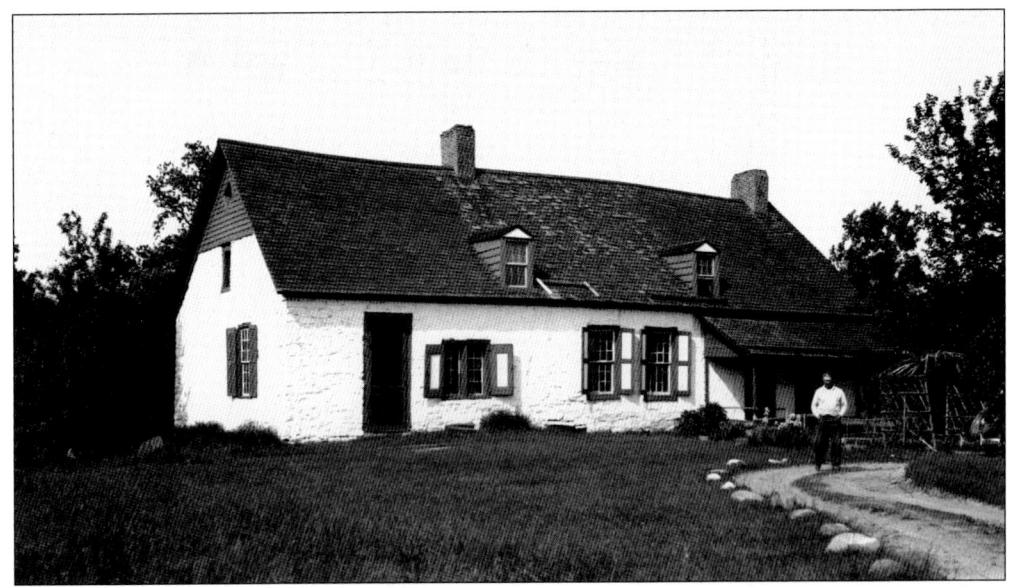

Anchoring the southern end of Flatbush is the Benjamin Ten Broeck house, one of the more important houses in the Hudson valley, having found mention in both *The Early Stone Houses of Ulster County* by Myron S. Teller and *Dutch Houses in the Hudson Valley Before 1776* by Helen Wilkinson Reynolds. The structure is a one-and-a-half-story stone house with clapboarded upper gables. The eastern and oldest section shows remains of a granary door. (Library of Congress.)

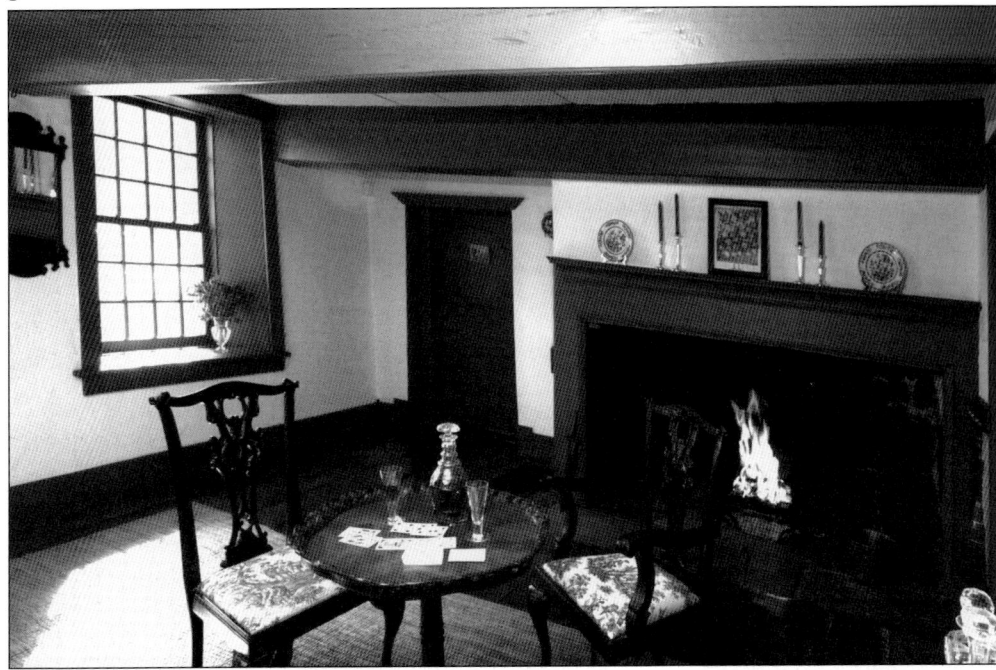

The center section bears an inscribed date of 1751 with the western and newest section carrying a date of 1765. Notable preserved elements are two casement windows, one with original glazing and shutters, probably installed by Myron Teller, and three fireplaces. A third casement window from the oldest part of the house was taken to Winterthur Museum and can be seen in the Ulster Room. (Rob Sweeny.)

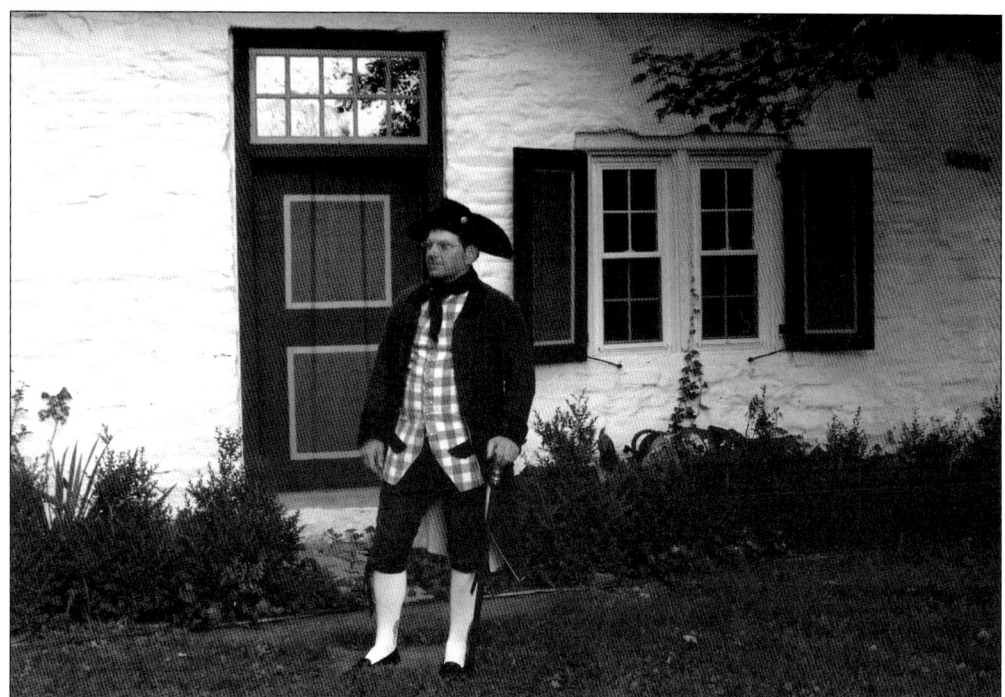

The Junior League survey says that the house began as a tenant farmer home on an estate. This is possible for the earliest third built by Johannes Maxmilion; however, the remainder of the structure's design and craftsmanship is consistent with that of a well-to-do landowner. It is unlikely that the house was a tenant home for very long. The door is a reproduction installed by the current owner.

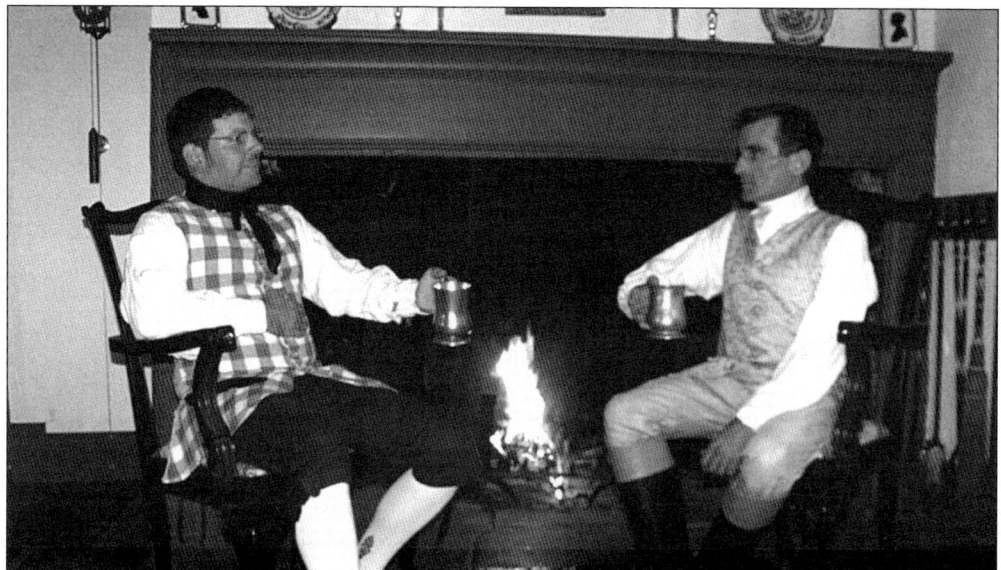

History comes alive when one plays an active roll. Here Johannes Snyder (left) and Edward Whittaker relax over a bit of grog. Whittaker manages farms for absentee Tory landlords. "It has been a sad and sorry year for the wheat crop," he writes them. It seems that for every wagonload headed to market, two have surreptitiously hit the road in search of the Continental army.

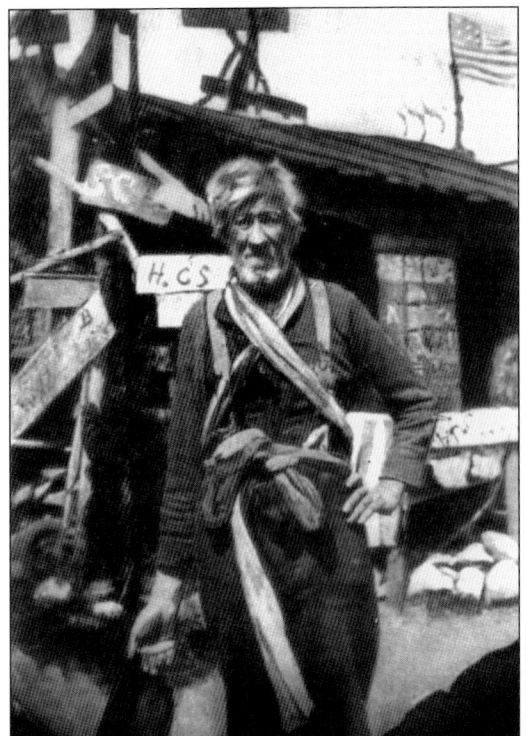

Tobias "Boots" Van Steenburgh was born in the old family homestead in Kingston city but spent most of his life in Flatbush. He was said to have been "friendly and harmless," nevertheless his eccentric ways brought him some local notoriety. Tales of him appeared more than once in newspapers of the 1870s and 1880s. In 1876, his photograph even appeared in *Harpers Weekly*. Boots was extremely patriotic and when he could not afford to buy a flag, he sewed his own. He apologized for not being able to make small enough stars. (Town of Kingston.)

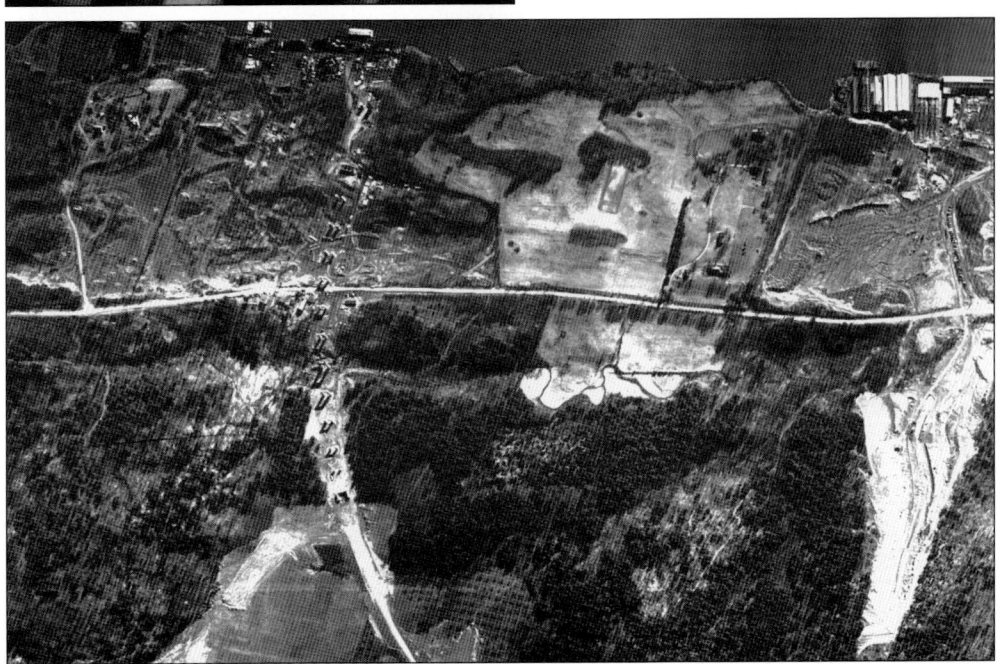

Look closely to see what all the construction is about. To the left of center are the brand-new piers that will hold up the Kingston Rhinecliff bridge. The bridge was constructed in 1955–1956 over the grounds of the former Goldricks and Rose brickyards. The bridge's overall length is 7,793 feet, and it opened to public traffic on February 2, 1957. The initial cost was $17.5 million, and it carried 7,630,370 vehicles in 2007. (Ulster town clerk.)

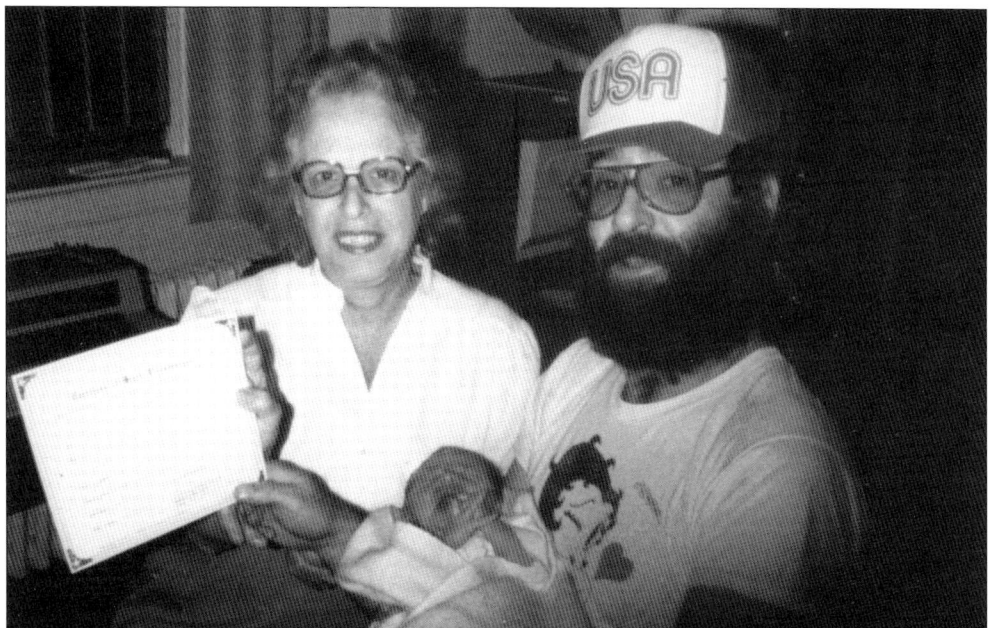

Delivered by his dad high atop the Kingston-Rhinecliff Bridge, Michael E. Garrity II entered this world on Flag Day 1984, heralded by a chorus of construction jackhammers. Rhinebeck town clerk Fanny MacPhail is handing Michael's birth certificate to his father, Mike Garrity. Dad is quoted as saying, "It was an awesome experience. I am very proud that the good lord saw fit to deliver my son directly into my hands."

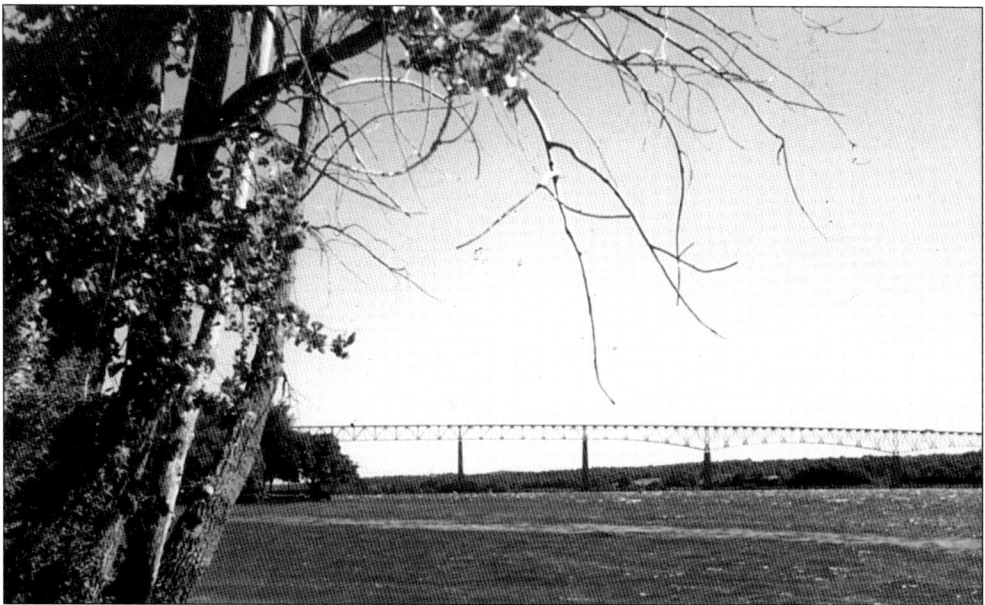

The elegant Rhinecliff Bridge is over a mile long and carries traffic across the Hudson River between Ulster and Dutchess Counties. On July 10, 1947, the New York State Bridge Authority authorized designer David Bernard Steinman to proceed with preliminary designs and surveys. Steinman's original plans called for the bridge to be of a suspension design and located approximately two miles south of its present location.

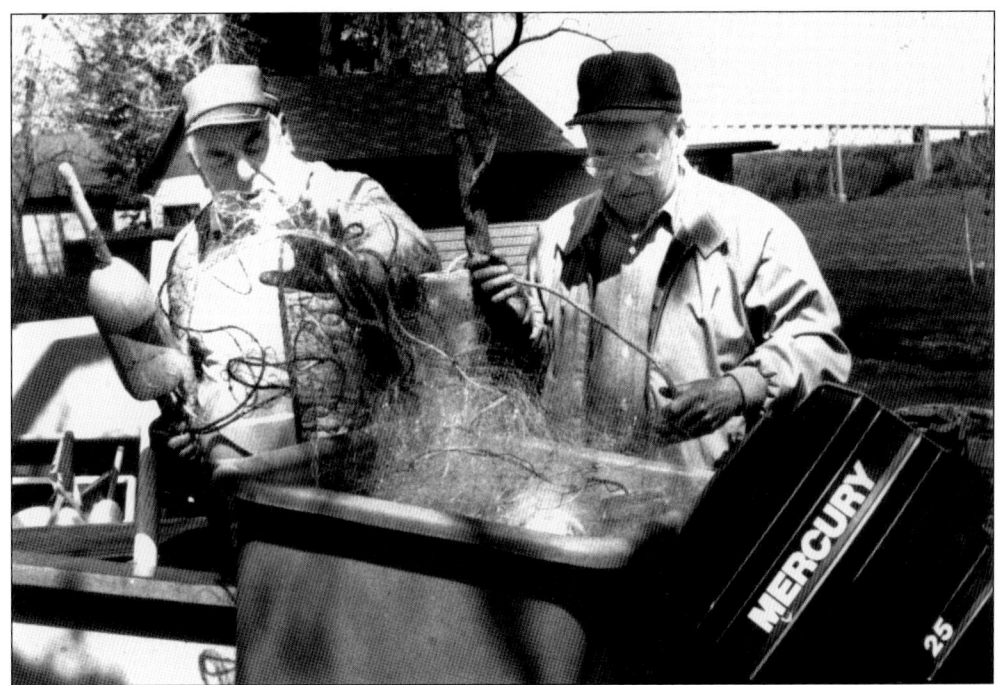

When forsythia and serviceberry blossom it is time to cast nets for shad. The season runs until the lilacs bloom. Former Rondout harbormaster Mike Turk is taking his brother Tommy fishing. Shad, the largest member of the herring family, is smoked or pickled and used to make salmagundi. This tasty Dutch invention was designed to keep well on long voyages. It was a staple aboard ships in the days of Capt. William Kidd. (Bob Haines.)

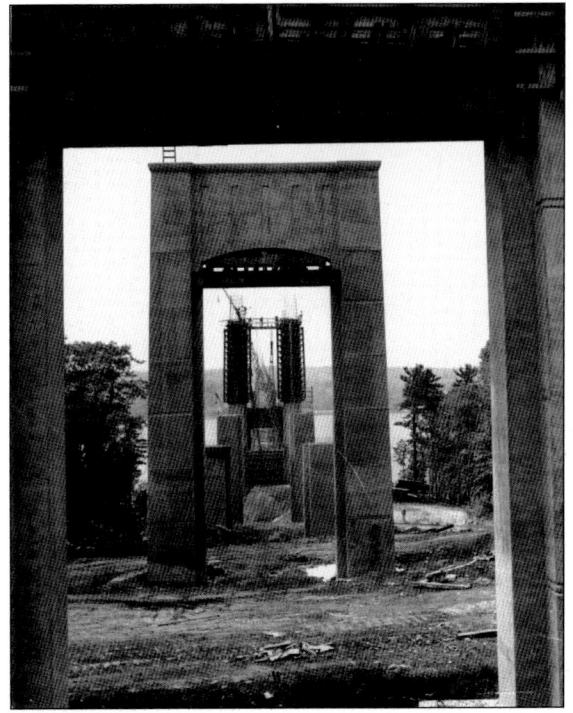

The Rhinecliff Bridge piers are under construction in 1953. In 2003, the New York State Bridge Authority wished to restore an access road and dock through the former Rose brickyard property, which had been foreclosed for taxes in 1941. The archaeologist for the project could not determine where the brickworks had been. Luckily a newspaper story alerted descendants of the former owner. They came to the rescue and pointed out building sites and dockages. (Bob Haines.)

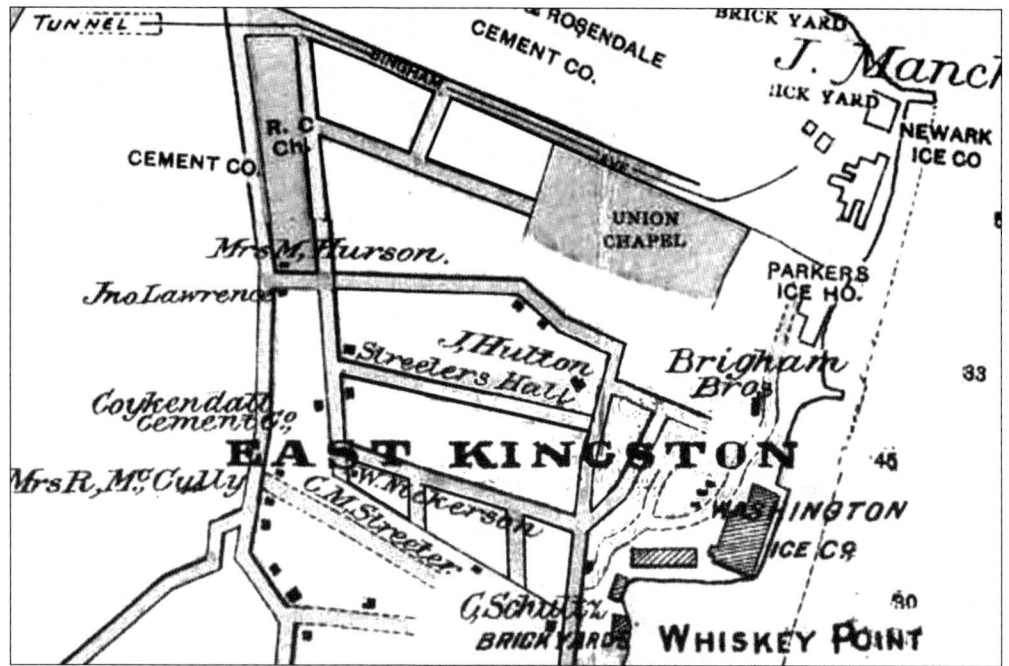

Identified as the Flatbush Precinct lots in 1874, two years later the same area was mapped into 278 lots called the village of East Kingston and was still owned by John Hutton Jr. Brigham Avenue covers the tracks of the horse-drawn railroad that led through the tunnel to the cement works quarries. The Newark Ice Company, owned and operated by the cement company, provided winter work for the men and horses. (Town of Ulster.)

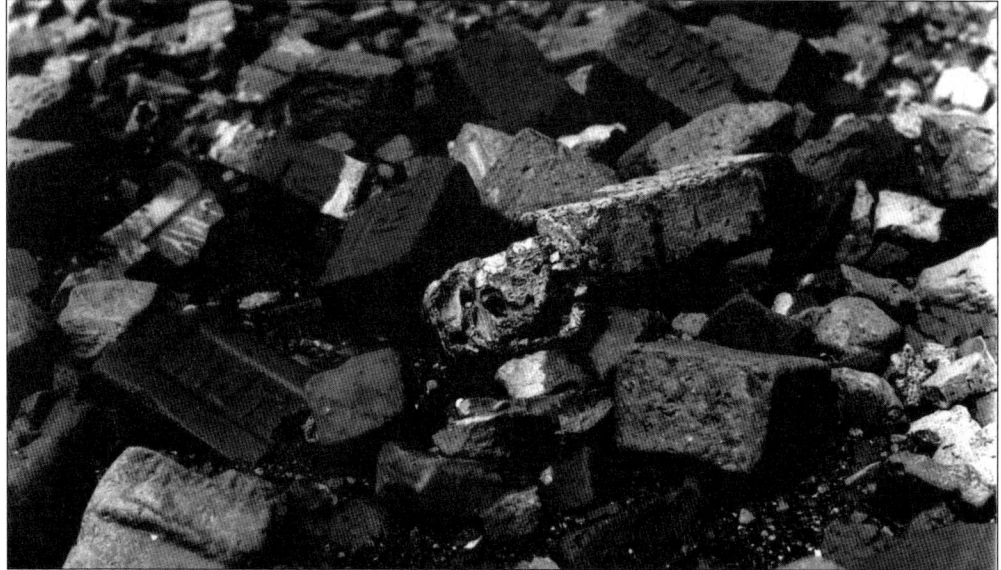

Living most of his life in the brickyard village where he was born at home in 1925, Pat Clausi spent much of his working life making bricks and cement. In 1946, he started at Star Brick (now Charles Ryder Park) as automation came in. When Star ceased operations, Clausi moved downriver to Hudson Cement, until it closed in 1981. Today Clausi keeps East Kingston's history alive with his scrapbooks, artifacts, and memories. (Susan Wick.)

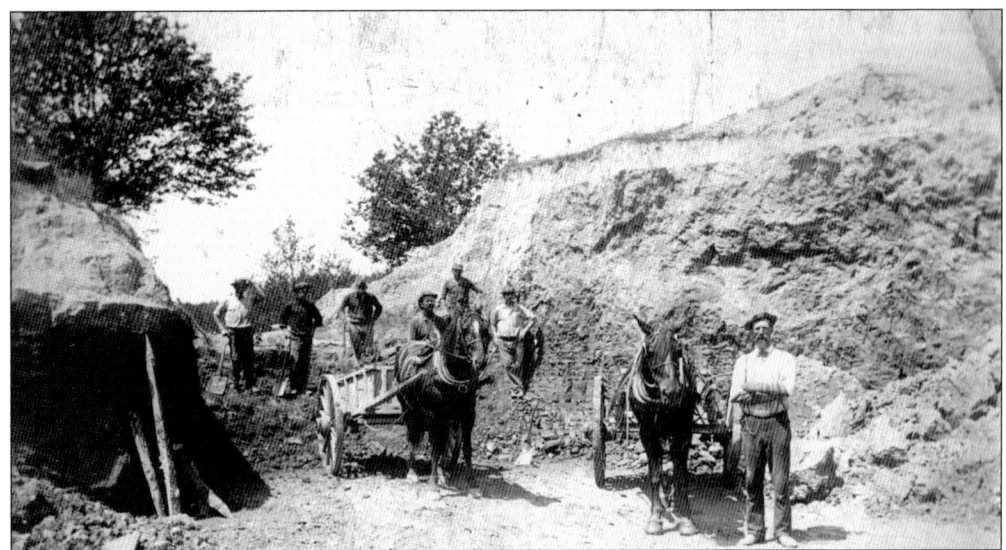

Most brickyards had their own clay banks but those in East Kingston were blessed with deposits of blue clay—clay with superior firing and strength characteristics. It was mixed with regular clay in carefully measured amounts. As deposits were depleted, wagons and men had to haul the raw material from somewhat greater distances. This led to the use of horse-drawn railroads and later locomotive-drawn versions. (Hudson River Maritime Museum.)

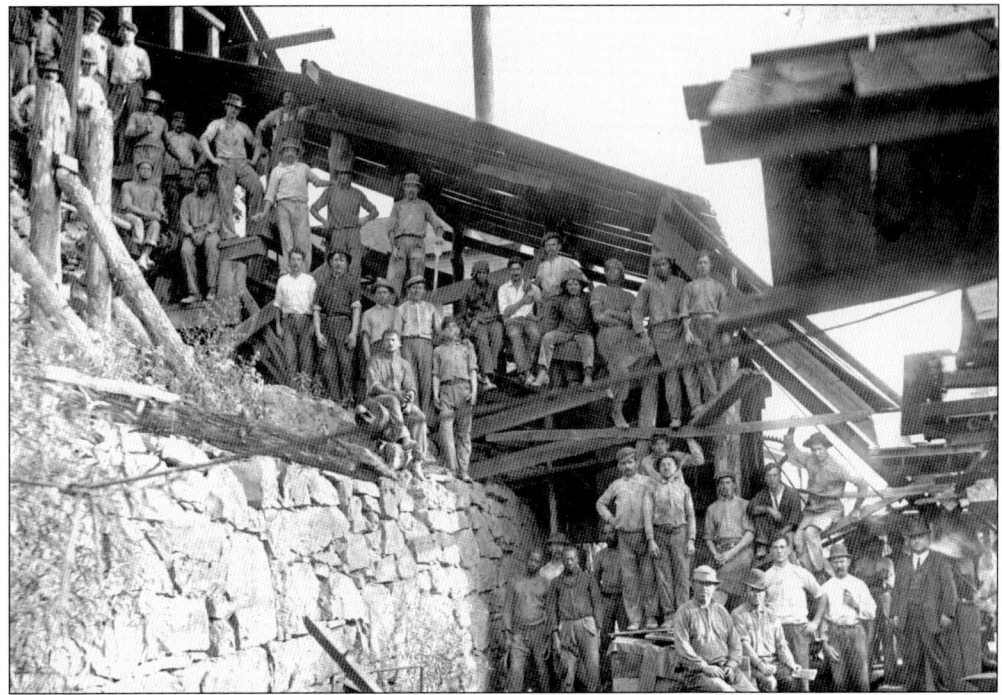

This is one shift at the Lynch brickyard around 1900: 43 men and their supervisor (at right). Italians, Irish, Germans, blacks, and others worked closely together, often trusting their lives to their partners with little thought of racial differences. A close inspection of the photograph will also show boys. No women are shown, however, their time for workplace equality had not yet arrived. (Hudson River Maritime Museum.)

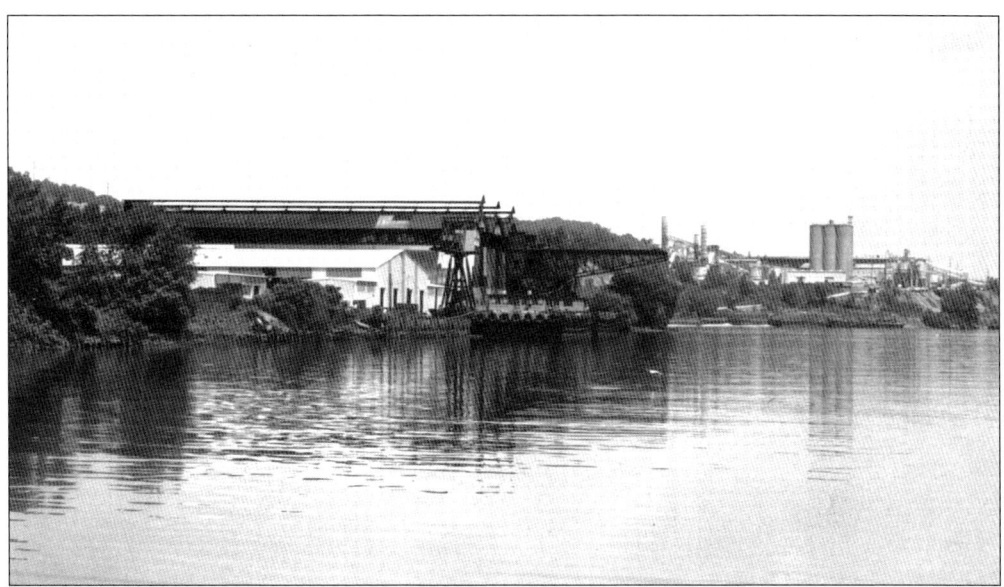

In the foreground is the Hutton brickyard and to the rear is Hudson Cement. The year is 1969 and the cement industry is still alive, served by both a railroad and river barges. Major complexes like these and many smaller ones once lined the western shore of the Hudson River leaving the slopes of the eastern shore for the estates of landed gentry. (Bob Haines.)

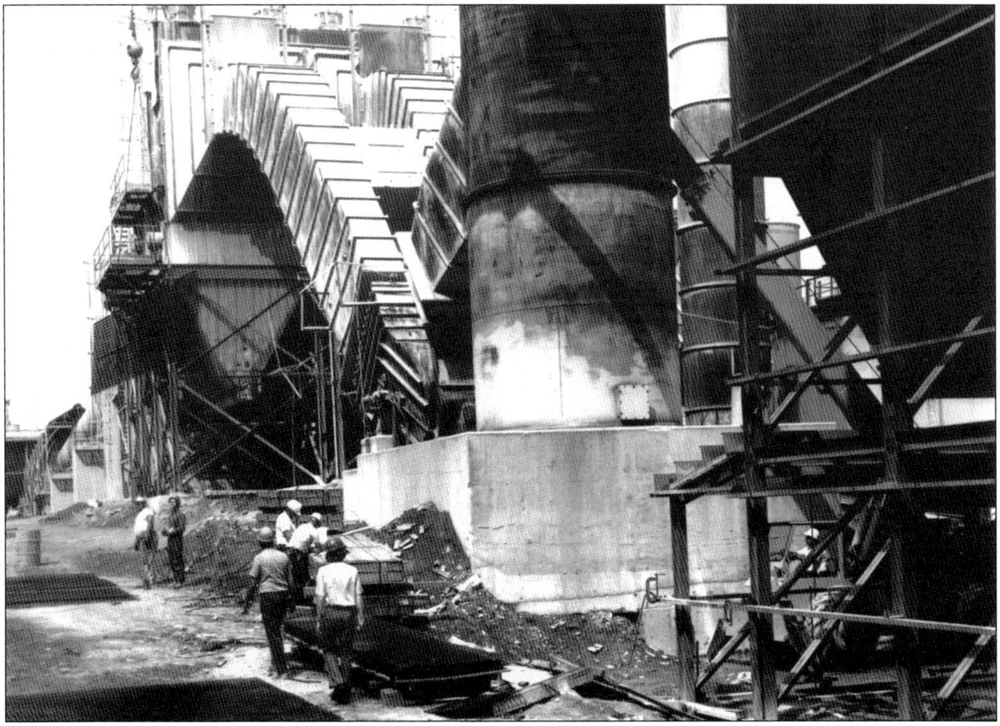

Here massive dust collectors are installed at Hudson Cement in the mid-1970s. The cement kilns burned trainloads of coal and generated both soot and stone dust that were potentially detrimental to the environment and to workers' health. This was a successful effort to minimize that problem. (Bob Haines.)

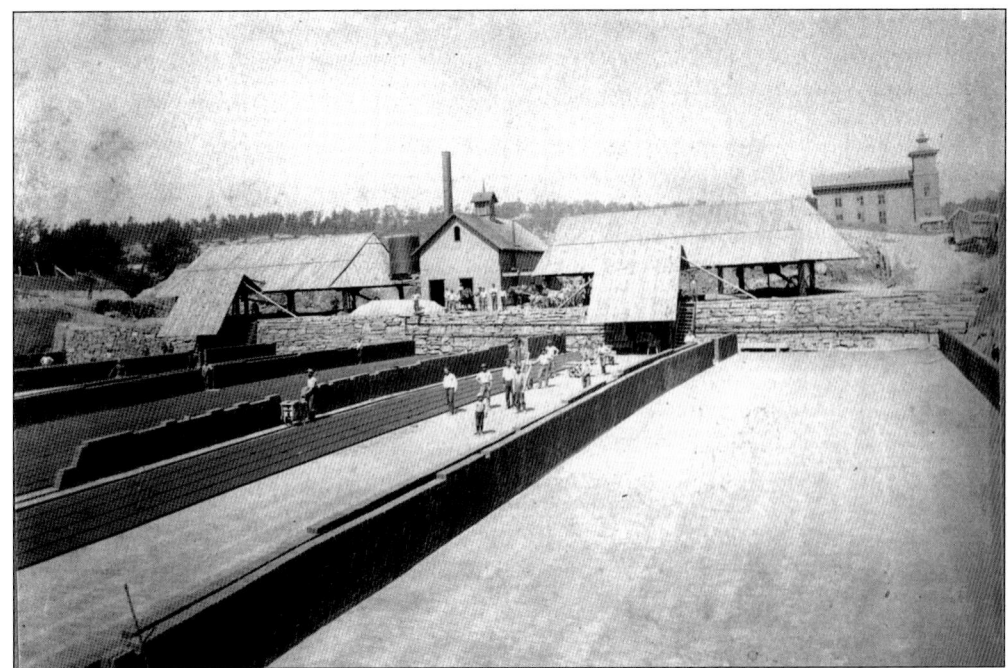

The Brigham brickyard drying yard is seen around 1900. After mixing and molding, the bricks were laid out by the thousands to air dry before being fired in high-temperature kilns made of the bricks themselves. The lines where bricks have been picked up can be seen at the right. Clay is still delivered by horses (rear), but under the chimney stands a powerhouse to run the two sets of mixing machinery. (Hudson River Maritime Museum.)

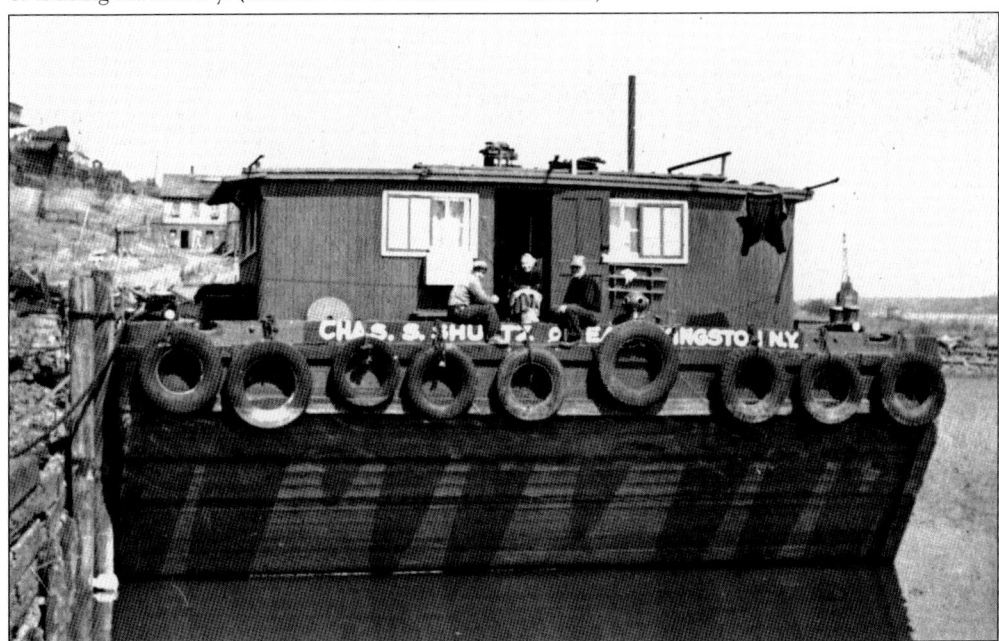

The Charles S. Shultz Boat Company of Kingston supplied both tugs and barges to transport bricks down the river to the large cities. It appears that this barge is home to a family as evidenced by the people—one young and two middle aged—the curtains, and laundry hanging to dry. (Pat Clausi.)

During the heyday of the brickyards, children were let out of school just before noon for their lunch hour. They would hurry home and pick up their father's lunch pails to carry to the brickyards as the noon whistle blew. Many carried extra pails for men who had no children currently in the school. Vince DeLuca carried Ed Post's pail and was paid $1 a week, plus Ed would share his desert with Vince. Here Vince shows his father's pail. There were three sections, the bottom for hot food like soup or stew, the center for potatoes and similar warm food, and the top for dessert.

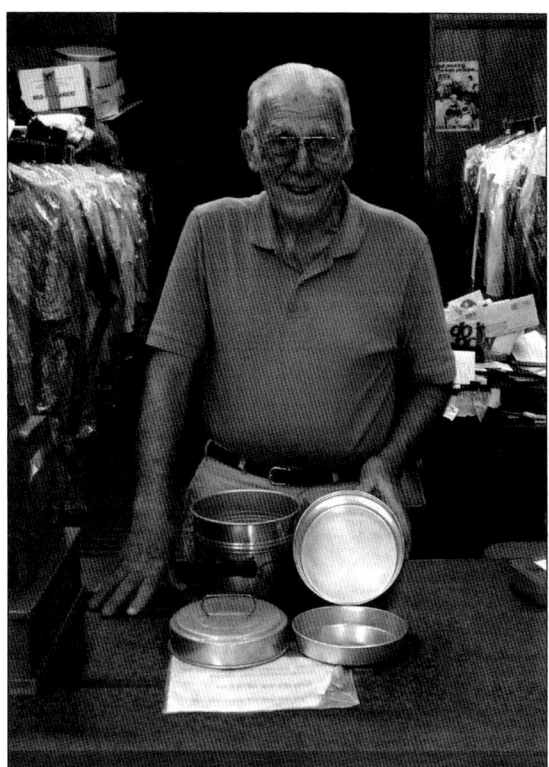

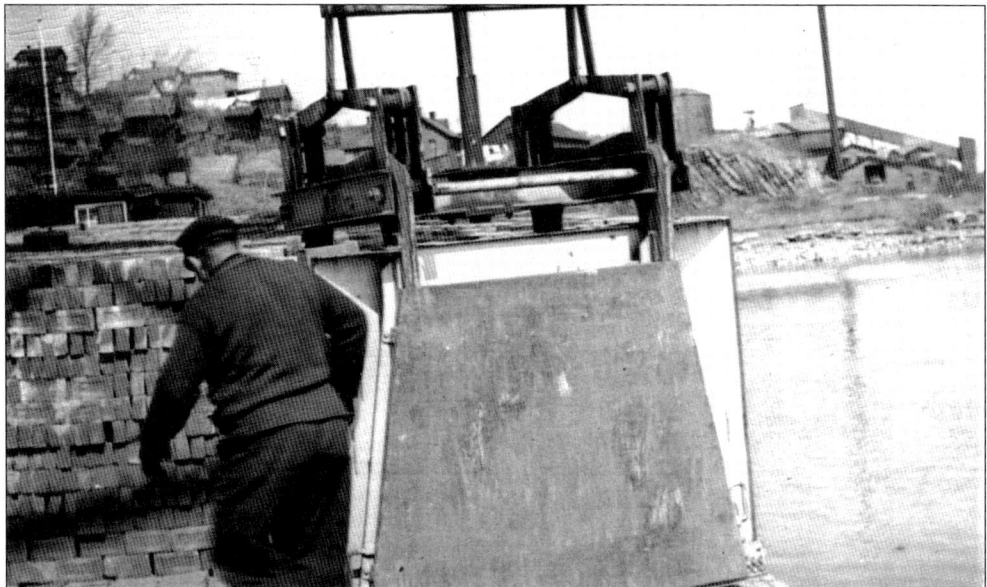

In the early days of brick making, men would roll flat wheelbarrows of finished brick up or down (depending on the state of the tide) ramps onto barges. Others would unload and restack on the barges. This was very labor intensive. After machinery became more available, cranes were used to speed loading and removed the need for restacking. Here a special device places a full pallet of brick at a time. It needed only an operator and a man to position it. This is at Hutton brickyard. (Pat Clausi.)

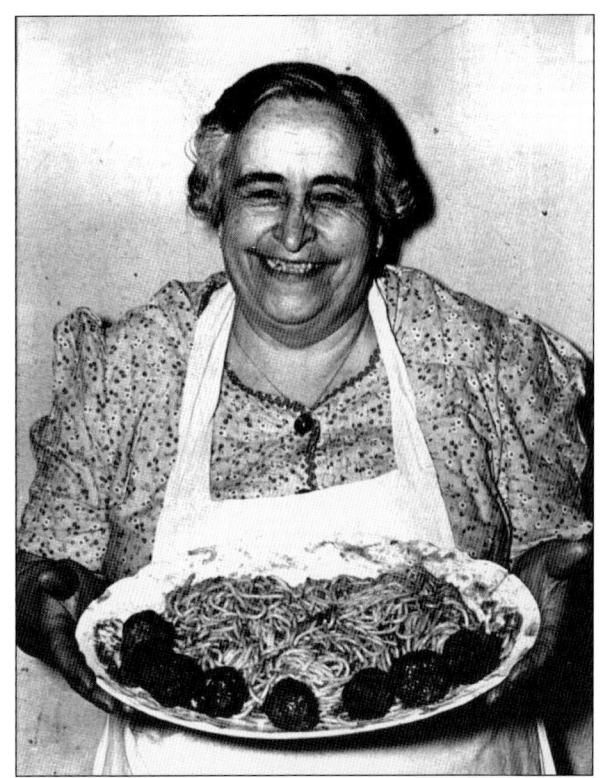

Angeline Berardi "Mama" Fiore ran Fiore's Bar and Grill with her husband. The locals called it the "five-and-ten." Mama was known for her massive plates of spaghetti. Large bowls of marinated hot peppers sat on the bar as free appetizers. The more of these one ate, the more the taps flowed. Local teenagers brought her small game and she would host free rabbit dinners for the neighborhood. (Pat Clausi.)

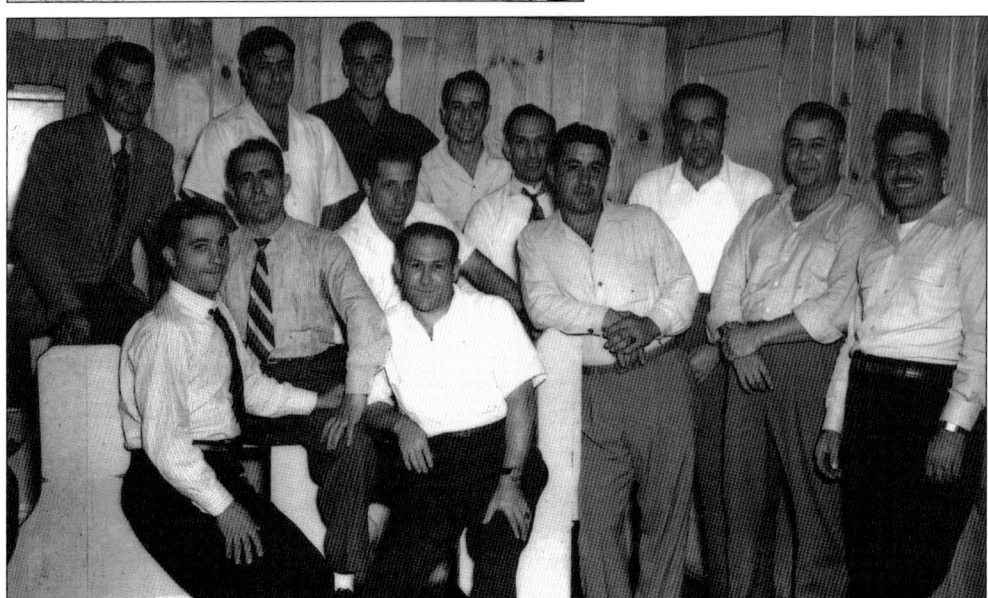

This is the 1951–1952 championship murra (morra) team lounging at Tommy's Restaurant on High Street in Kingston. From left to right are (first row) Charles Tiano, Joseph Mitchell, Thomas Berardi, Joseph Guido, and Michael Pugliese; (second row) George Fay, John Mauro, Joseph Fiore, Thomas Clausi, Michael Tiano, Charles Machione, Julius Chick, and James Gallo. Morra was a game known in ancient Rome as micatio. It is a contest of skill and prediction still played in many nations, particularly Sardinia. (Pat Clausi.)

Tall and debonair with an infectious smile, Harold "Bo" Jones was a gentleman. Born and raised in East Kingston, Jones was also a first-rate promoter. In the 1920s, he organized and managed the Goldenrods, Kingston's first and only black baseball team. A fountain of community spirit, Jones was especially concerned about making life good for the children. There were no strangers in Jones's life, only friends he had not met yet. (Mrs. Geraldine Blake.)

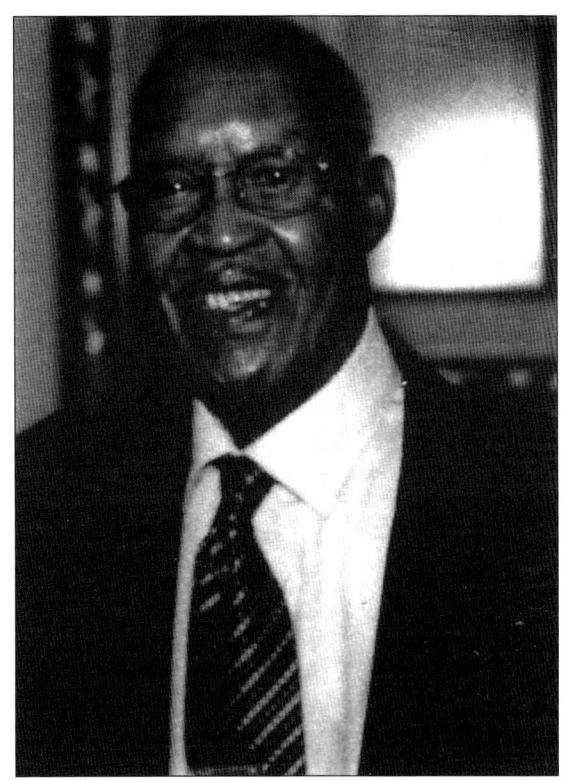

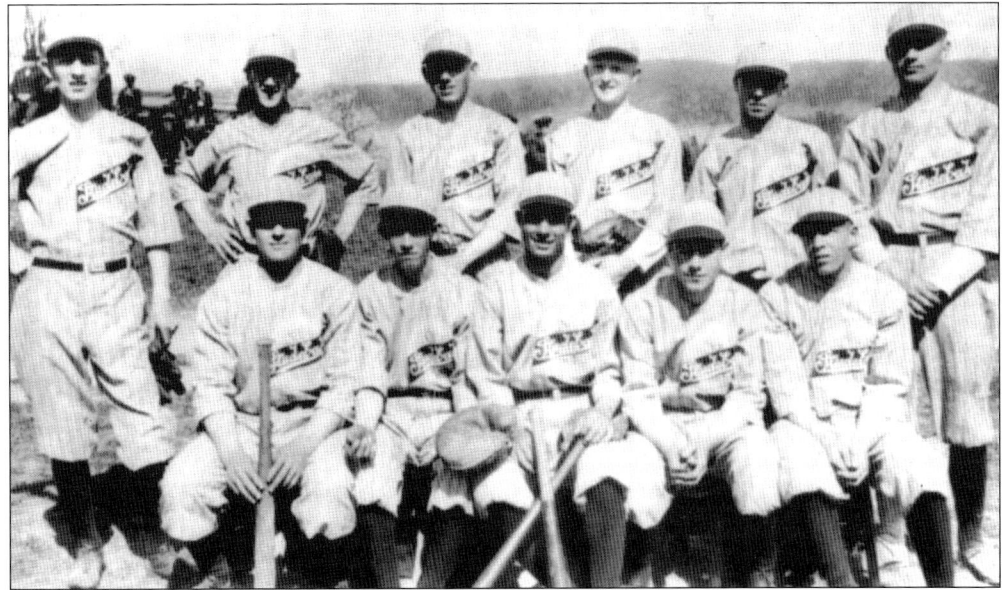

This is Studebaker's baseball team of East Kingston. This was one of several ball teams hosted by the hamlet. They even had a basketball team, which was the Catholic Youth Organization champions in 1952. From left to right are (first row) John (Jack) Watzka, William (Bill) McNally, Louis "Coke" Tiano, Francis "Cap" Moran, and Leo Vertetis; (second row) Thomas (Tommy) Davitt, Frank Smith, Marty Carr, John (Johnny) Hurson, Frank Flanigan, and Dewey VanBeuren. (Pat Clausi.)

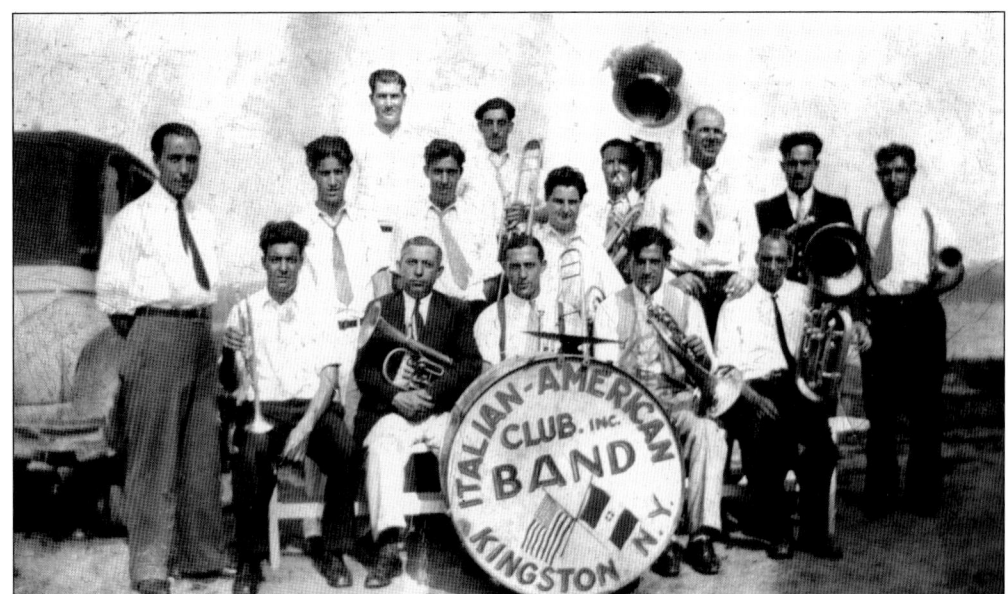

Sal Castiglione (left) poses in 1931 with his East Kingston band. They practiced in the basement of (what is now) Pat Clausi's house until the church hall was built. Seen from left to right are (first row) Joe DeLuca, Frank Castiglione, and Frank DeLuca; (second row) Al DeLuca, Sam Golazano, Mickey Mazzuca, John Emmet, Tom "Chick" Carpino, and Frank Tiano; (third row) Jim Maccaline, Brosh Coniglio, unidentified, Chief Fuscardo, and Frank "Shorty" Mitchell. (Vince DeLuca.)

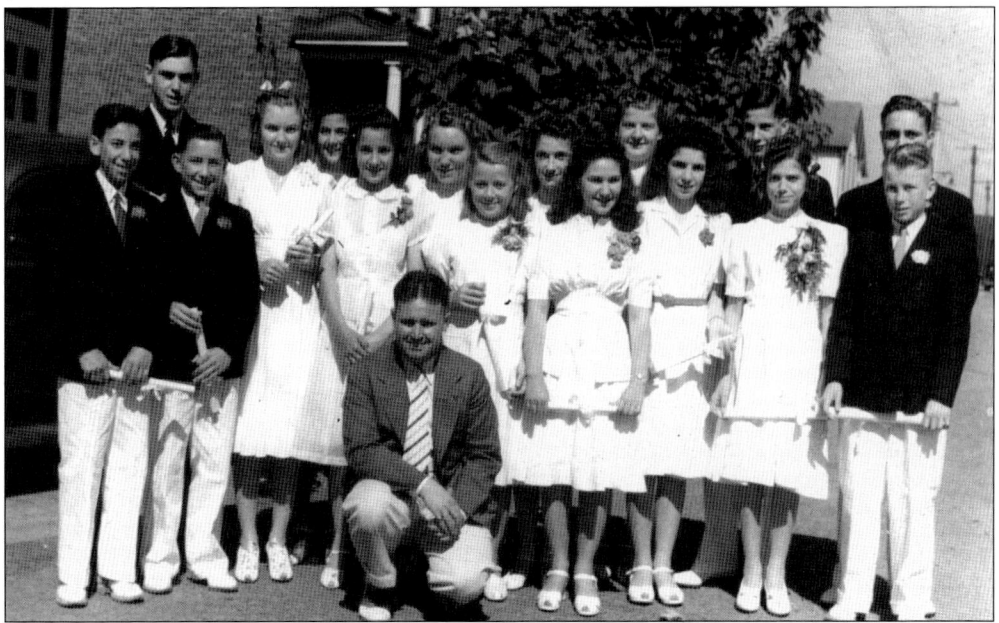

The 1940 East Kingston School graduates are seen here. In 1937, these students made front-page news, going on strike to protest the removal of two favorite teachers. The betrothed couple was rumored to have kissed in the coatroom. This displeased several trustees. Led by Dolly Fiori and Peggy Clausi, the children marched the streets for a month singing songs of protest. After an election of two new trustees, the teachers were reinstated. (Vince DeLuca.)

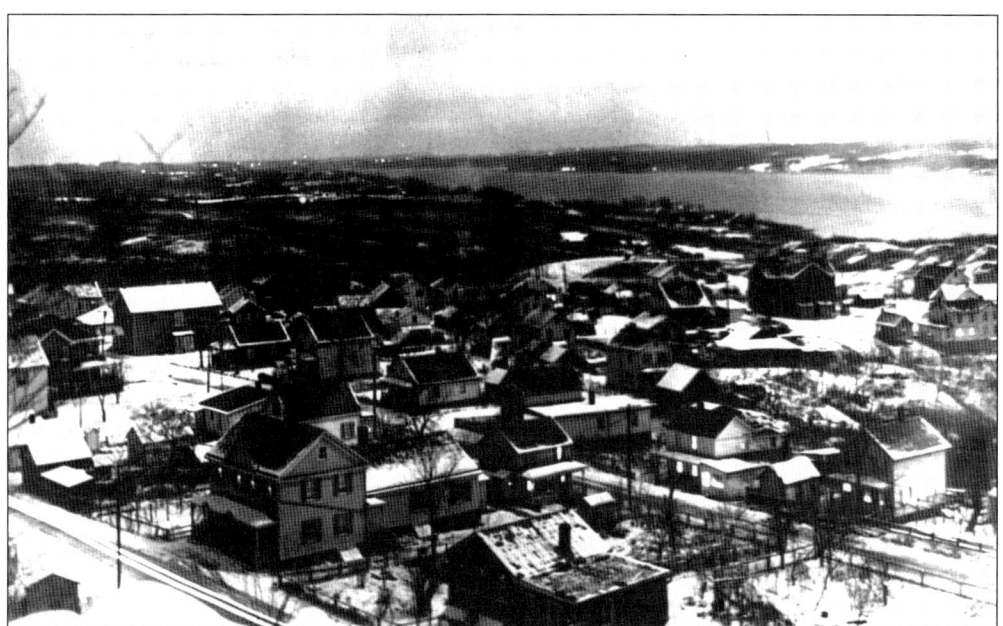

This c. 1890 view of East Kingston shows a mix of middle-class houses and smaller homes. At the far right is the school. East Kingston was a brick, cement, and ice industry town inhabited by European immigrants. The village was created from lands of John Hutton on February 16, 1876. To the far rear is the pathway of the horse-drawn railroad from the Hudson River to the clay banks. (Pat Clausi.)

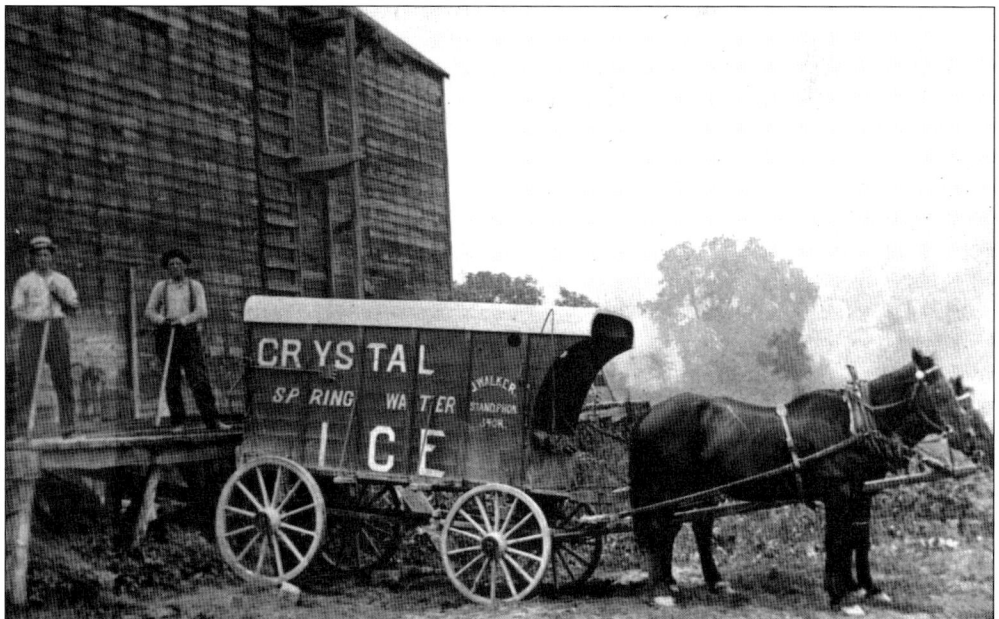

Seen here is a typical ice delivery wagon from around 1890 used by small icehouses. When the ice industry is mentioned, many picture huge icehouses lining the banks of the Hudson River from the salt line to the north country. There were also many small interior icehouses that cut from lakes, ponds, and streams. Some of these are still extant, for example a small version on Main Street in Ruby. (Town of Kingston.)

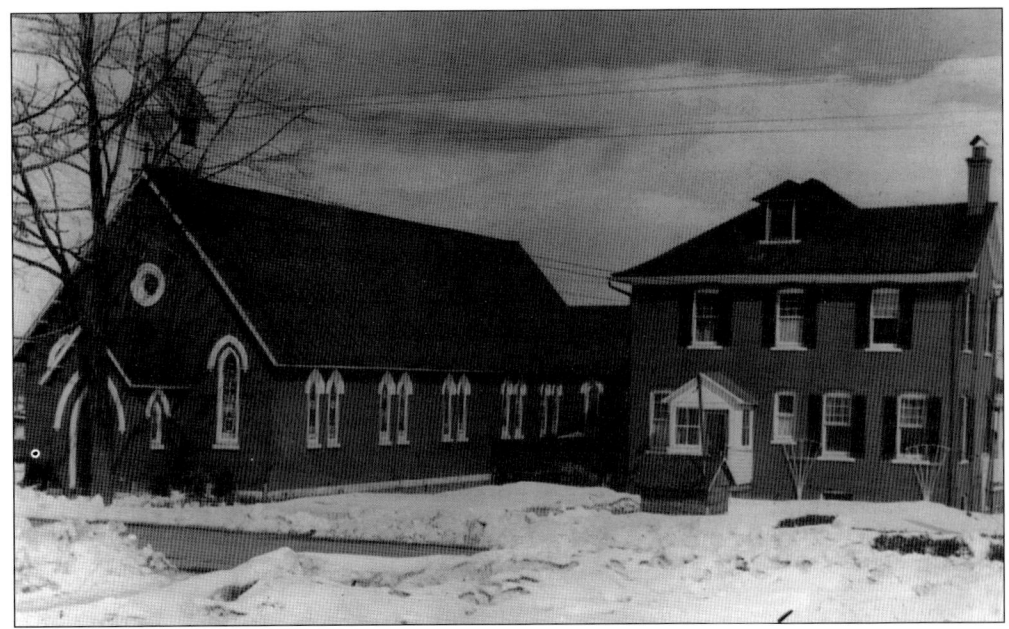

St. Coleman's Roman Catholic Church was established to serve the spiritual needs of the large catholic population of East Kingston. This photograph was taken in the 1930s, but the structures and faith of the parishioners remain largely unchanged. The East Kingston Methodist Church was active during the days of brick and cement but now stands silent. St. Coleman's is the surviving church of the two. (Pat Clausi.)

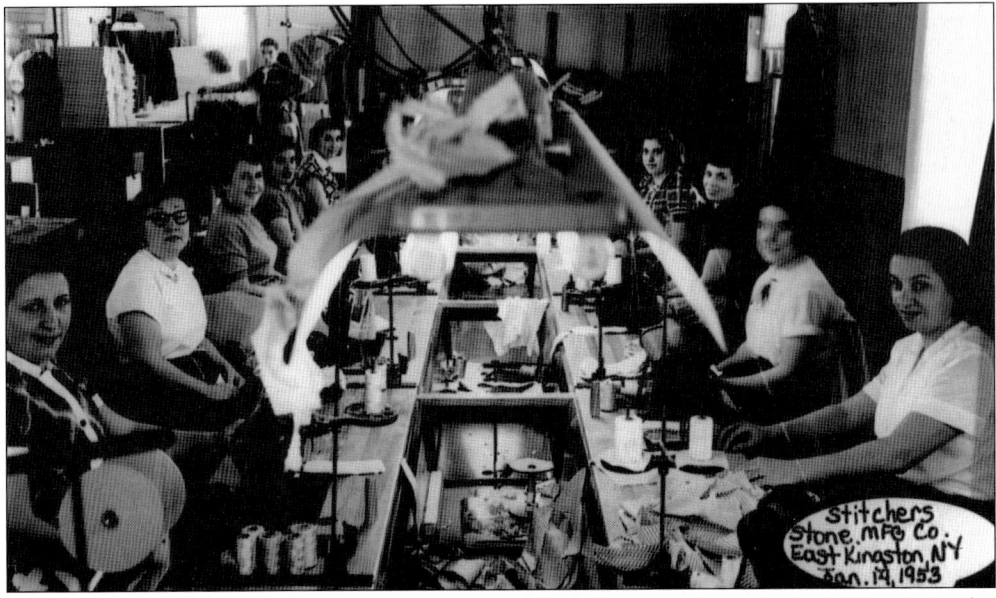

The Stone Manufacturing Company was active in East Kingston through the 1950s. A similar photograph of a larger room shows three rows of tables and machines. The company made men's shirts and Judy Bond blouses for the New York City market. Seen here are, clockwise beginning at the left, Frances McCullough, Gertrude Mitchell, Marie Puglese-Miller, Betty Alecca, Angie Shabot, Eva Gardecke Clausi, unidentified, unidentified, and Emma Tiano Berardi. (Pat Clausi.)

There were two benevolent organizations in East Kingston, St. Liberata's and St. John's. They both provided supplemental income for the sick and eventually merged. Vince Deluca described them as precursors to HMOs. The statue holds donations of money pinned there by the faithful during the annual celebration. (Pat Clausi.)

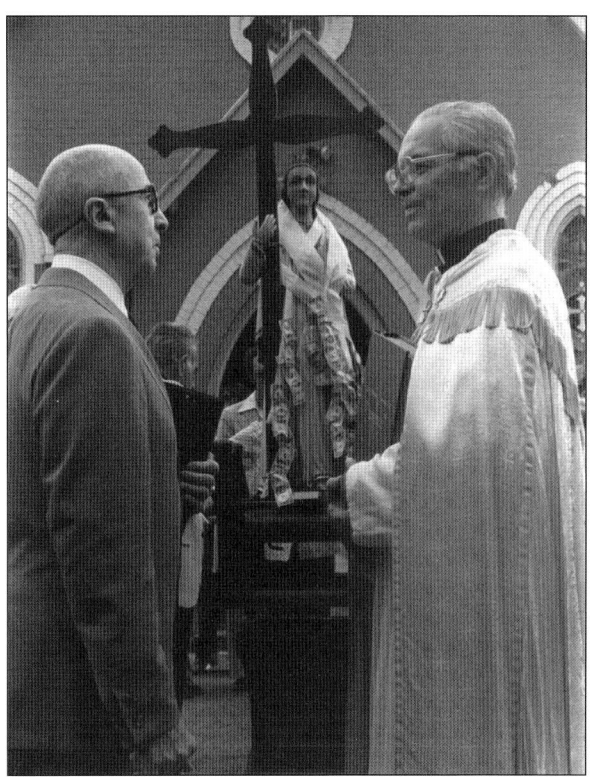

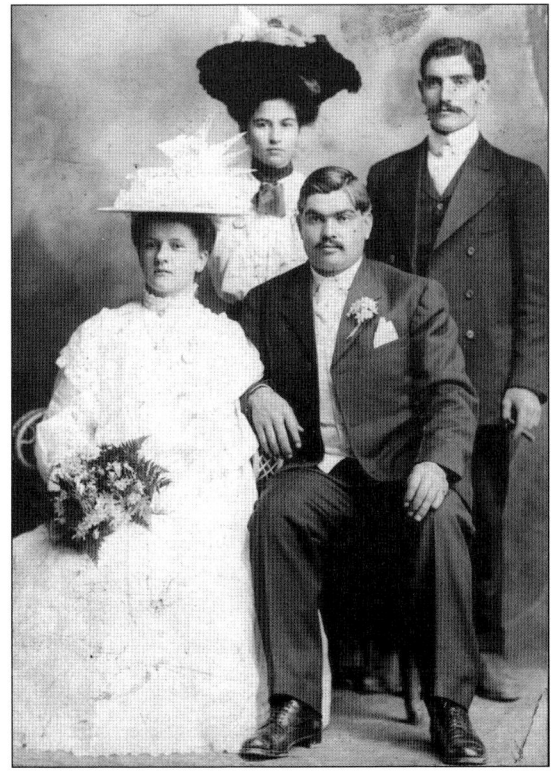

This is the wedding portrait of Irma and Michael DeCicco, who were married on January 18, 1908. The attendants were Mr. and Mrs. Belisto. Michael DeCicco served as justice of the peace for the town of Ulster from 1914 until 1924 and again from 1927 until 1935, and they had a daughter named Eva. (Town of Ulster historian.)

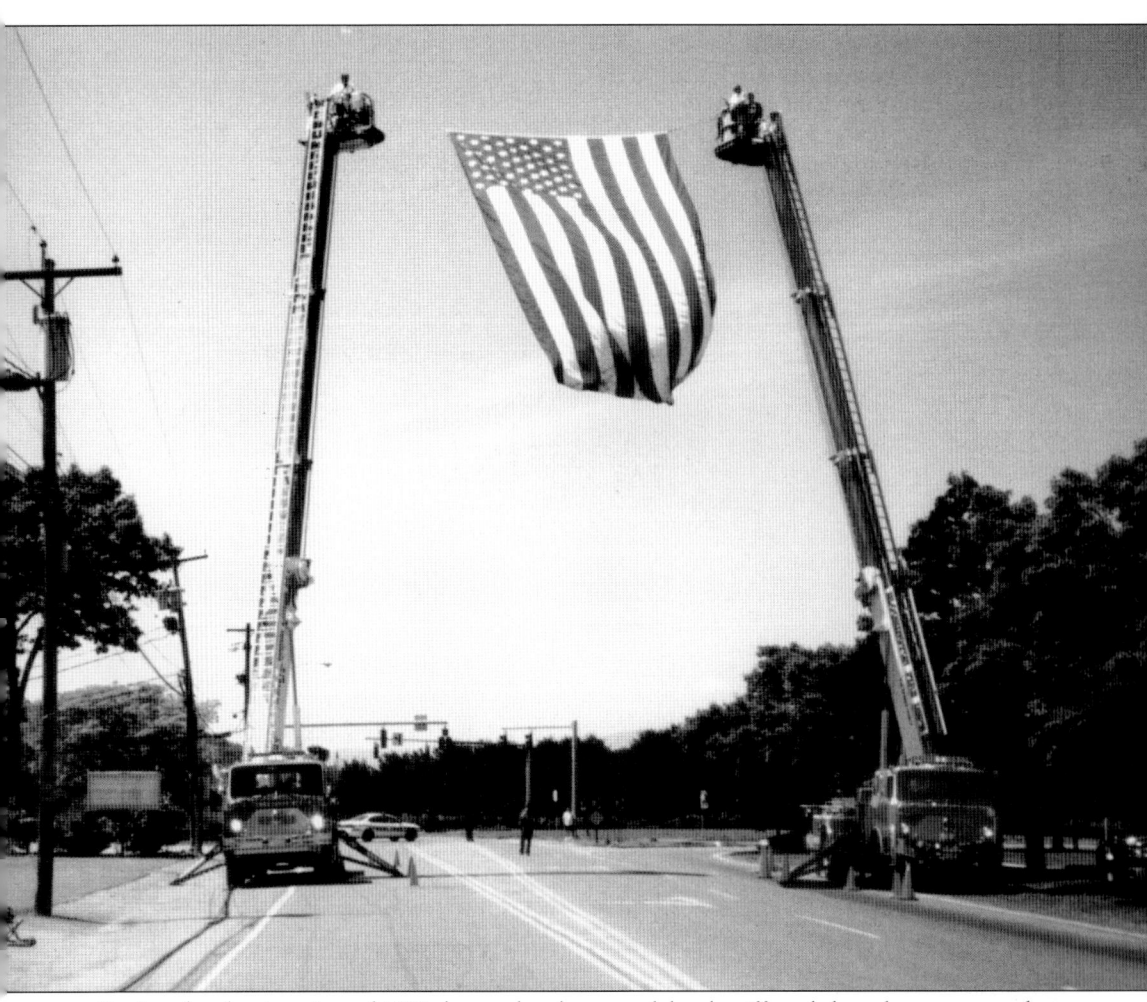

During the election riots of 1879, due to the absence of the sheriff, and the subsequent sundering of the Town of Kingston into two separate political entities, public safety in the form of police protection became imperative to the town fathers. Ulster immediately formed a constabulary of four men. By 1890, Kingston employed two deputy sheriffs, one justice of the peace, one justice, one constable, one "police," and two police of the election. Ulster employed seven constables, three deputy sheriffs, two "police," one police justice, and five justices. In the image above are the sibling Mack tower ladders of Ulster Hose Company No. 5 and the Bloomington Fire Department hoisting the colors high above the parade route on Flag Day 2003. Bloomington is situated in the township of Rosendale abutting the southwestern corner of the township of Ulster. They provide fire protection for Eddyville by contract. (Mac and Peg Tinnie.)

Seven
SERVING THE COMMUNITY

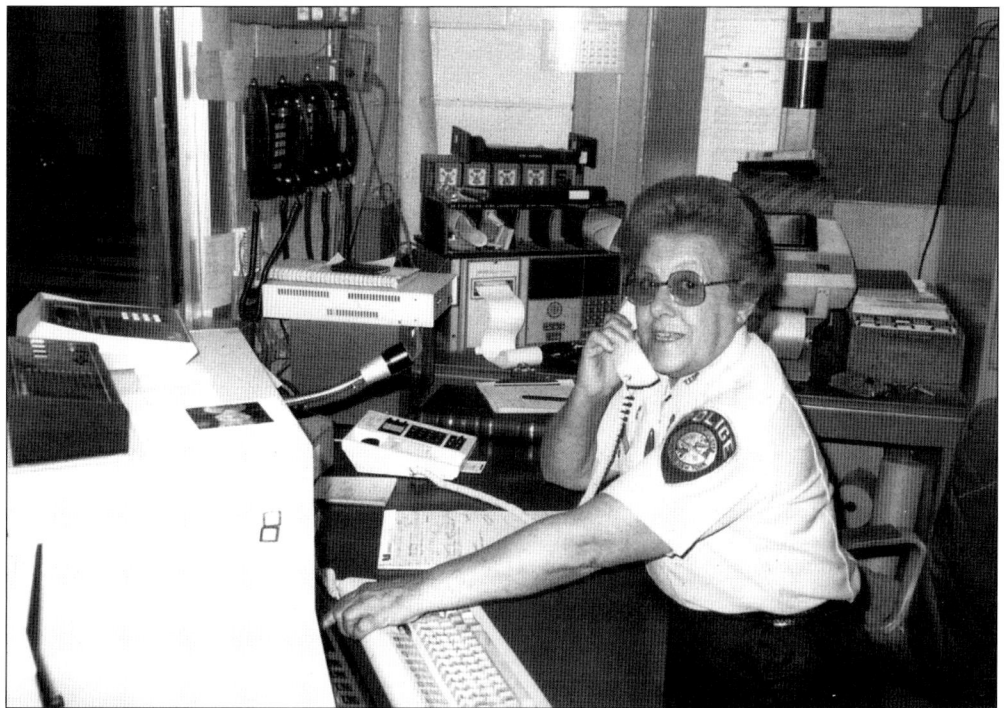

Town of Ulster Police Department senior dispatcher Delores Guido takes a call in 1987. Two decades later in 2007, the next generation's senior dispatcher Stacey Hommel and her eight capable assistants handled 9,301 complaints from the public and 5,647 incidents discovered by officers on patrol. This averaged out to 41 incidents and over 51 units dispatched per day and resulted in 1,243 arrests for crimes and violations. (Ulster Police Department.)

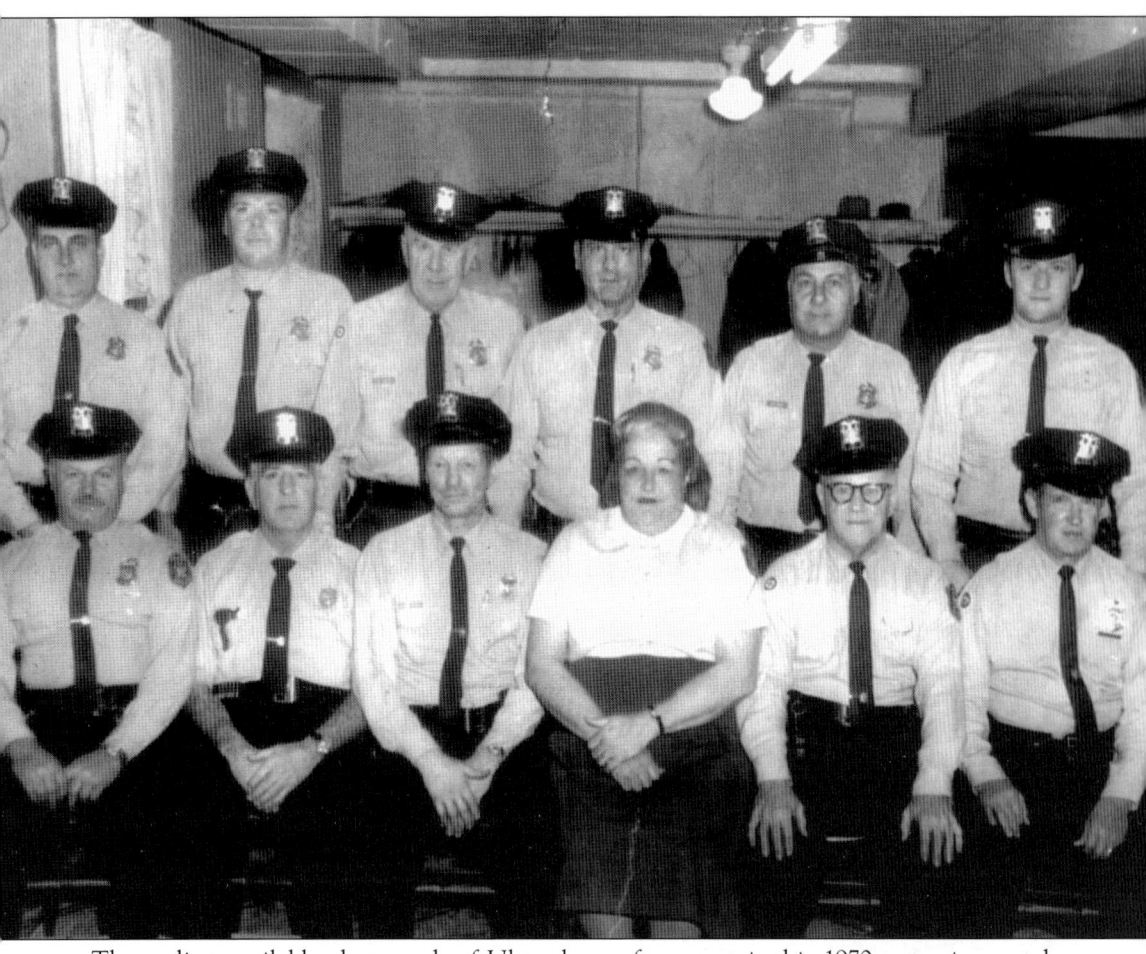

The earliest available photograph of Ulster law enforcement is this 1970 group image taken during the last year of the Town of Ulster Constabulary. The names that go with the faces are, from left to right, (first row) Nick Marino, Joe McNierney, Hap Felton, Mary Stokes, Calvin Schwartz, and Leo Robinson; (second row) Ralph Hayner, Mac Tinnie, Norm Cornitz, Don Crispino, John Costello, and Skip Stobel. Chief Myer Levy, followed by Danny Miller, brought the constabulary to a higher level of service and professionalism by beginning the complicated process of state accreditation. In 1974, the constabulary consisted of only five men and had a budget of $60,000. Don Koeppen became the sixth officer in 1975. After conversion to a police department, Ulster Police Department ran with three shifts of five men each. Because of budget constraints, the men worked at first for low pay and with minimal equipment. In June 2002, the department received full accreditation. (Mac Tinnie.)

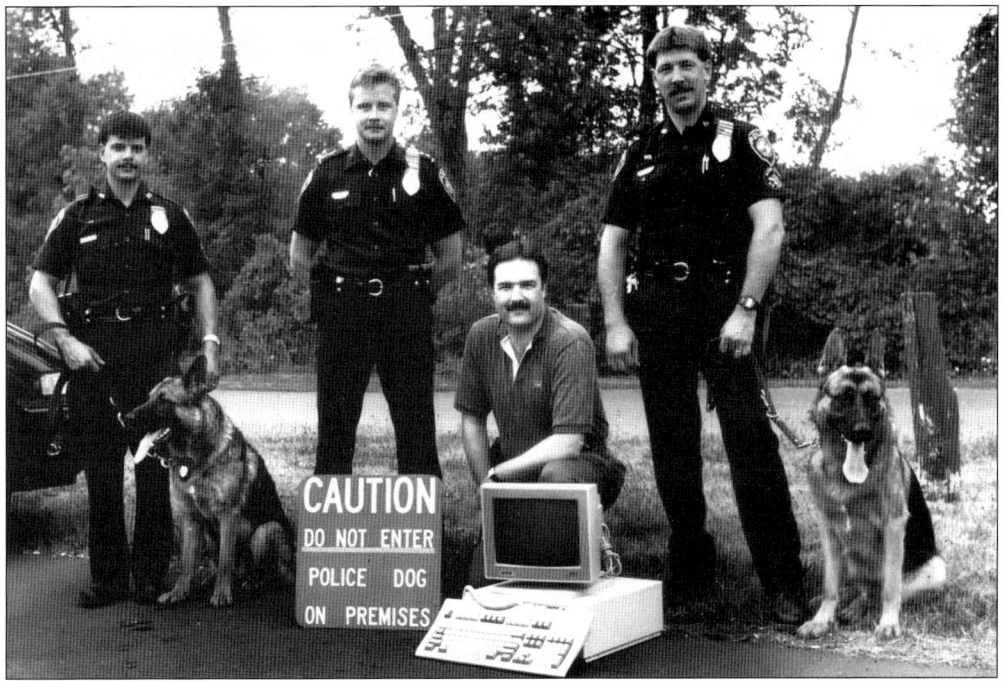

The 1990s ushered in the computer age for Ulster Police Department. Here from left to right are patrolman Joe Sinagra with his dog Nico, patrolman and future chief Danny Miller, IT specialist Don Ryan, patrolman Billy Smith, and Zak. The year was about 1993 and the chief of the department (not shown) was Bill Slover. (Ulster Police Department.)

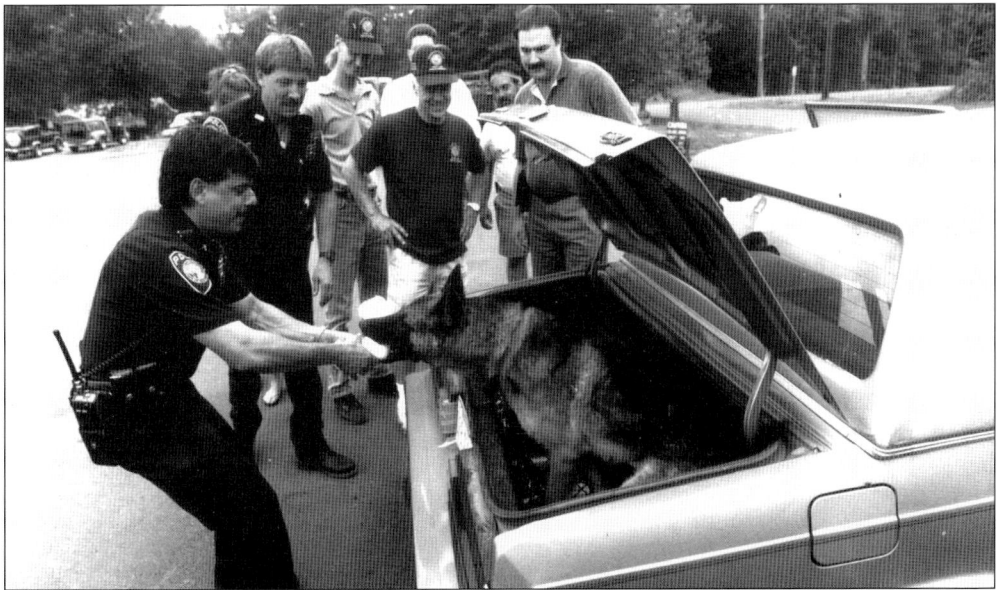

The year 1993 brought more than computers to the department. It also marked the beginning of the K-9 Program with three certified dogs. A fourth was added in 1997. Many of the dogs have passed on, but the unit remains active today with the newest dog, Dak, a patrol and narcotics specialist, and his handler Joseph Garvilla. Above are patrolmen Joe Sinagra and Billy Smith demonstrating Nico's prowess. (Ulster Police Department.)

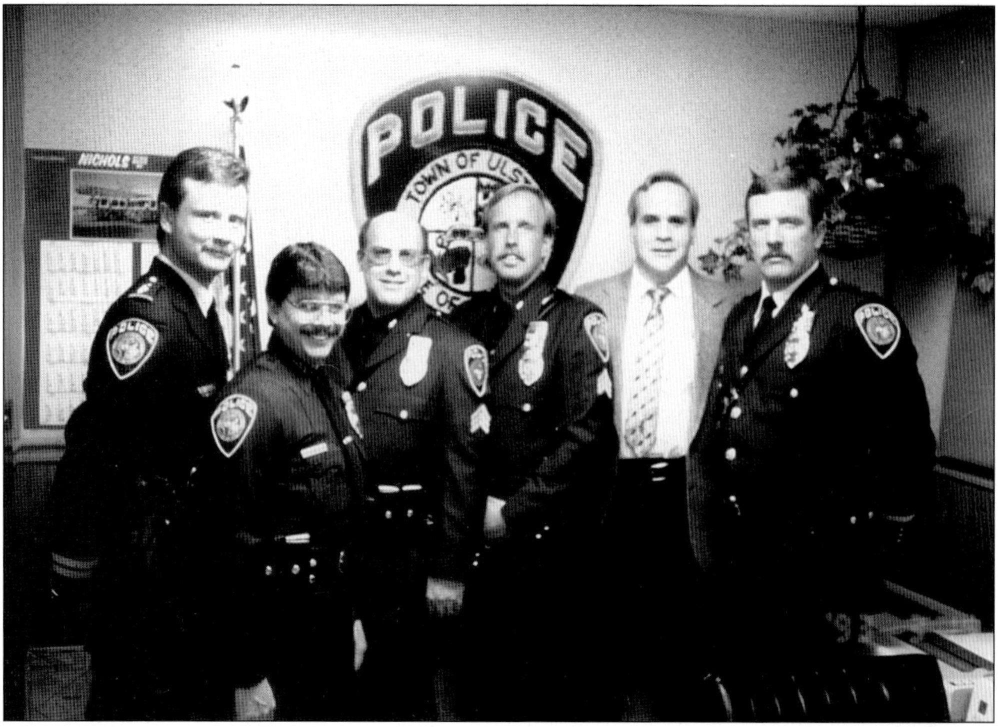

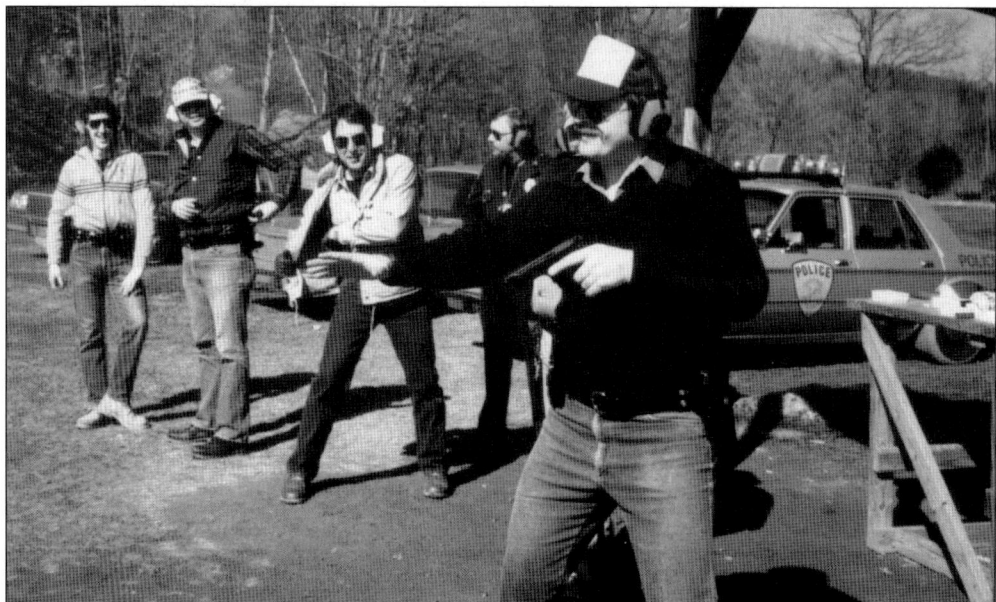

This is a late-1990s scene inside the new station at the town hall. From left to right are officer and future chief Danny Miller, officer and future deputy chief Joe Sinagra, Sgt. Steve Kuraffa (now a police chief in Vermont), Sgt. Donny Short, unidentified, and officer George Turner. (Ulster Police Department.)

Good police work requires much training. This is a 1991 session at the firing range in Ruby. Members are, from left to right, Paul Kesick, John Miller, Al Helman, FBI certified firearms instructor Don Koeppen, and Rod Purvis. (Ulster Police Department.)

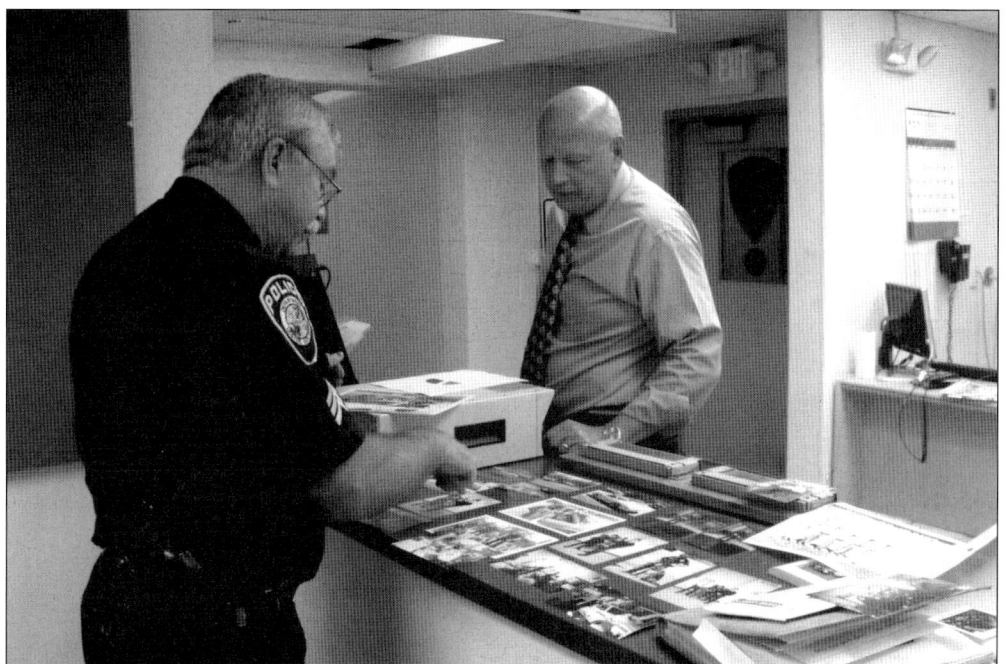

In August 2008, Sgt. Don Koeppen and Chief of Police Paul Watzka look over the department's photograph collection in preparation for creating this chapter. It was a lot of fun as they reminisced and discovered their roots. Thank you gentlemen! Thanks also to Deputy Chief Joe Sinagra, Lt. Matt Taggard, and IT specialist Nick Monaco.

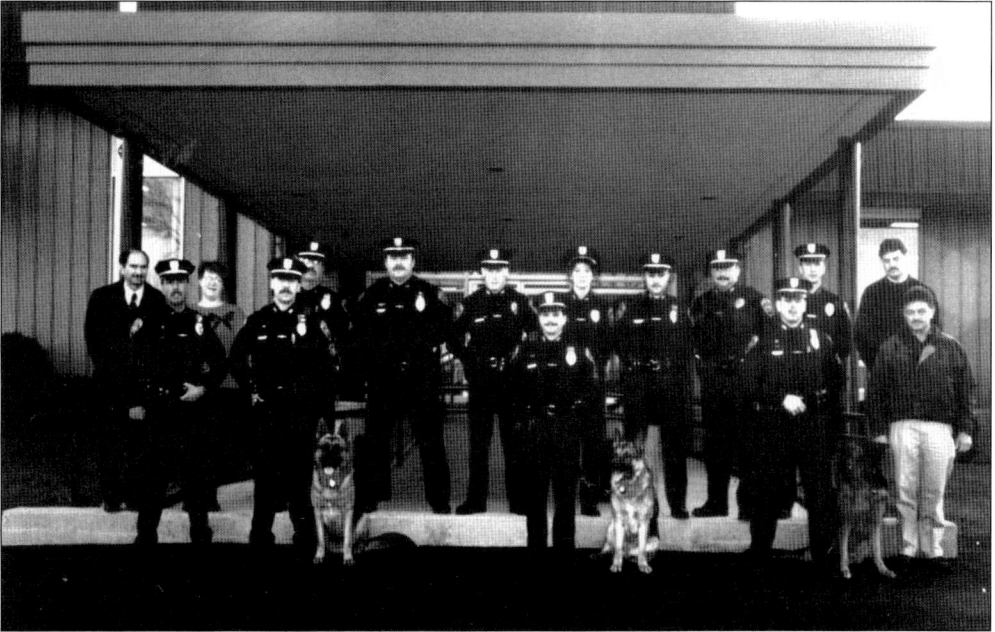

In this photograph from about 1993 are, from left to right, (first row) Donny Short, Billy Smith, Zak, Joe Sinagra, Nico, Matthew Taggard, Brix, and Gerry Kelder; (second row) unidentified, unidentified, Don Koeppen, Rod Purvis, Pete Palin, Rachel Zimmerman, Jimmy Kilfoyle, Gerry Brainert, unidentified, and Bobby Reynolds. (Ulster Police Department.)

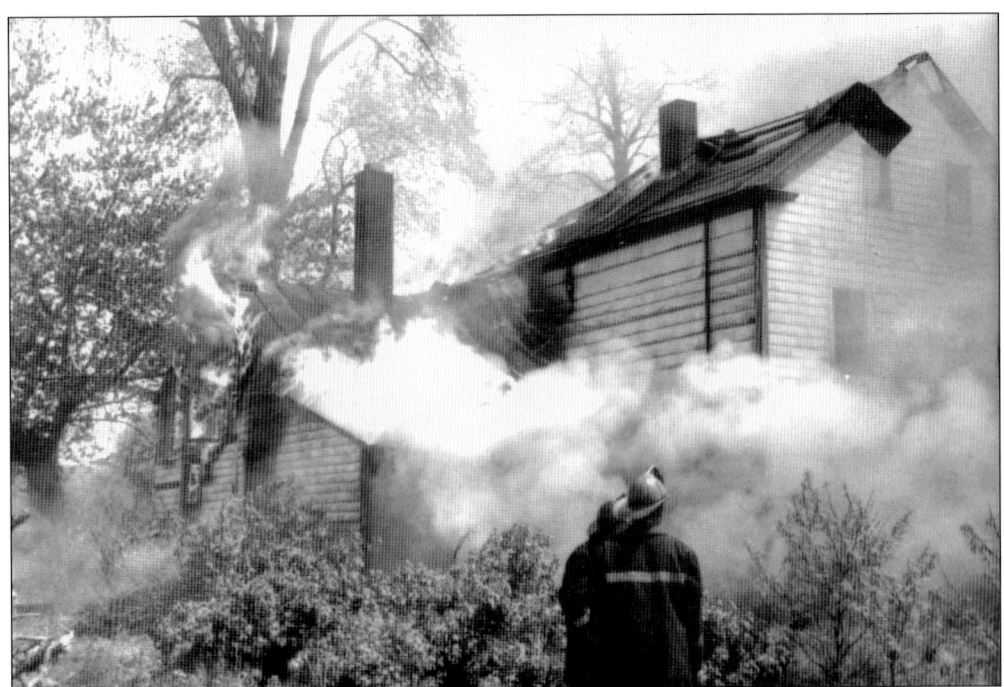

Public service is not limited to the police. High on the list of critical personnel in rural areas are the volunteer firefighters. The township of Kingston, being by design rather small, proudly hosts one fire department. Ulster, with its wider-ranging geography, is home to four. There was originally another fire department in the town of Ulster. The Eddyville Fire Department was incorporated in the original commercial center of the town, Eddyville. (Town of Kingston.)

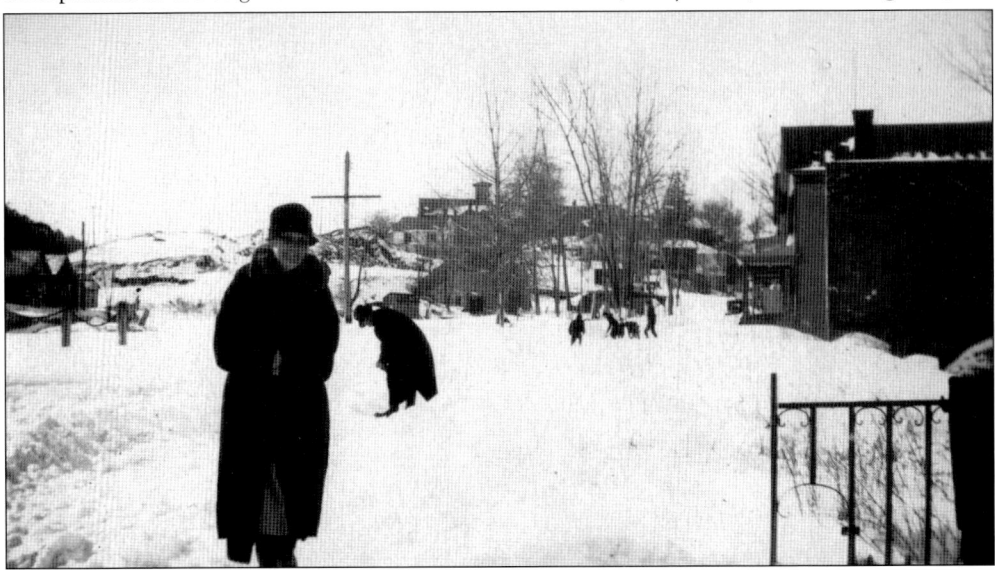

Legal filings indicate April 28, 1926, as the actual date of incorporation. Apart from one newspaper photograph of the principals, the authors were unable to find further mention of the company. The authors do know that the St. Remy Fire Department provided protection to Eddyville after its organization in 1931 at least until 1945. The Eddyville station and hall are located near center right in this winter 1926 image. (Martin Jordan.)

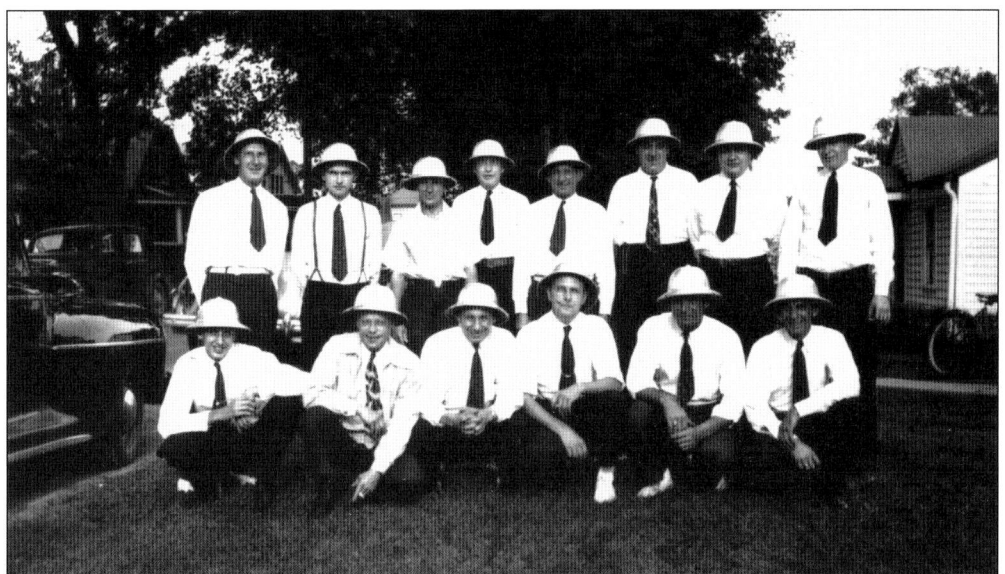

By early 1940, residents clamored for fire protection in the town of Ulster. The city of Kingston engines were simply too far away. Albert Montavani and John Osterhoudt, with only drive and determination to help them, set forth to make this dream a reality. Twenty-one men signed on, and using Osterhoudt's personal Packard, they responded to emergencies with rakes, brooms, fire extinguishers, and a first-aid kit. This photograph shows the 1945 crew dressed in their civilian defense helmets. (Town of Ulster historian.)

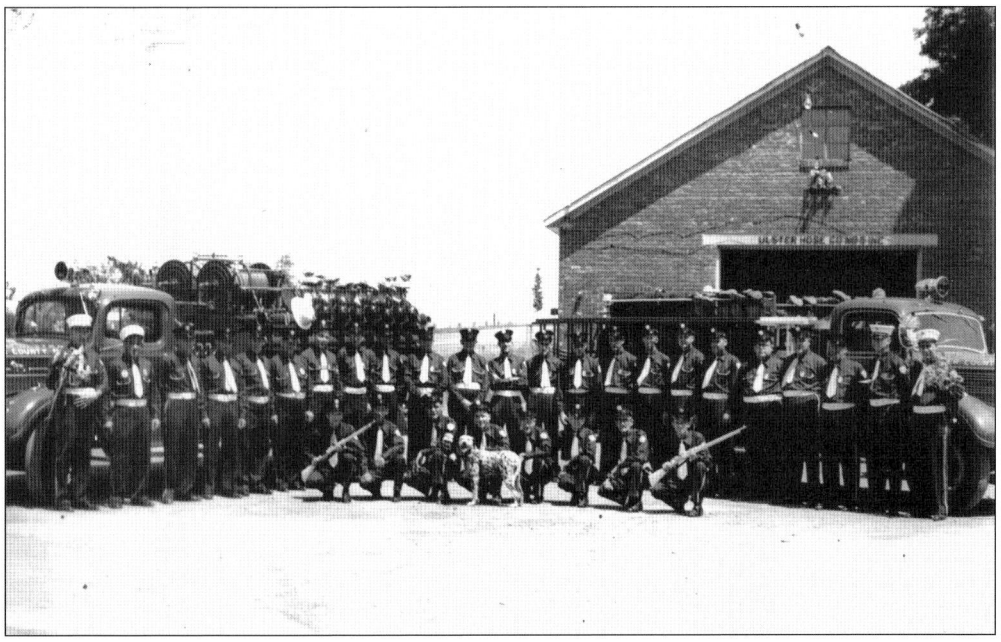

On March 9, 1944, the department held its first-recorded meeting. Officers were elected and official service began. John Osterhoudt was president and Albert Montavani was fire chief. The assistant chief was William Williams Sr. There were six commissioners. Underwriter's sanction came in December 1945. This photograph shows the department around 1948 at its newly constructed station. (Ulster Hose Company No. 5.)

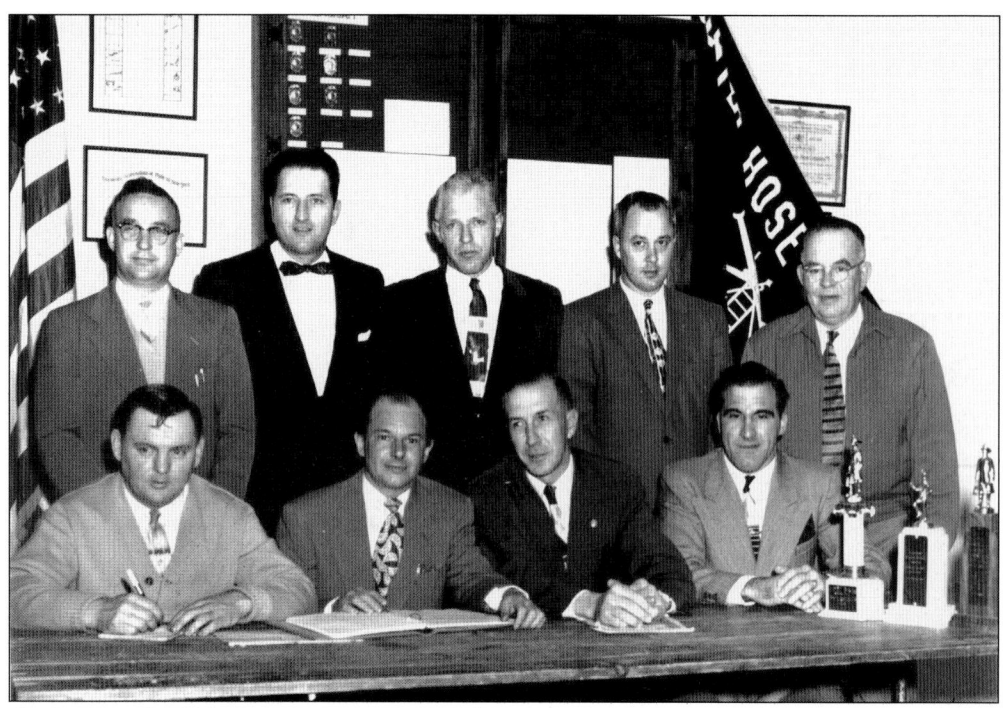

On January 6, 1945, the company purchased a 1936 Chevy truck from Phelan and Cahill for $200. A 275-gallon oil tank was cleaned and mounted on the truck along with a portable pump and several lengths of 1½-inch hose. Perhaps they had visions of one day hosting the county firemen's convention. This possibility came to fruition in 1957, and Ulster Hose Company No. 5 continued to grow steadily. (Ulster Hose Company No. 5.)

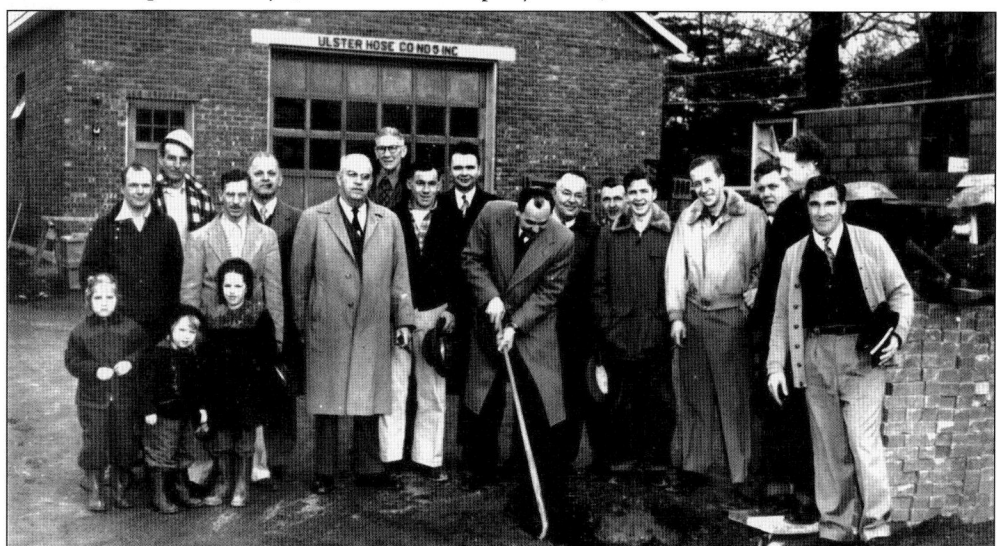

Through hard work and generous contributions from town residents, the company was able to burn its mortgage on October 29, 1950. The station was already too small. Resident Burt Chambers donated land for an addition and ground was broken in September 1953. Chambers is in the long coat. Also shown are Ed Fischang (left), Bill Harbig (rear), Gerry Woodbine, Al Kilmer, Don Reid, and Ernie Petersen (right). (Ulster Hose Company No. 5.)

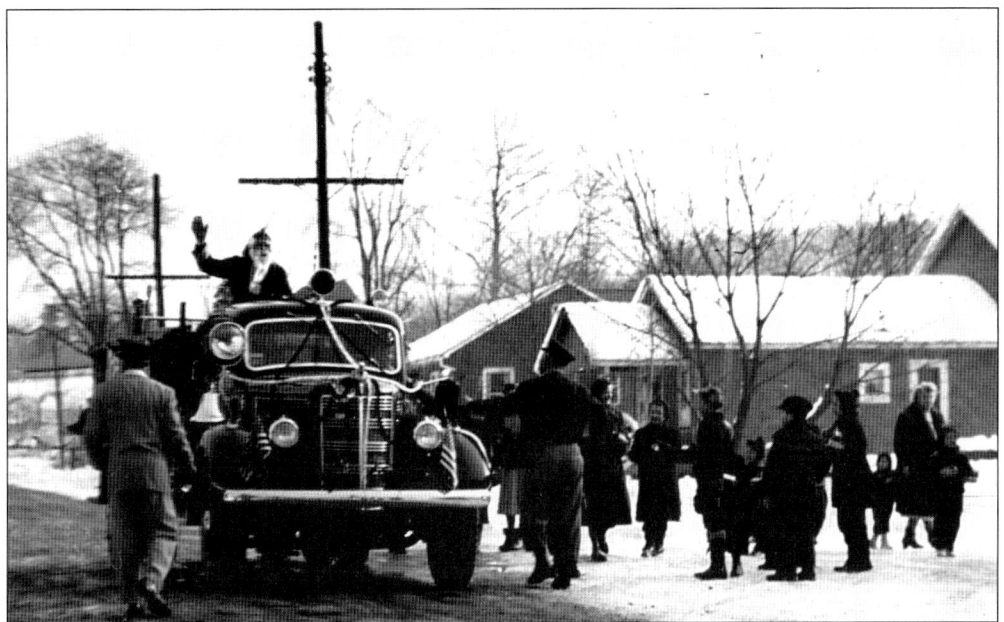

In December 1947, the members of Ulster Hose Company No. 5 showed the residents of Vincent Street their brand new 1947 Mack pumper. This was Ulster's first genuine fire engine and proudly bore the designation "Engine 1." It had a state-of-the-art 500-gallon-per-minute fire pump and 500-gallon water tank. It looks like Santa needed a ride and his friends happily lent a hand. (Bill Williams.)

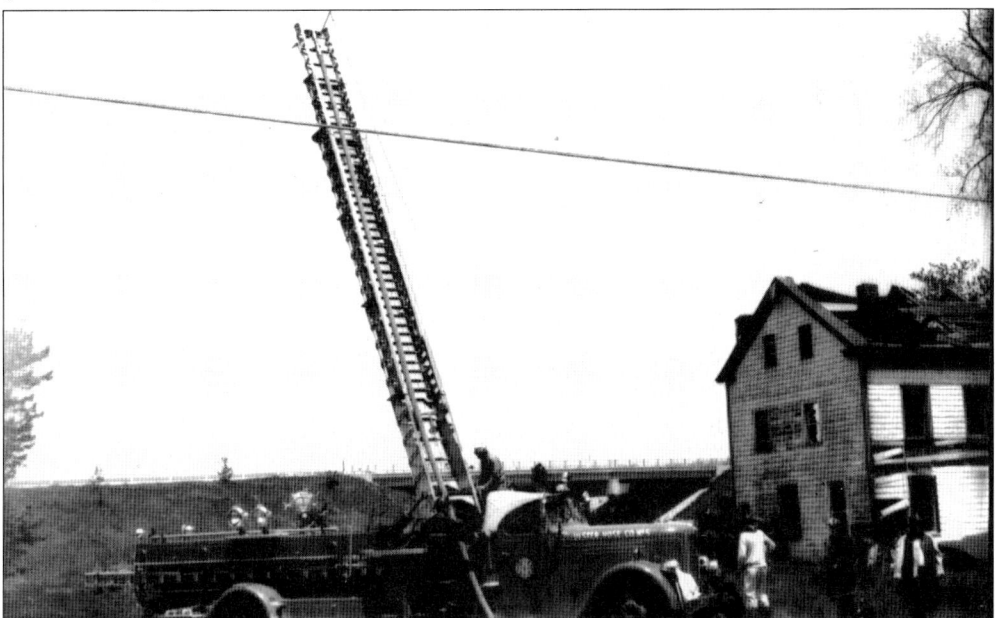

In 1967, Ulster Hose Company took delivery of a 65-foot Peter Pirsch aerial ladder truck from Pearl River. The truck was purchased with district monies. This was a good year for apparatus. On March 13, a local firm donated a tanker truck to the department. Shown above is the first drill for the new ladder. The date is May 28, 1967, and William Fischang was fire chief. (Town of Kingston.)

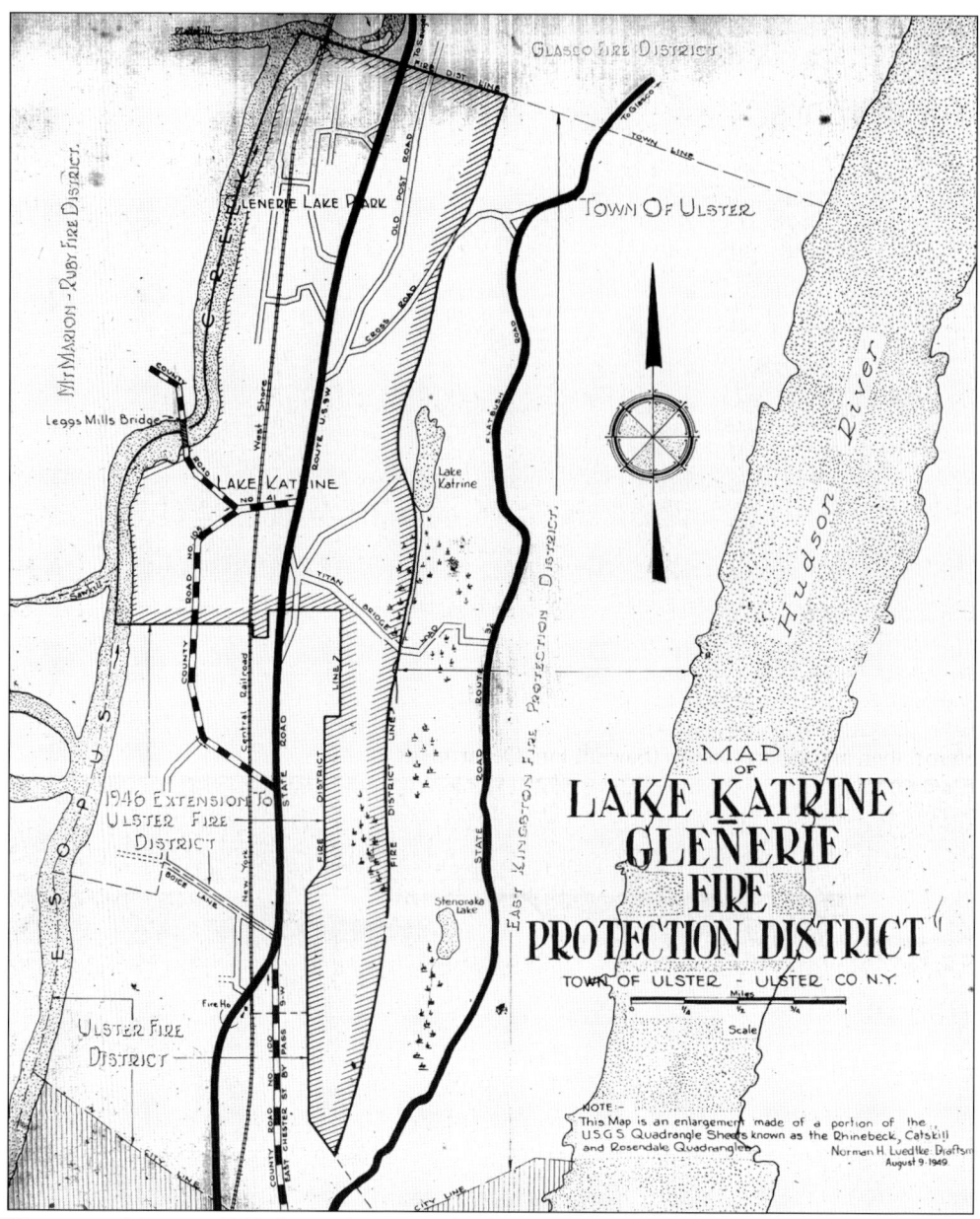

This map of August 1949 shows the original Ulster Fire District, a 1946 expansion, and a new Fire Protection District. Loosely, a fire district is covered by a government-sanctioned agency funded (at least partially) from a taxable base, and a fire protection district is protected by an agency that contracts with the township. Ulster had been accepting members from Lake Katrine since January 1947. On October 26, 1959, the Ulster Hose Company No. 5 district was officially expanded to cover the Lake Katrine and Glenerie Fire Protection District. During the summer of 1962, the department began to consider building a second station. They purchased land near Glenerie that year. Construction contracts were awarded in June 1966, and the station was complete on February 13, 1967. Today Ulster Hose Company No. 5 has a new main station, over 90 personnel, and 10 pieces of apparatus. They responded to 1,095 incidents in 2007. (Ulster County clerk.)

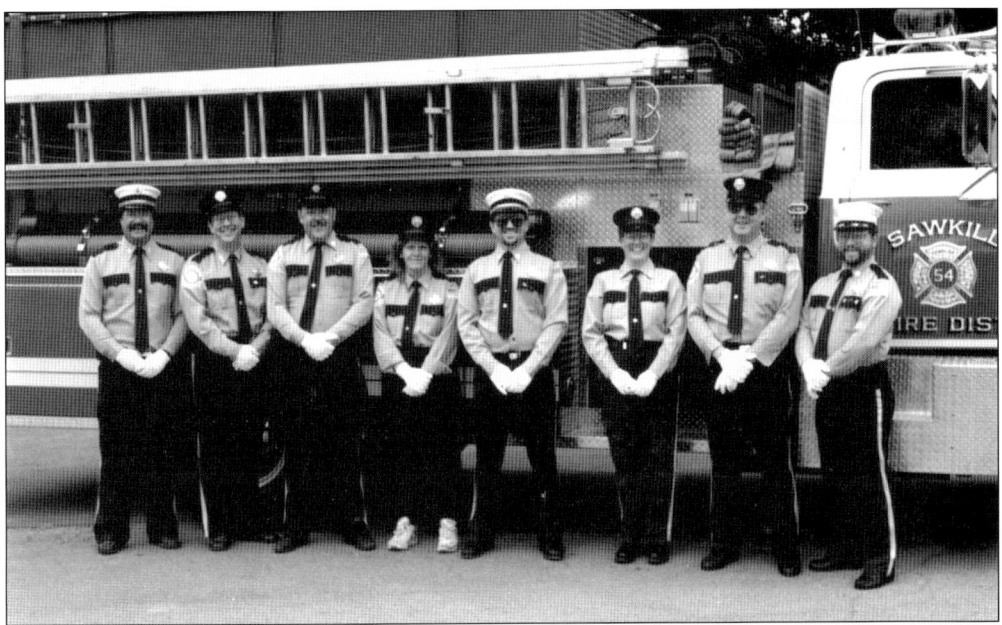

Kingston Township was just as progressive as its child. It followed Ulster's lead and established its own fire department in October 1951, under the leadership of Chief Harry Siemsen. The photograph above was taken on May 28, 1998. Firefighters shown with E5420 are, from left to right, Jim Crowley, Art Gardiner, Dan Luby, Dianne Hoffman, Chris Conklin, Paula Boice, Bob Steinhilber, and Brian Cesear. (Sawkill Fire Department.)

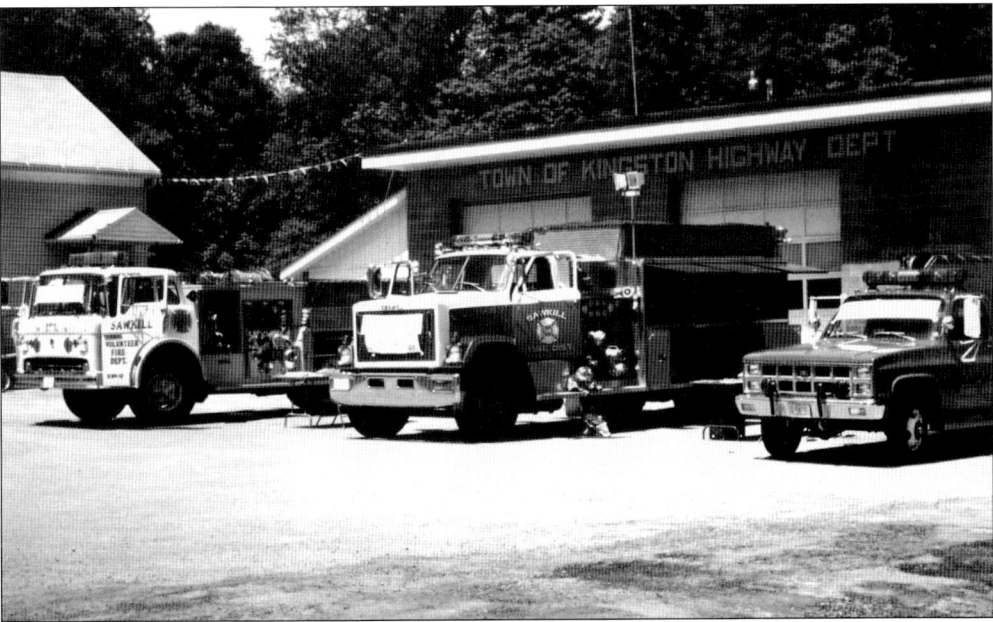

This was the Sawkill fleet in 1988. From left to right are 5410 a 1975 Ford engine, 5420 a 1985 GMC Brigadier tanker with a 1,000-gallon-per-minute pump, and 5430 a GMC rescue. The engine has since been replaced by a 3D-HME 1,250-gallon-per-minute engine and the rescue with a Ford F-550 Super Duty 500-gallon-per-minute minipumper/rescue truck. The trucks are positioned in front of the town highway garage for the park dedication. (Sawkill Fire Department.)

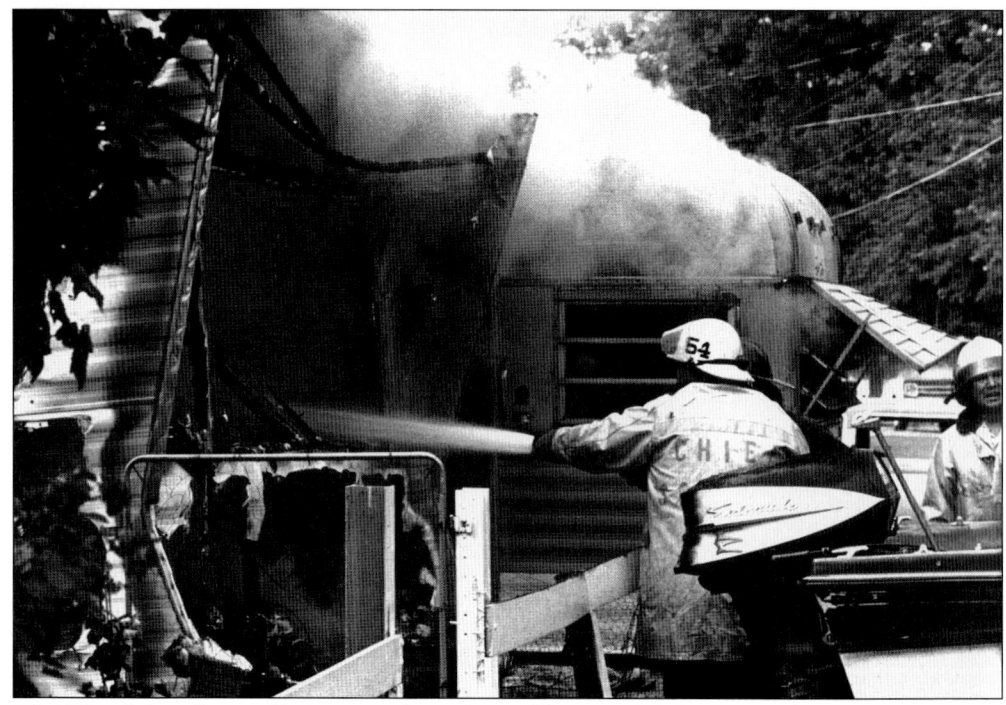

Chief Frank Brogden and Bob Howard attack a stubborn mobile home fire in Boices Trailer Park on June 17, 1983. The fire, possibly caused by a cigarette in a chair, spread quickly and destroyed an adjacent travel trailer and boat. A dog in the trailer was killed and the porch of another trailer suffered fire damage. The operation was complicated by a leaking propane tank, which caused respiratory difficulty for three firefighters. (Sawkill Fire Department.)

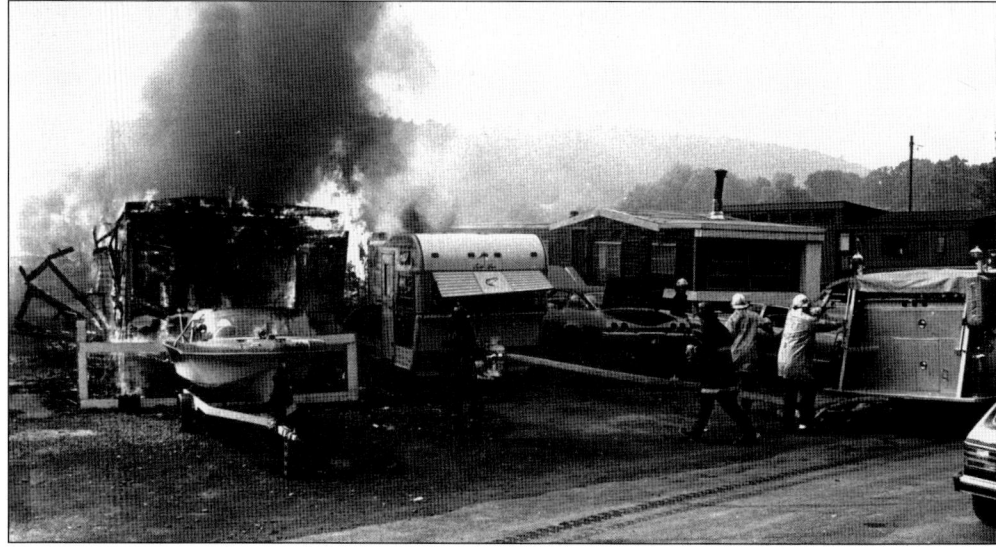

Firefighters Paul Leedeck of Sawkill, Kevin Kesick of Ruby, and Craig Applio were taken to Benedictine Hospital where they were treated and released. Here the first arriving unit pulls hose and checks for trapped occupants. Flames were already exiting the roof when they arrived at 4:23 p.m. Without their intervention, the fire would have engulfed all of the vehicles and structures in the photograph and then some. (Sawkill Fire Department.)

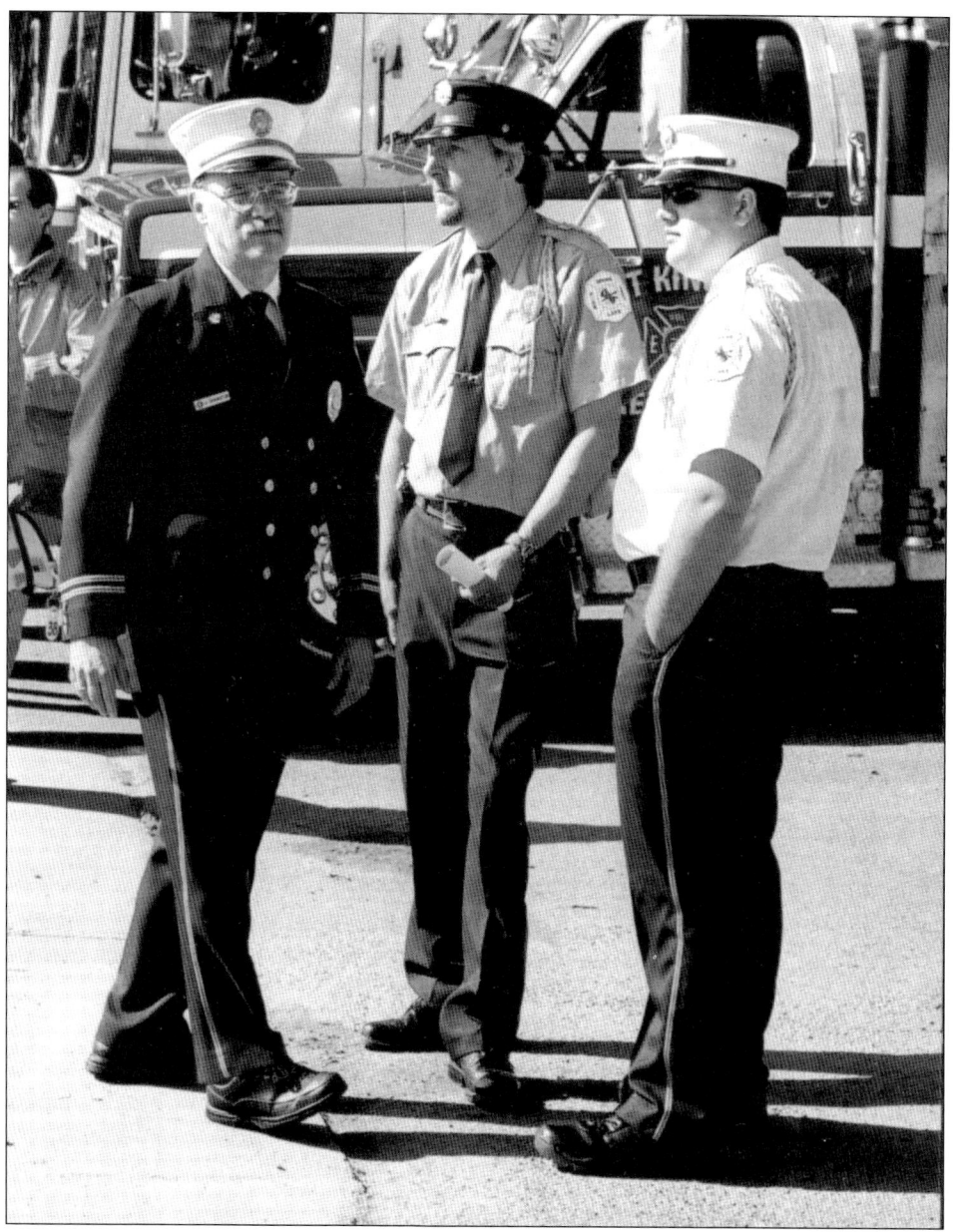

Prior to December 1956, the residents of Ulster Fire District No. 1 primarily relied on the kindness of the Kingston Fire Department to respond to emergencies in the area, even though it was outside of their district. After two disastrous fires around 1953, local residents asked the town board to establish their own fire district. The board readily agreed. On September 21, 1955, the Ulster Hose Company No. 1 Inc. (to become the Spring Lake Fire Department in March 1957) was formed. On September 27, 1955, the organizational meeting of the fire company was held at the Spring Lake Beach House, and the first officers were elected. There was still no firehouse or apparatus, but newly elected captain (the title was quickly changed to chief) Tom Dragotta and his crew were on their way. The year 1956 brought about great progress. Land was purchased, construction begun, and in December the first piece of apparatus arrived. Thanks to Jeremiah McDonough for historical insight. (Spring Lake Fire Department.)

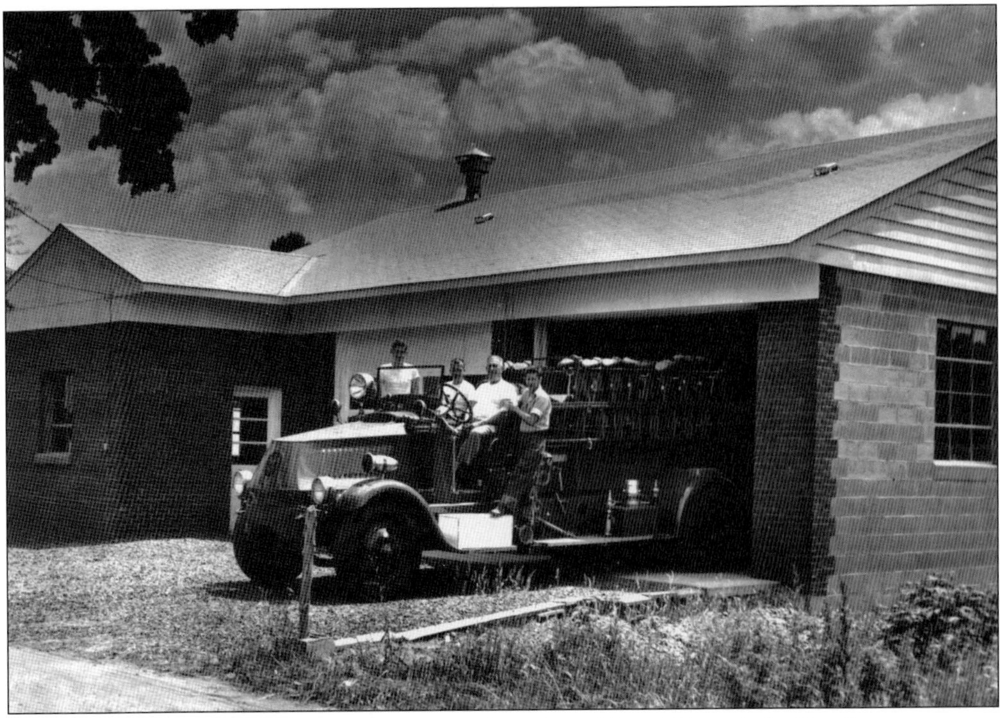

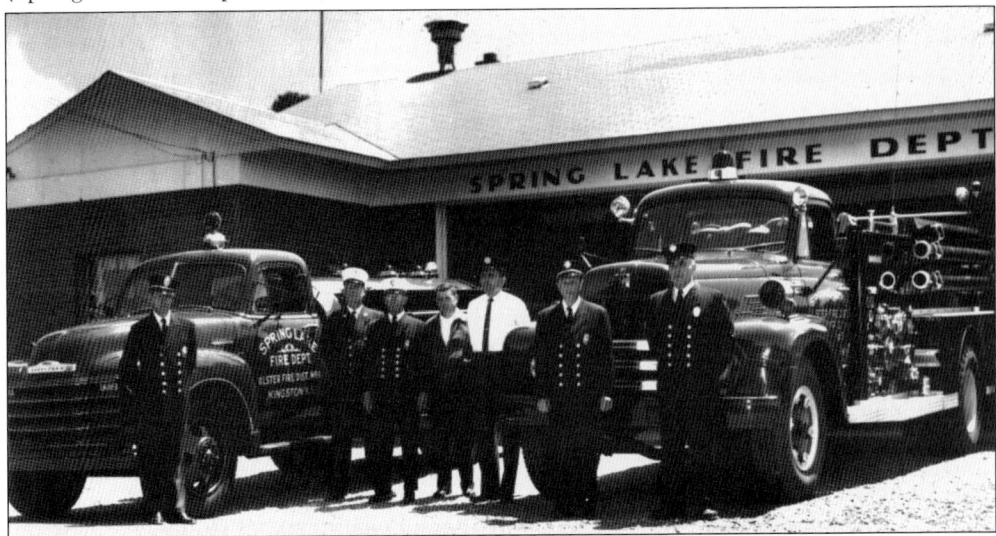

The first truck, a 1928 Mack pumper, was purchased used from Tilson Lake Fire Department in December 1956 for $500. It was first used on December 23 to help Santa Claus deliver candy. Chief Bob Pardee is at the wheel. The station was completed in May 1957, and the men trained heavily. July 8 of that year was the first official day of operations for Spring Lake Fire Department. (Spring Lake Fire Department.)

In September 1958, the company purchased a used tanker. Clayton Elmendorf converted it into the tanker show above on the left. In November of that year, the company took delivery of a new American Lafrance pumper with a 750-gallon-per-minut pump and 750-gallon tank on an International chassis. The 1928 Mack was traded in. The updated fleet is shown above. Chief Pardee and Assistant Chief Elmendorf are in white hats. (Spring Lake Fire Department.)

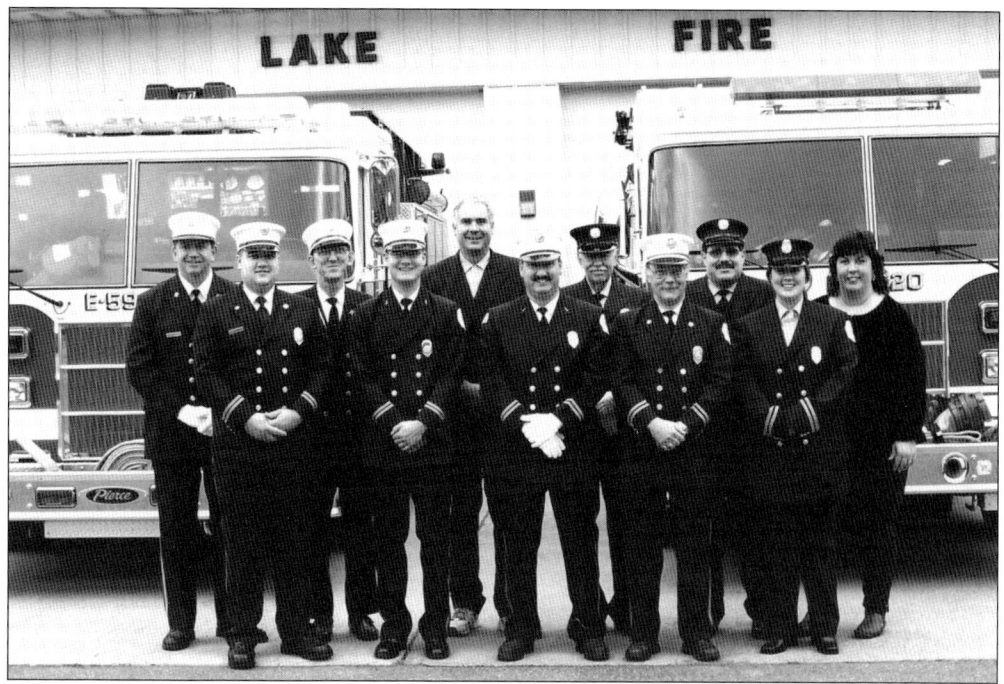

Spring Lake's 50th anniversary in October 2005 is seen here. From left to right are (first row) Jeremiah McDonough, first assistant chief; Chris Carey, lieutenant; Paul Alley, lieutenant; John "Doc" Cranston, chief; and Ashley Krom, firefighter; (second row) Jeremy Collins, second assistant chief; John Quick, commissioner; Jared Mance, commissioner; Ted Jones, life member; Bob Messina, firefighter; and Stephanie Messina, firefighter. The photograph was taken in front of E59-30 and E59-20. (Spring Lake Fire Department.)

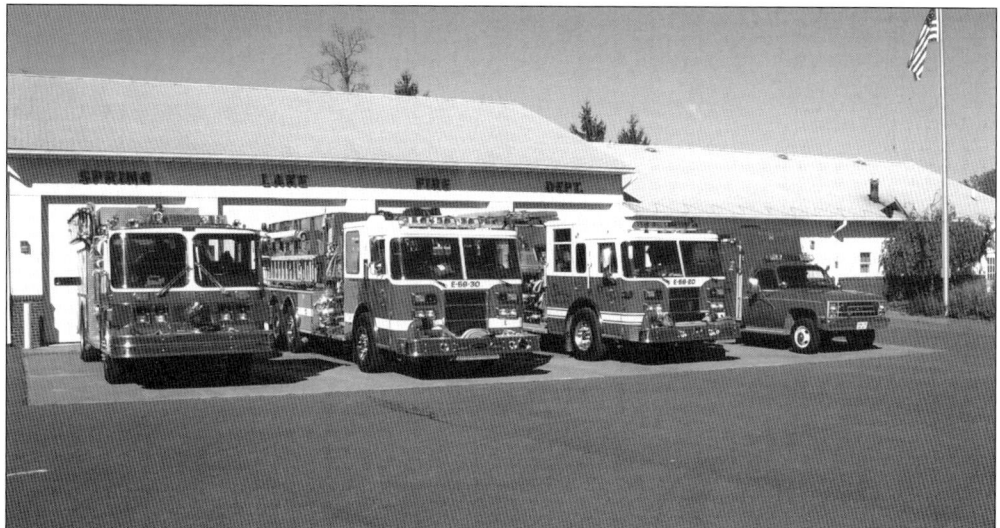

Seen from left to right are E59-10, a 1986 Hahn pumper; E59-30, a 1996 Pierce pumper/tanker; E59-20, a 2002 Pierce rescue pumper; and R59-40, a 1989 Chevy rescue. This picture was taken in October 2005 in preparation for their 50th anniversary dinner program. All of these trucks are still in service except for R59-40, which has been replaced with a Ford F-350 rescue truck. Not pictured is car 59, a 2000 Dodge Durango, the chief's vehicle. (Spring Lake Fire Department.)

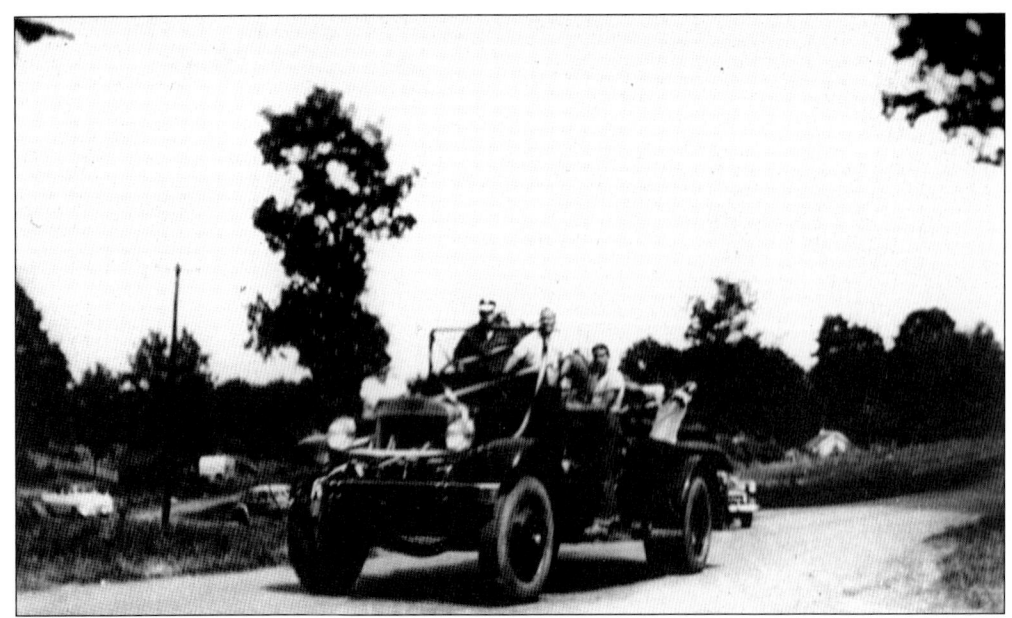

In 1946, the inhabitants of Ruby and Mount Marion came together to form a joint fire department. Plans were made, a pair of twin trucks was ordered, and two nearly identical stations were constructed. One of the stations was near the post office in Ruby, and the other was near the four corners in Mount Marion. This is the Ruby truck coming to its new home in 1946. (Ruby Fire Department.)

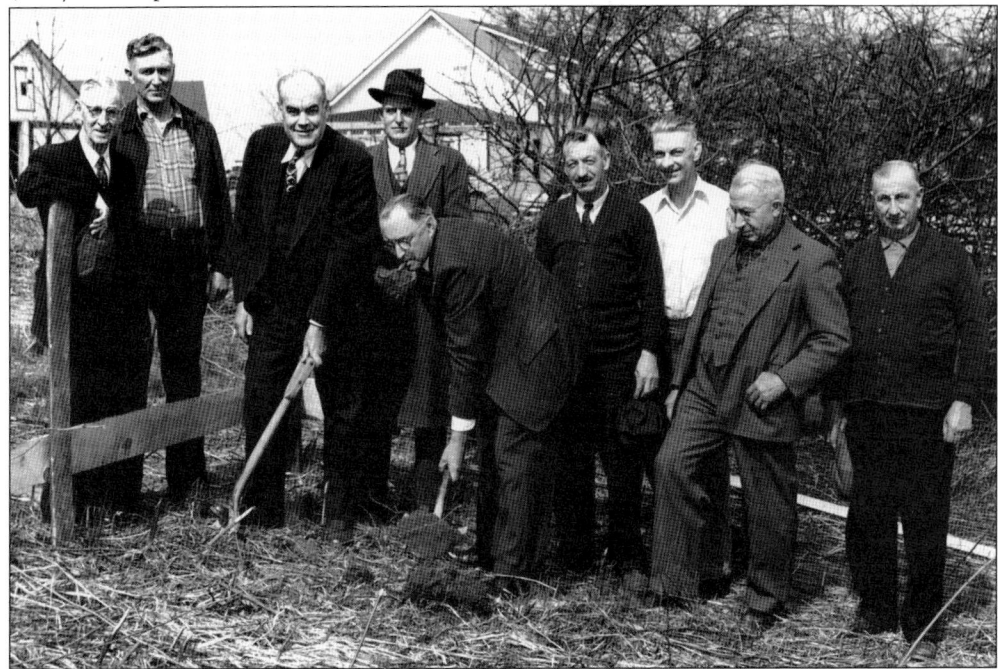

Mount Marion–Ruby Fire Department members break ground for the Ruby station in 1946. From left to right are Mr. Werner, Jake Scheffel, Peter Boice, Roy A. VanBenschoten, Vernon Felton, G. Adams, H. Schmidt, G. Shank, and W. Snyder. This station remained in service until it grew too small in the 1970s. (Ruby Fire Department.)

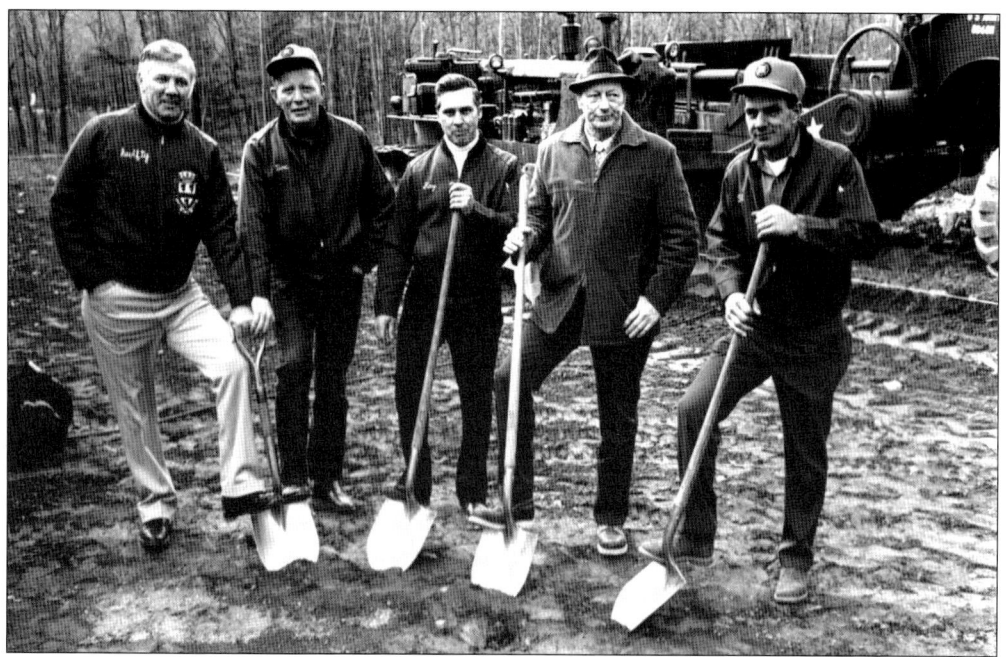

The last scene was repeated in 1975 by the next generation of volunteers when ground was broken for a new three-bay station. This station has a large commercial kitchen and community meeting room where a myriad of functions are held year-round. Department members helped with construction and managed to pay off the mortgage in just 15 years. From left to right are Reginald Swift, Hugo Dachenhausen, Ray Scheffel, Harold Felton, and Bill Scheffel. (Ruby Fire Department.)

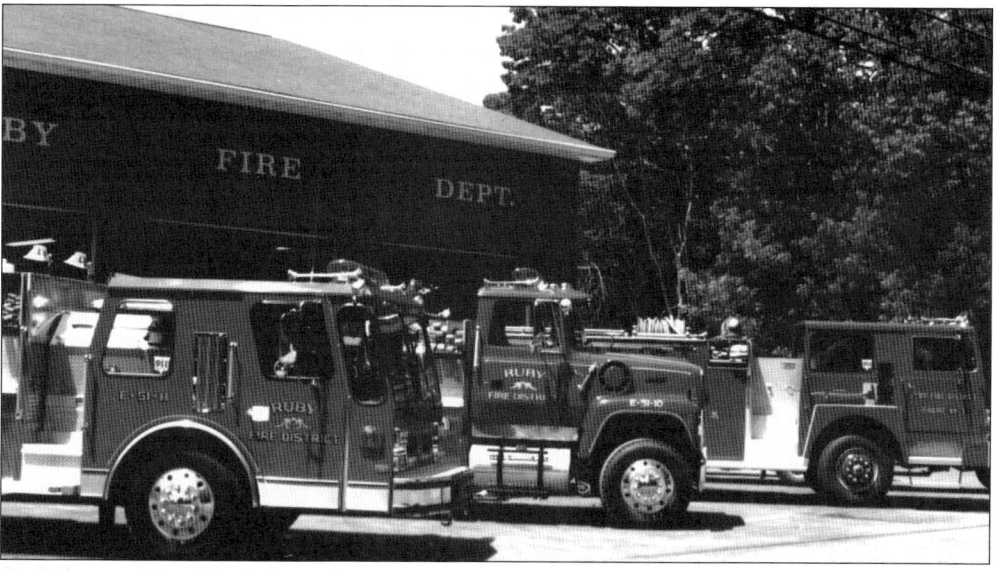

On February 24, 1972, Ruby and Mount Marion became separate entities, but continue to have a close working relationship. This is the roster of Ruby apparatus in 1996. E5111 is a 1988 E1 1,250 pumper and 5110 is an E1 1,500-gallon-per-minute pumper/tanker. Both are still in service as is M5130, a four-wheel drive 750-gallon-per-minute minipumper; a six wheeler brush apparatus; and a Ford Explorer medical fly car. (Ruby Fire Department.)

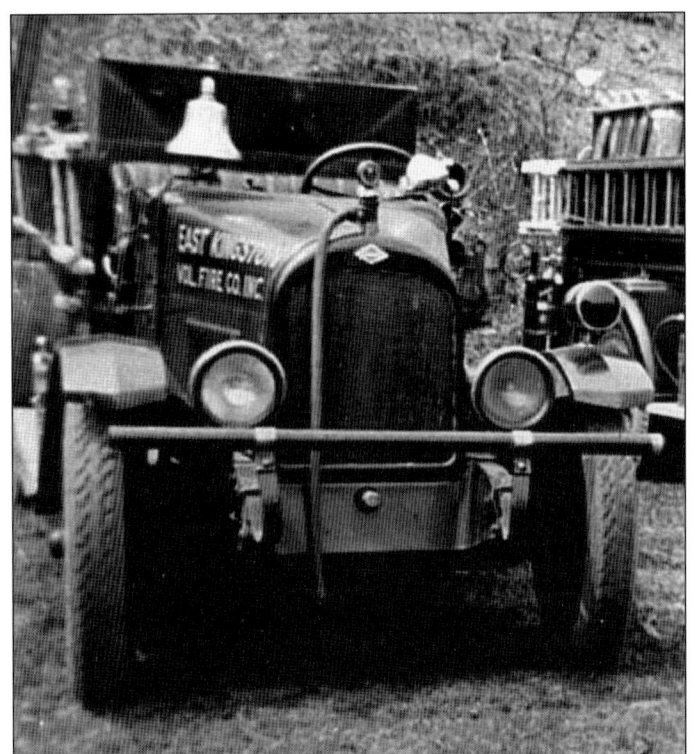

The East Kingston Fire Department was founded in August 1949 by the hard-working men of the brickyard community. The hamlet was a thriving community and needed fire protection. The charter officers were department president Ed Feldman and Chief James Costello. The first piece of apparatus was a 1927 Larabee pumper and was housed in Fiore's garage until a fire station could be constructed. The old garage is now a residence. (East Kingston Fire Department.)

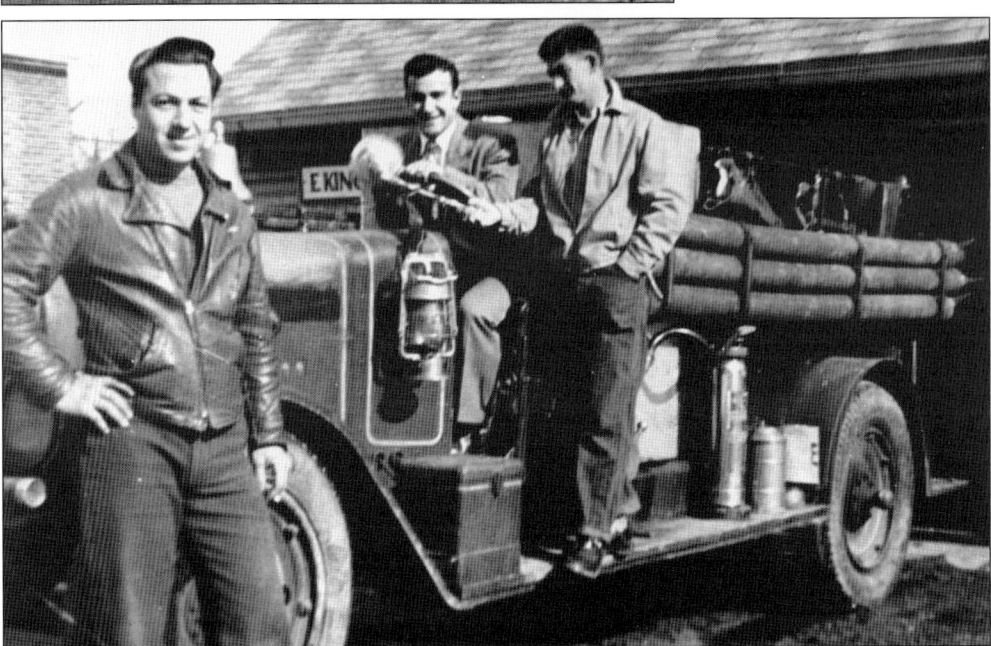

In 1949, charter members put the Larabee into service. East Kingston Fire Department is a member-owned fire protection district and contracts to the Town of Ulster for its services. They operate out of two stations. Station No. 2, on Ulster Landing Road, was built in 1975 and houses T2515, a 1986 GMC tanker; E2516, a 1990 E1 pumper; plus emergency medical service equipment and a 6,000-watt generator. (East Kingston Fire Department.)

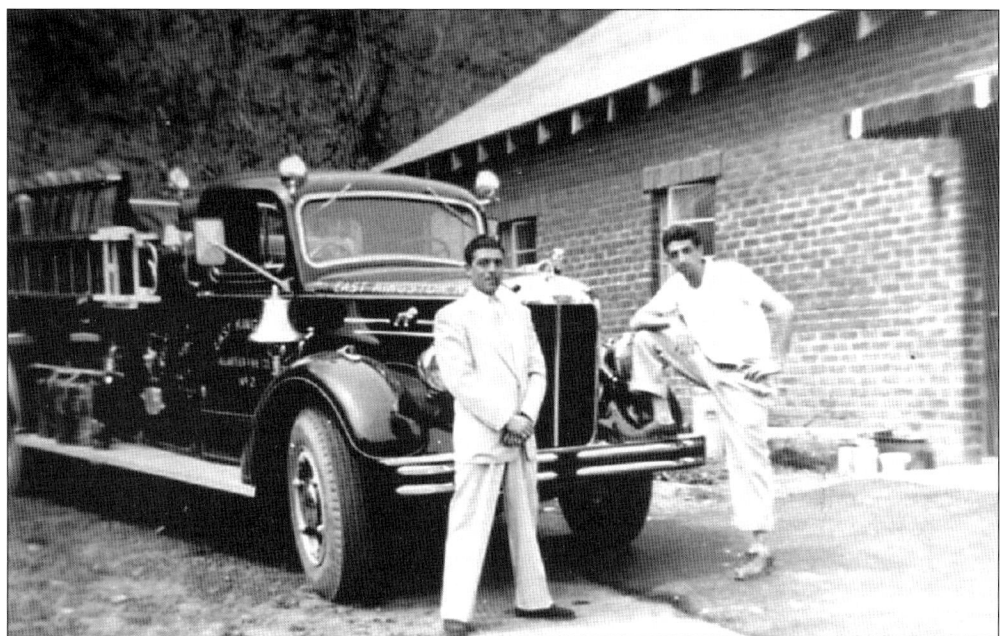

Station No. 1 (headquarters), built on Main Street in 1950, is home to E2517, a 1999 3D pumper with a 1,250-gallon-per-minute pump and a 1,000-gallon tank; medical equipment; and a 9,000-watt generator. The image above is a 1951 Mack pumper that was East Kingston's first new piece of fire apparatus. Mike Quarantino is at the left and Chief Lou Clausi is at the right. (Frank Rittie and East Kingston Fire Department.)

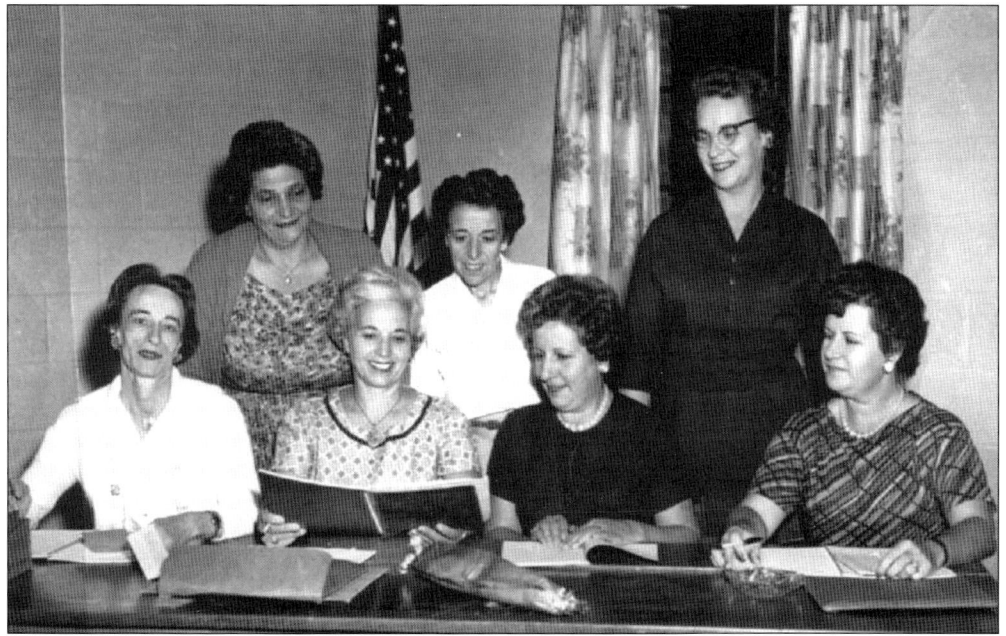

No fire department would be able to function without its ladies auxiliary. This is the East Kingston Auxiliary in 1961. From left to right are Evelyn Hunter, Eva Post, Mary Nardi, Dolly Quarantino (of school strike fame), Fran McCullough, Thelma Clausi, and Lillian Rittie. (Frank Rittie and East Kingston Fire Department.)

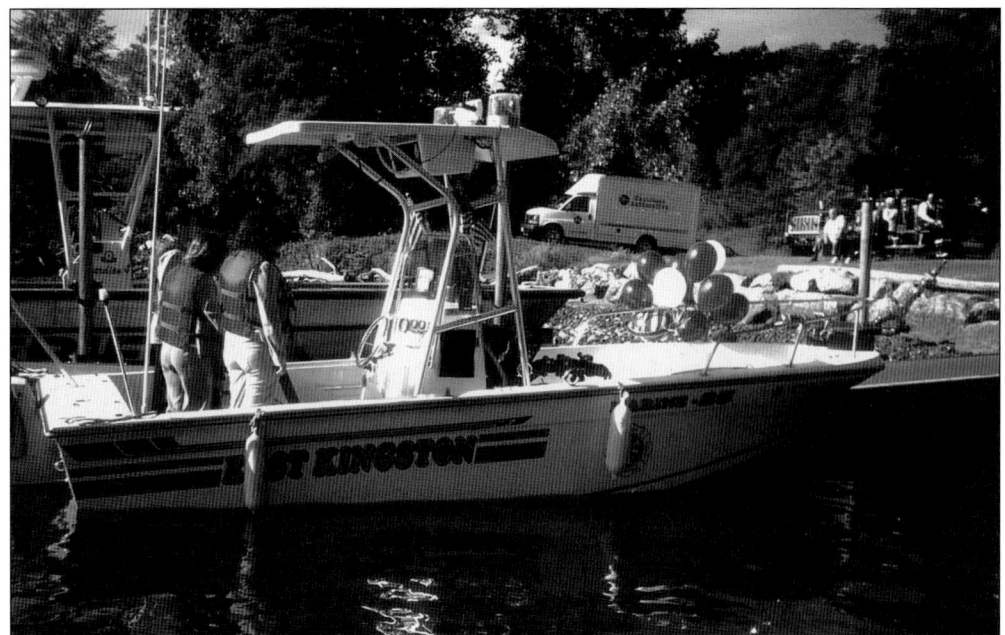

East Kingston covers a long stretch of the Hudson River, including the part under the Kingston-Rhinecliff Bridge. Marine 25 is their fire/rescue boat. It has an onboard pump and master stream device plus a full compliment of water-rescue equipment. A boathouse at Charles Ryder Park was begun in 2005 with assistance from the Town of Ulster Highway Department and completed in 2006. (East Kingston Fire Department.)

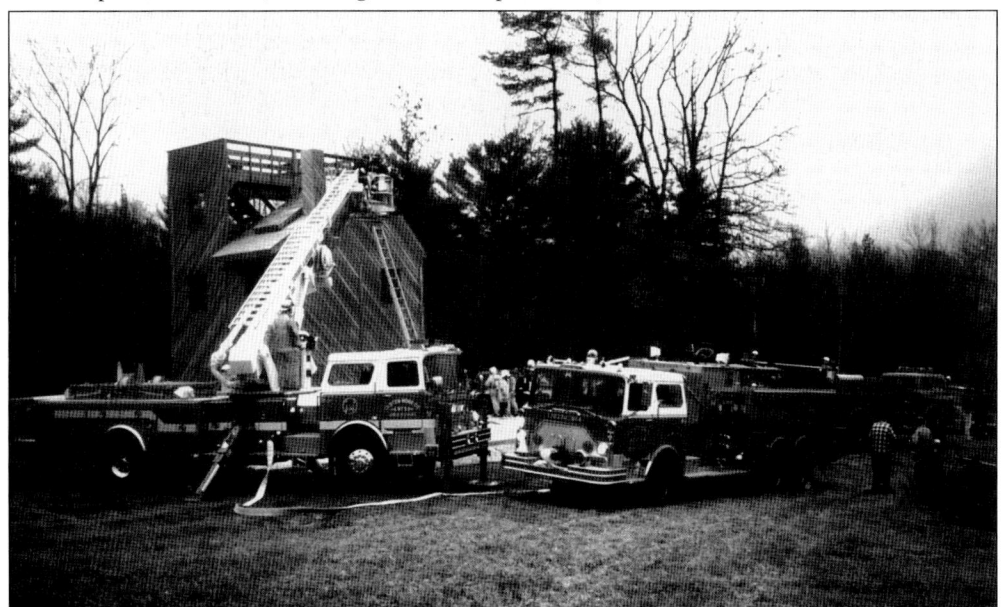

The Ulster Fire Training Center is located on Ulster Landing Road near the Kingston-Rhinecliff Bridge. The center was the creation of Frank and Maryanne Rittie of East Kingston. Frank is a New York State fire instructor and past chief of the East Kingston Fire Department. Membership is open to all volunteer departments in Ulster County. On another part of the property is the Ulster Police firing and qualification range. (Ulster Police Department.)

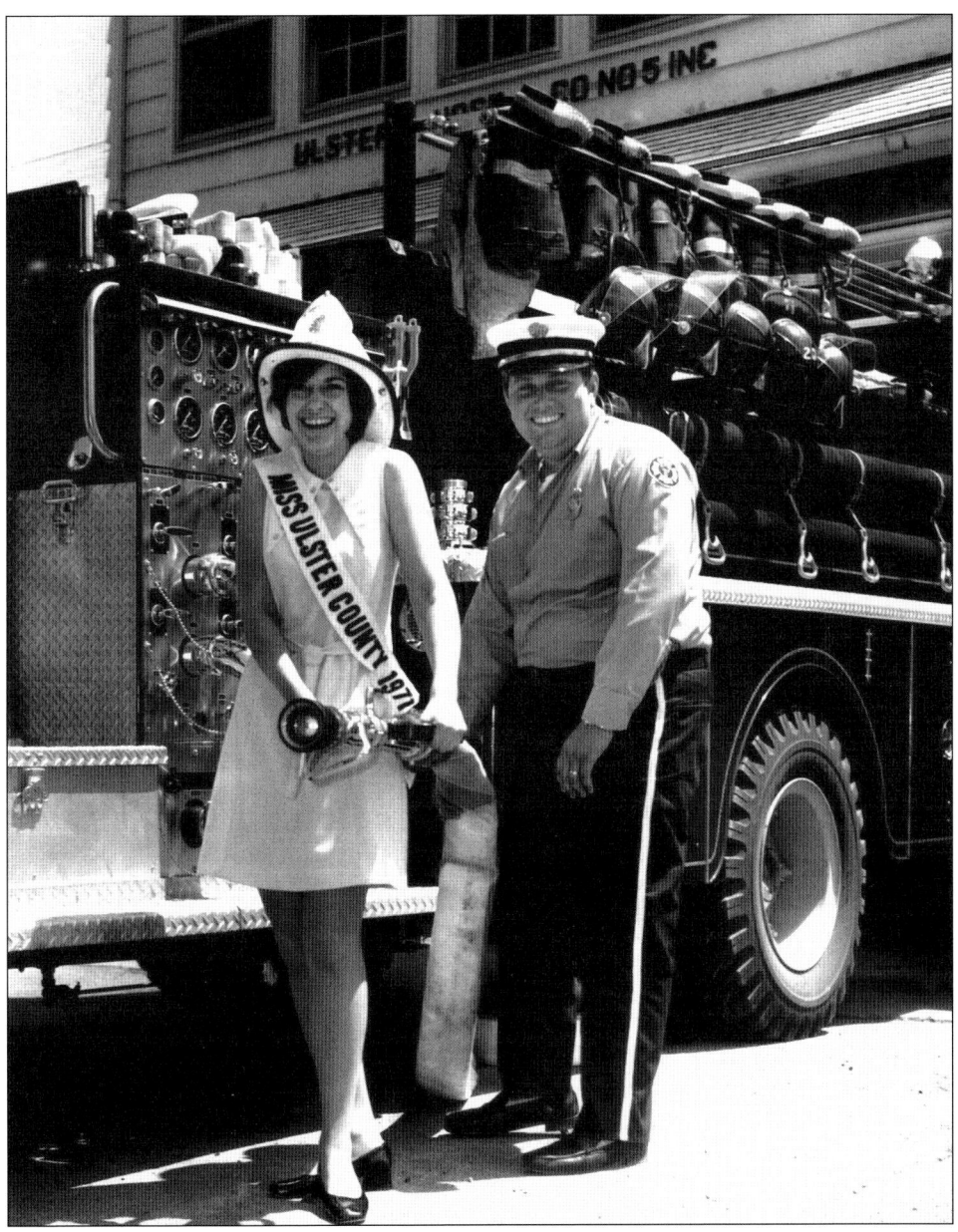

It is early fall in 1971 and Ulster Hose Company No. 5 fire chief Bill Williams poses with Miss Ulster County Patricia Czarski in front of headquarters on Ulster Avenue. Czarski was a 1971 graduate of Kingston High School and lived in Lake Katrine at the center of Ulster Hose Company's territory. They both appear to be enjoying the autumn sunshine. The pageant itself originated in 1956 as the Miss Saugerties Pageant. Crystal Jobst Scriber was the winner that year. In 1967, the pageant evolved into the Miss Ulster County Scholarship Pageant. Susan Schoonmaker, a 1967 graduate of Rondout Valley Central School and a daughter of Mr. and Mrs. Elmer Schoonmaker of High Falls, was the first winner of that event. She was also voted Miss Congeniality by her peers. Susan is now a doctor of chiropractic medicine. Finally in 2005, it grew once more to include both Ulster and Dutchess Counties and is now named the Miss Apple Valley Scholarship Pageant. (Ulster Hose Company No. 5.)

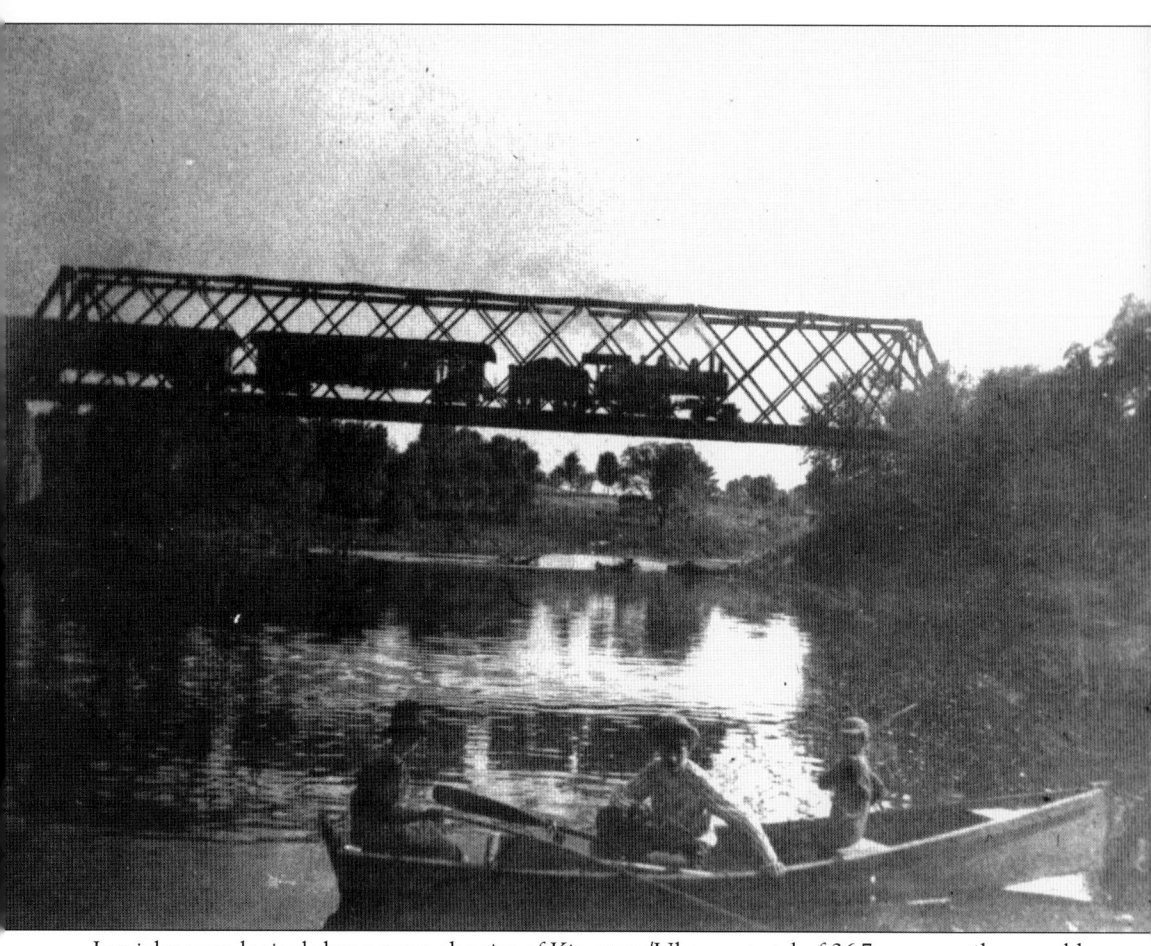

It might seem logical that a town the size of Kingston/Ulster, a total of 36.7 square miles, would be well served by the railroad boom of the latter half of the 19th century. Not so. In fact, although four major railroads passed through the townships, only two had stations therein, and those were single stations, one moderate in size and the other tiny. The towns did, however, host two horse-drawn short lines serving local industry and almost became home to a commuter trolley line to the city. The apparent dichotomy can be explained by noticing that the township virtually surrounds the city of Kingston, which was a major junction for these railroads. The Ulster and Delaware Railroad, Wallkill Valley Railroad, and Ontario and Western Railway all terminated in the city and the New York Central West Shore Line passed through with a large union station in midtown. (Town of Kingston.)

Eight
Railroads Pass Through

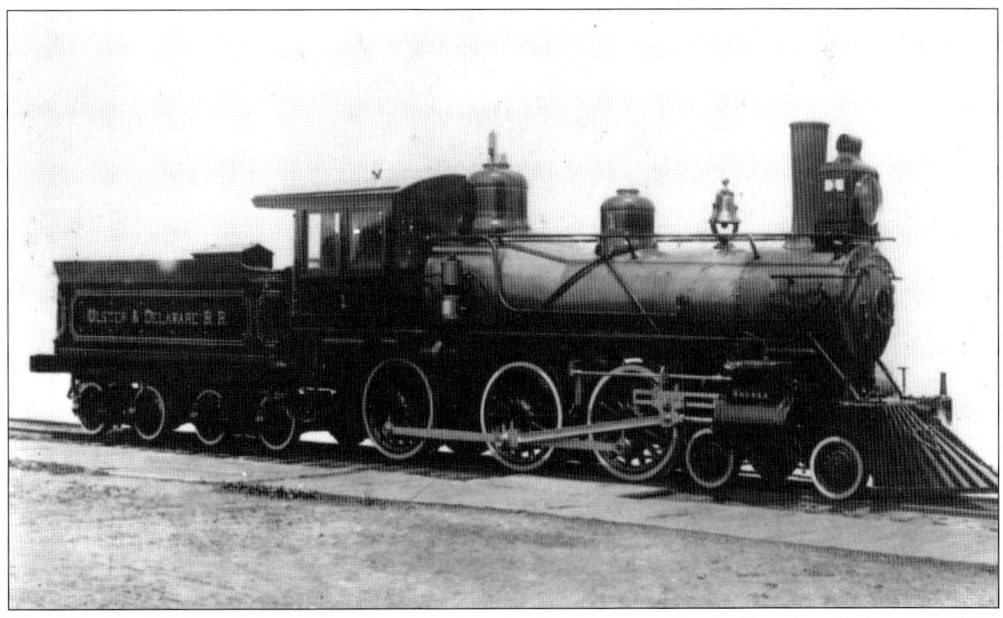

The Wallkill Valley Railroad track crossed only about one and a half miles of the township, while the Ontario and Western Railway traversed only about 1,000 yards on its way to points south. The Ulster and Delaware Railroad had a single tiny station in the townships. That was the Stony Hollow station. Above is Ulster and Delaware locomotive No. 1 beginning service in 1898. (Town of Kingston.)

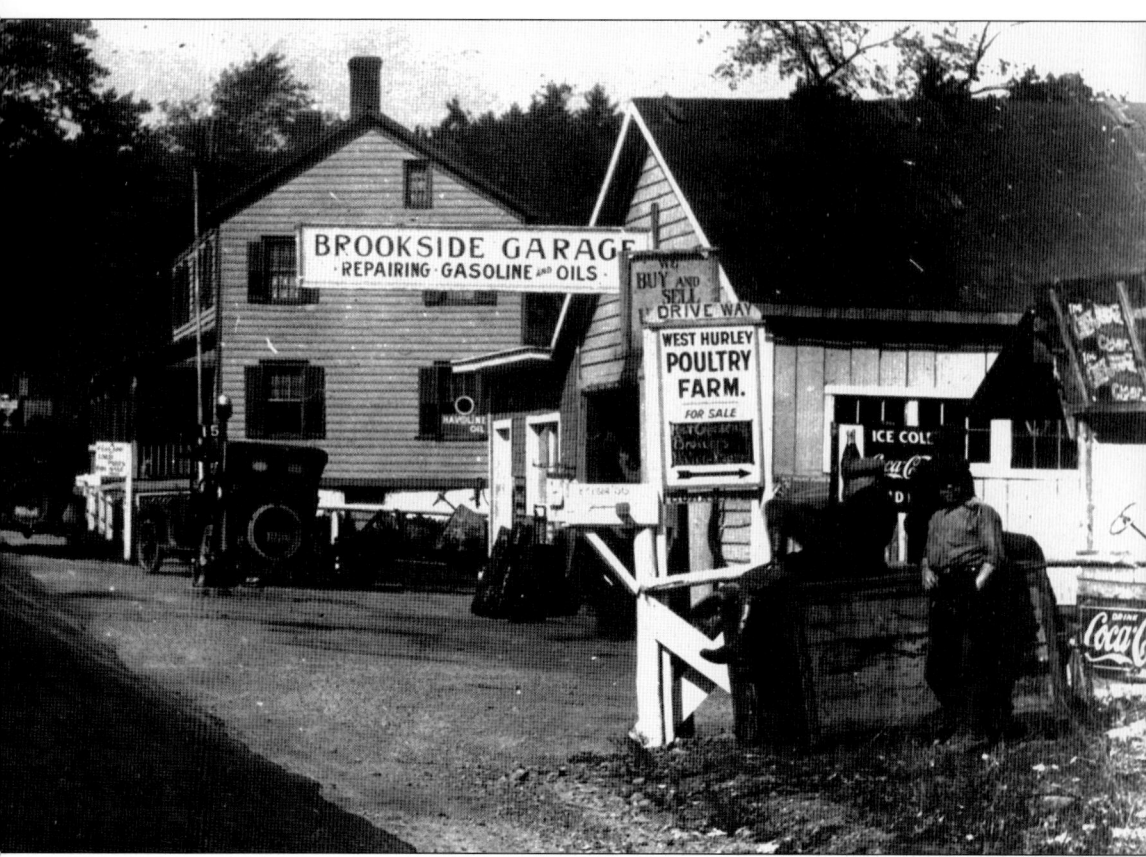

Sadly, there appear to be no photographs of the Stony Hollow station. There is however, an Edison movie showing the station. Stony Hollow was a simple station and shelter serving the local farmers, woodsmen, and stonecutters. The station was painted a cream color around 1900. One can see two stills captured from the newsreel in John Ham's book about the Ulster and Delaware stations. With the coming of the Ashokan Reservoir project in 1913, both rail and vehicular traffic through Stony Hollow increased greatly, and the grade crossing was replaced with a viaduct to allow slow-moving construction vehicles to pass over the rails without interference of either by the other. Stony Hollow still exists. While most of the early buildings are gone, a few nice old structures are still extant. This is a c. 1929 photograph of Benson's Brookside Garage. The overpass was removed in the late 1980s, after the railroad discontinued service and the grade crossing was restored by the Catskill Mountain Railroad preservation group. The author recalls driving this route many times during his childhood. (Rob Sweeney.)

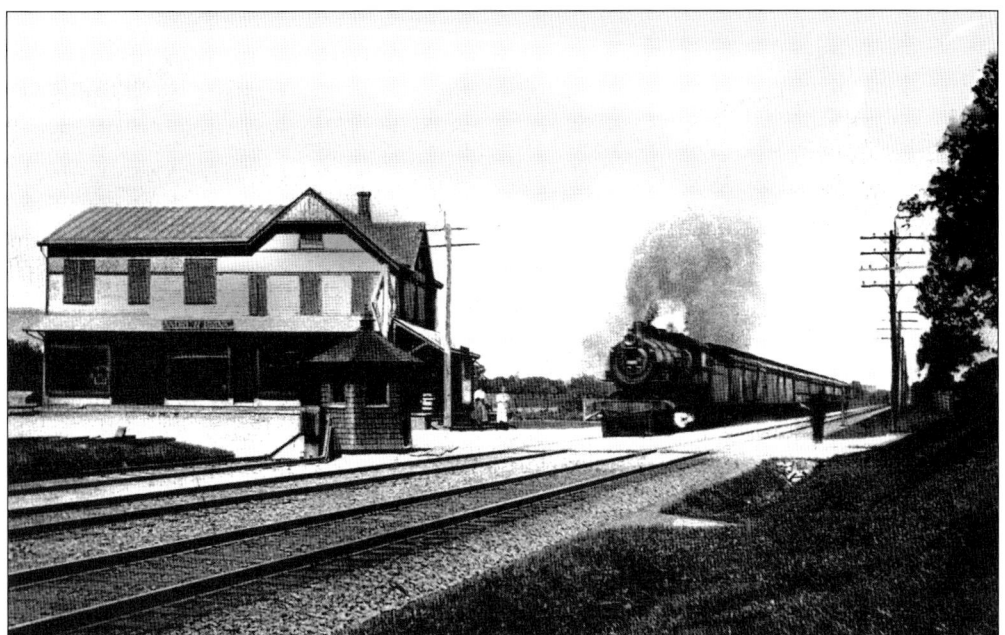

On the New York Central West Shore Line, the Lake Katrine station was located at the store of Andrew W. Brink sometime between 1889 and 1907. Often a station was combined with a general store and a post office. This is a staged photograph from about 1910 used on a postcard. The 2-8-0 consolidation steam engine pulls a consist of five passenger cars into the station while the flagman protects the crossing. (John Ham.)

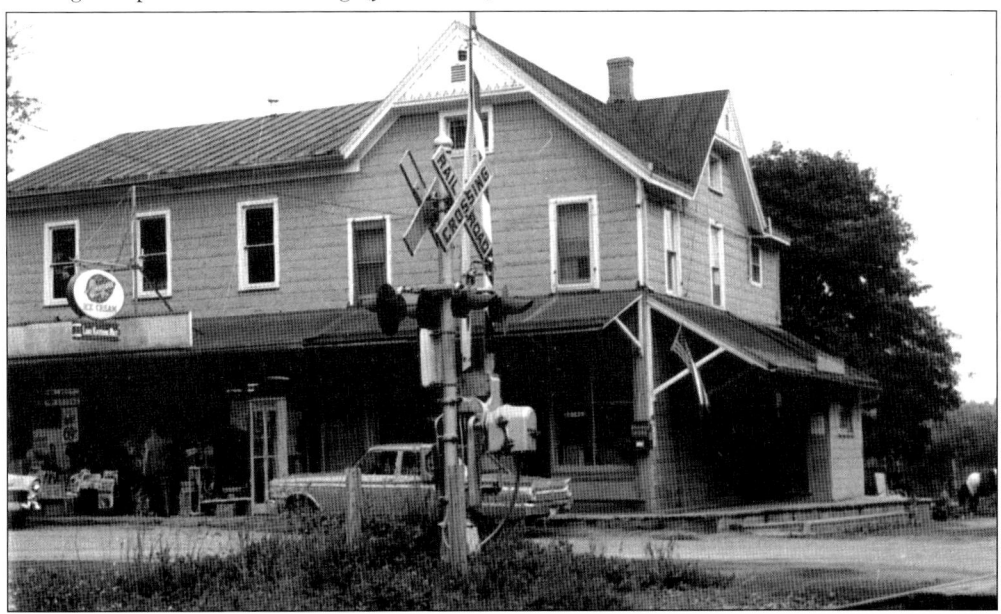

Sixty years later, the venerable Brink's store retains the same lines but is no longer a stop on the West Shore Line. The railroad abandoned passenger service in 1959 and removed one of the two tracks. The store and post office are still active. The crossing is guarded by a modern gate and signal system approved by the town in March 1926. The old multiarm communications poles are long gone. (Town of Kingston.)

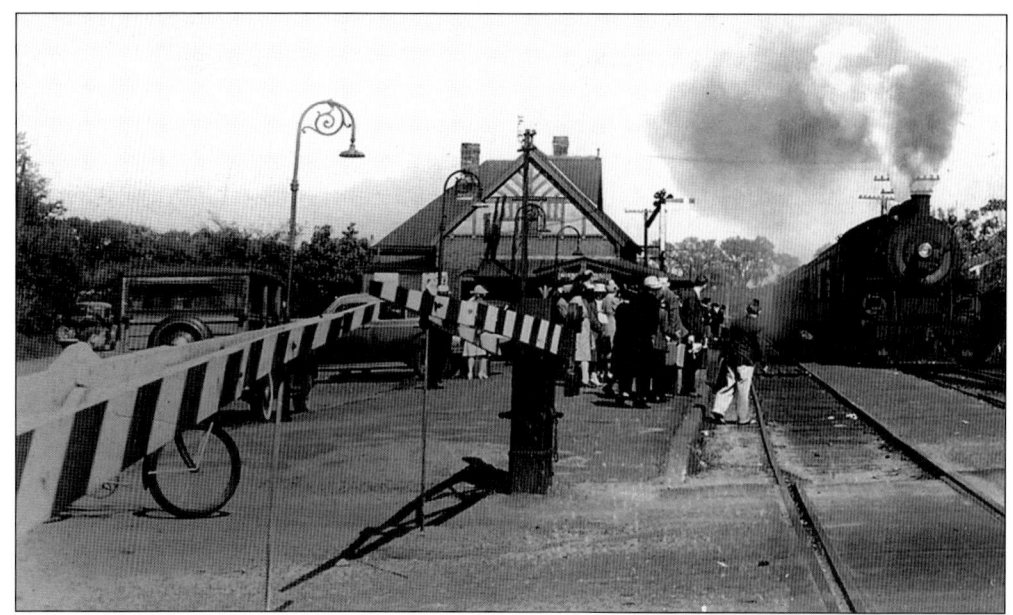

Three miles north of Lake Katrine was Mount Marion station. It was actually located just over the line in the town of Saugerties, but also served Ulster and Kingston residents. The date is likely the early 1940s. What a difference a generation makes. The fancy station is now complete with streetlights for the parking lot and gates at the crossing. There are also mechanical signals for the trains. (John Ham.)

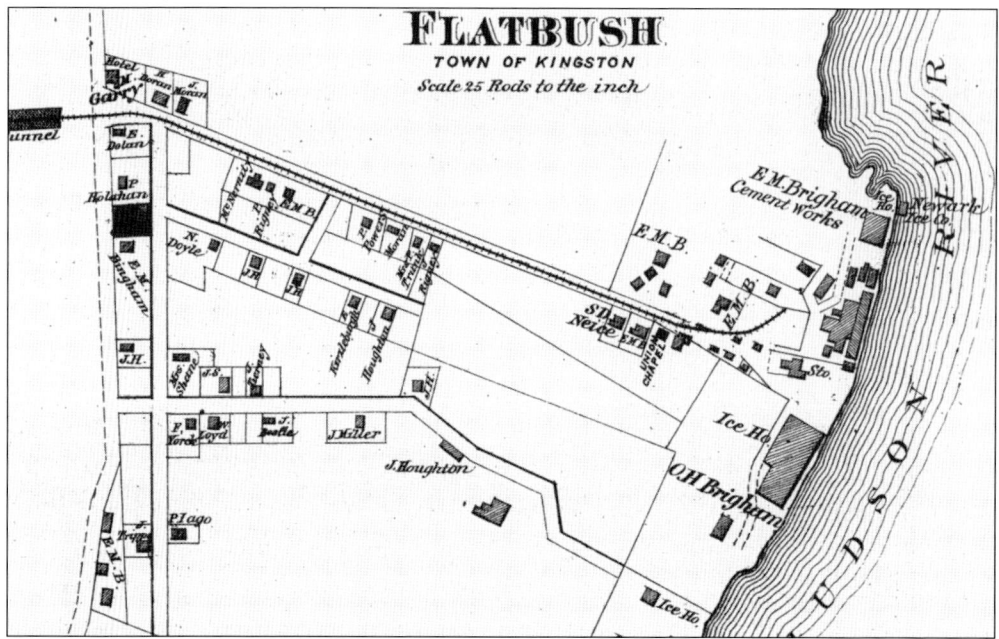

A vignette to the 1875 atlas of Ulster County featuring today's East Kingston shows the horse railroad of the E. M. Brigham companies. Brigham owned a cement company, brickyard, and the Newark Ice Company. The railroad followed a very straight path down a filled berm that would become Railroad Avenue in the 20th century. Horses drew small ore cars carrying limestone for cement and clay for brick making. (Donald Briggs I.)

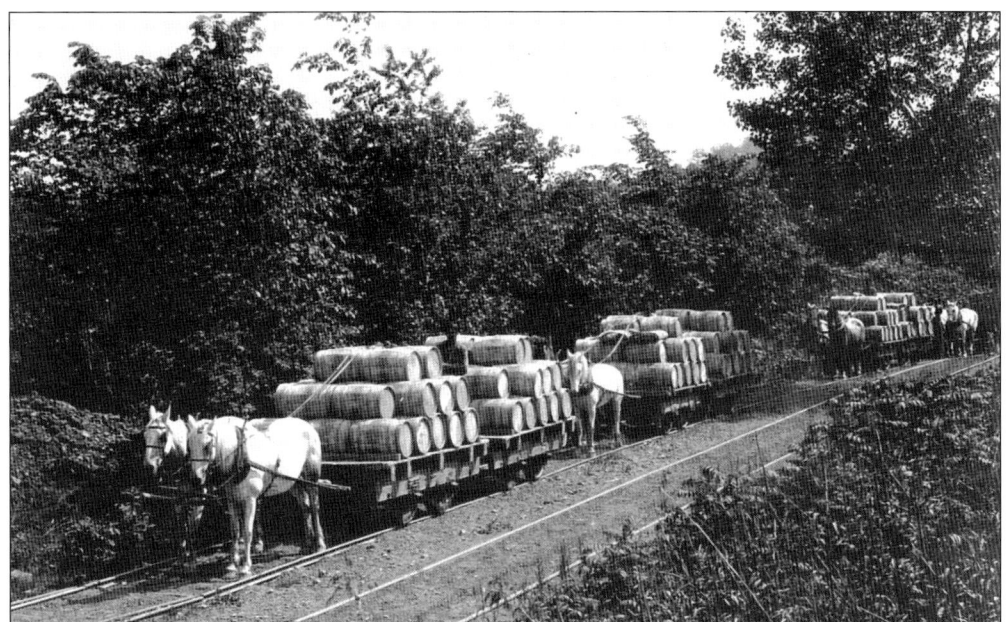

The Eddyville and Hickory Bush Horse Railroad was a joint venture of three cement companies. The road carried coal to the cement mines and barrels of cement to Eddyville. Each wagon carried 70 barrels and was pulled by mules or draft horses. The rail was light iron, about 15 pounds per yard, and was laid in the 1850s on the bed of a short-lived plank road. (Century House Historical Society.)

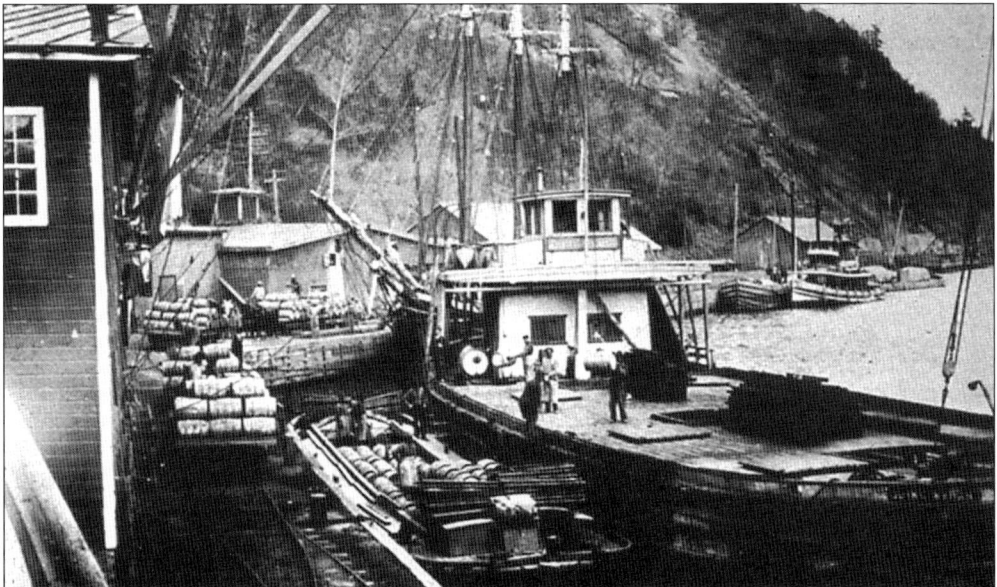

The Eddyville loading facilities are seen around 1900. The steam tug brought the cement-laden canal boats back to the tidewater lock of the Delaware and Hudson Canal, a quarter mile east. In the midground stands a sloop—possibly carrying coal for the machinery—in the background there appears to be one of the small steamboats of the Haber Boat Company. By 1910, Edward Coykendall had combined the three companies into the Consolidated Cement Company. (Century House Historical Society.)

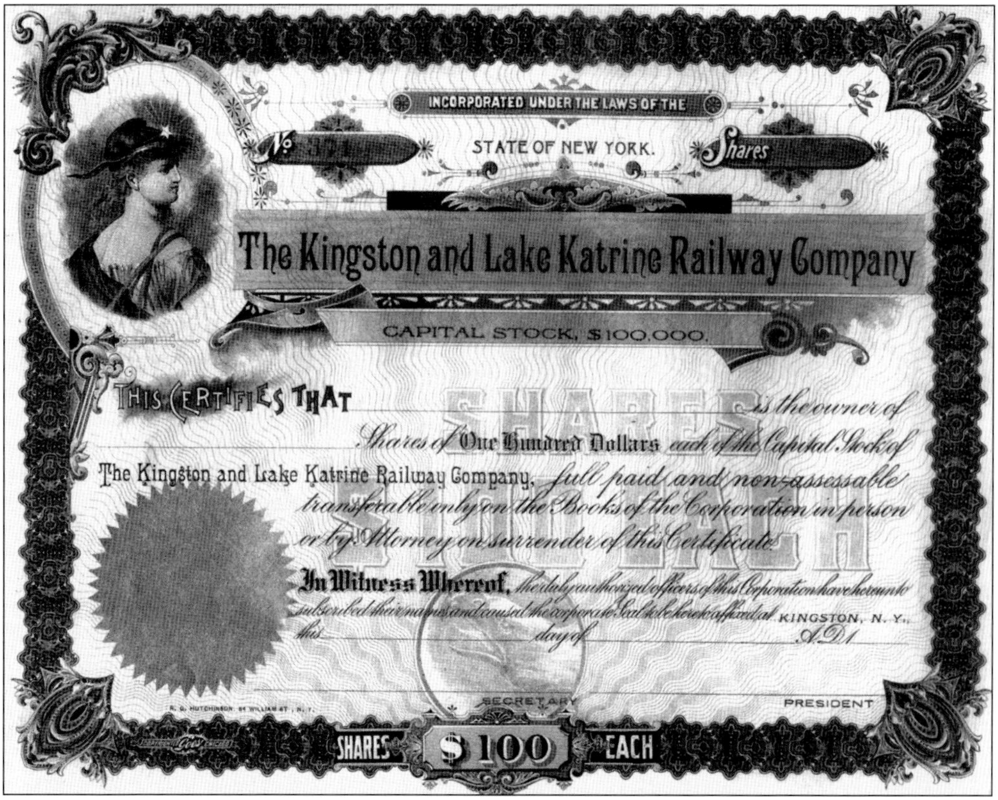

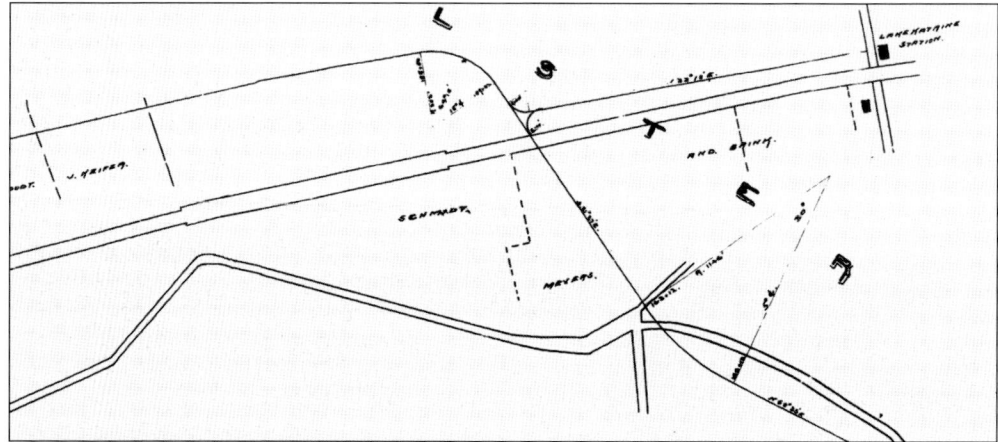

In 1896, ambitious individuals devised a plan to construct a four-mile horse-drawn railroad from the Kingston Union Depot in midtown Kingston to the West Shore Line station at Lake Katrine and on to the lakeside resort. The principals filed articles of incorporation on February 21, 1896. These were approved by the New York State Railroad Commission in June of that year and announced on July first.

The proposed line made a large loop around midtown before heading northward along Elmendorf Street toward Manor Avenue. At South Manor was a wye and a three-block spur to the end of Foxhall Avenue. The main line ran partially along Manor Avenue and then cross-country directly toward the Katrine station. A second wye, with a half-mile spur to the lake, was 1,200 feet short of the station. (Ulster County Archives.)

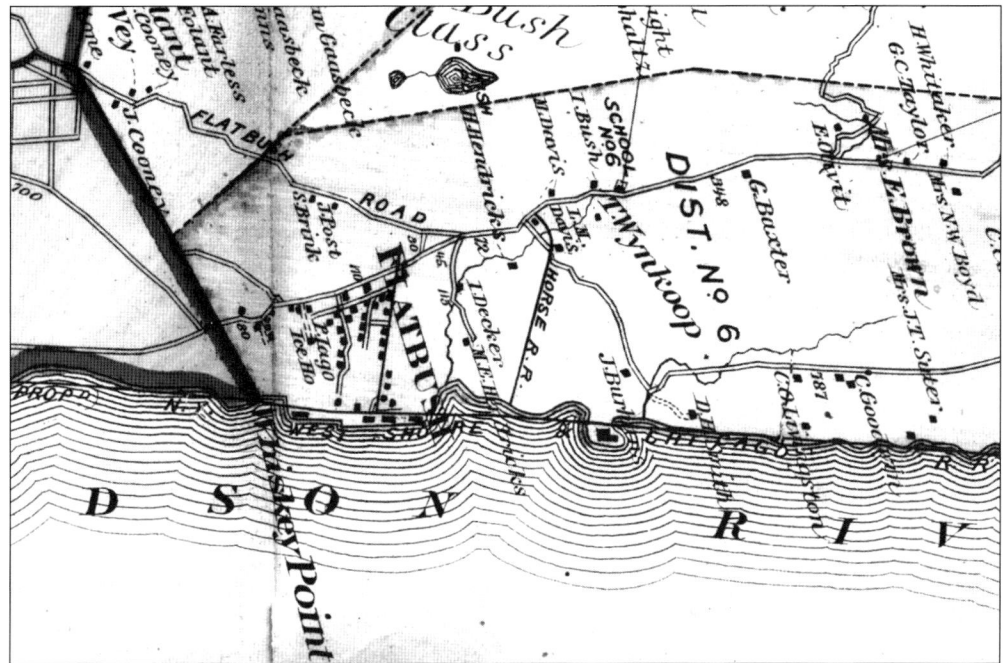

As late as 1875, Pullman, Porter, and the Pennsylvania Railroad had plans to build the West Shore Line along the actual shore, as is evidenced by this map. A special sessions act designed to protect the flourishing ice industry along the western shore from the devastating potential effects of coal soot, caused the actual rail line to turn inland at the salt line near Highland and remain there until reaching Albany. (Donald and Shirley Briggs.)

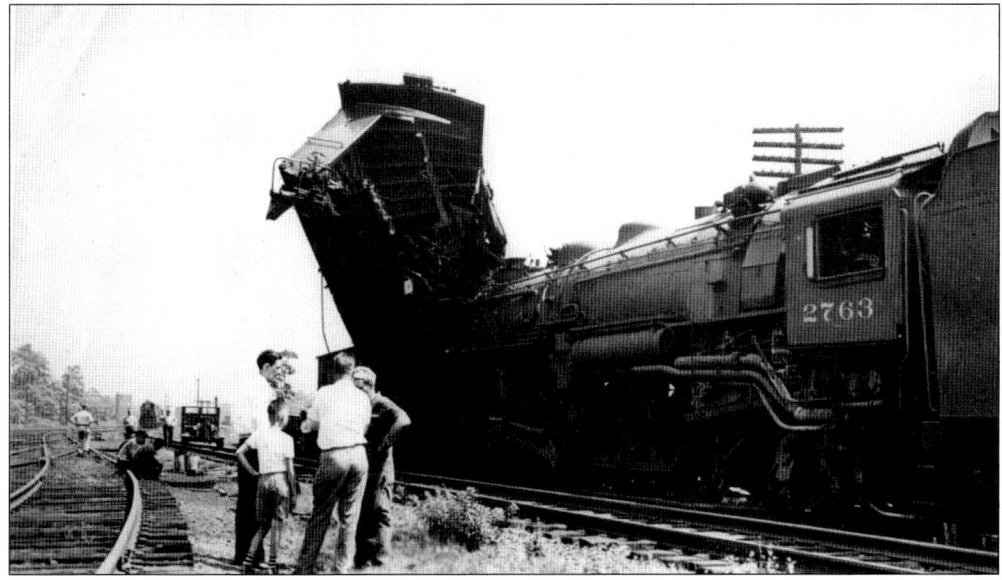

Although the railroads brought much prosperity and convenience to the towns, sometimes they also brought various levels of calamity. In July 1940, a train crew brought a freight into the north yard from the Wallkill Valley branch. Unfortunately, someone forgot to reset a switch to the through line. L2a Mohawk 2763 was next to enter the yard and could not halt its own 364,500-pound weight. The result was spectacular. Note the track car. (Bob Haines.)

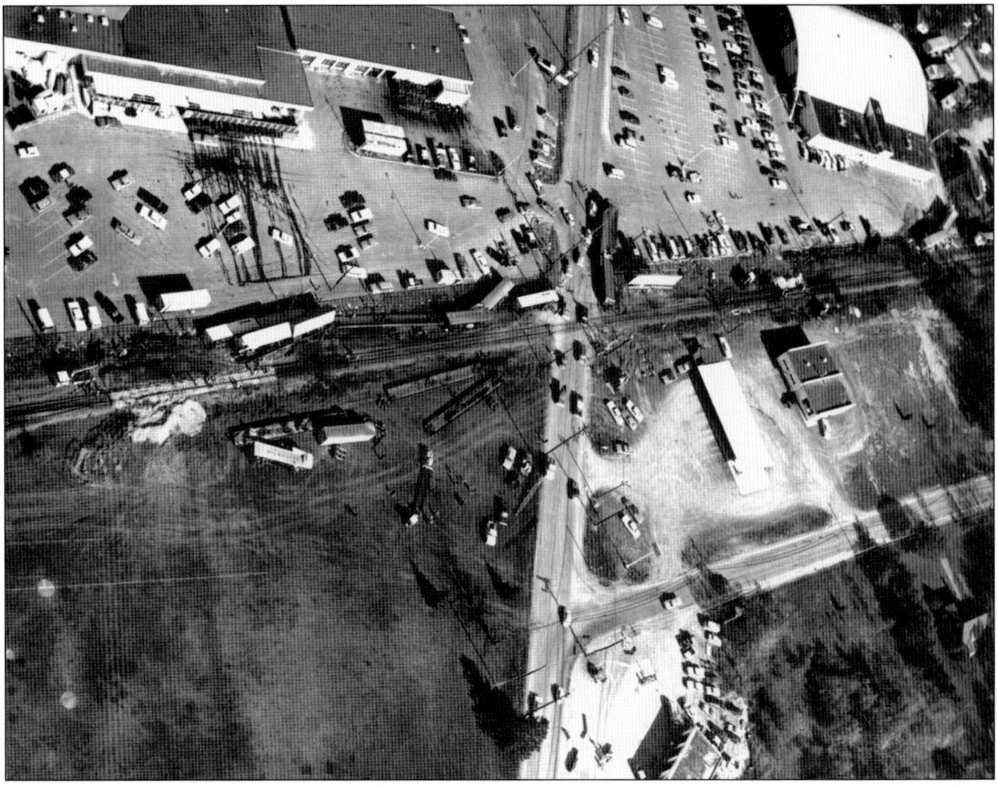

Almost 30 years later, on May 1, 1969, a similar calamity struck the New York Central's successor, the Pennsylvania Central, just outside of the same yard at Boices Lane. A close inspection reveals freight cars in the Shoprite parking lot and crews already rebuilding broken track to the west of the Montgomery Ward department store. The derailment was likely caused by what the locals called the railroad's notorious lack of periodic maintenance. (Bob Haines.)

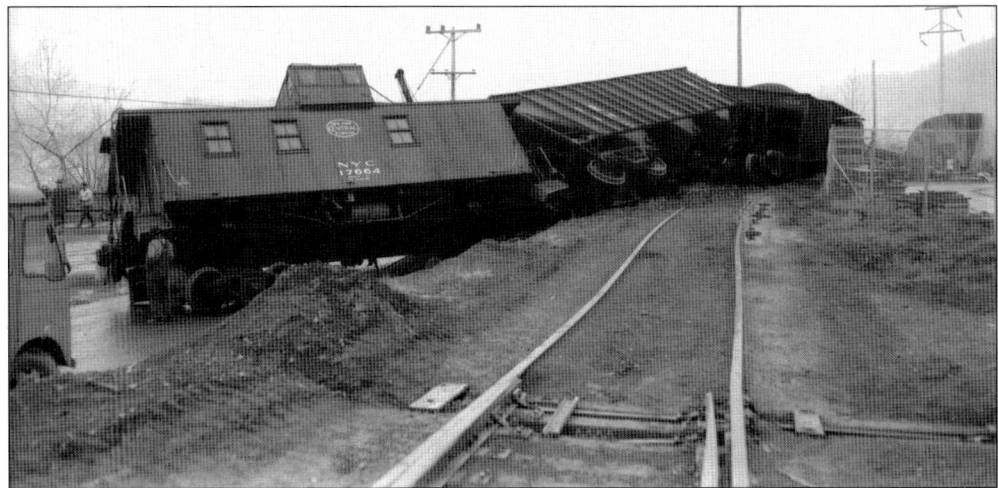

The New York Central was guilty of similar deferred maintenance on its Catskill Mountain branch (former Ulster and Delaware Railroad). This 1969 wreck occurred while the locomotive was pushing a train into Hudson Cement. The caboose landed on North Street. Fortunately the cars could be easily set back onto their trucks and the coal reloaded. (Bob Haines.)

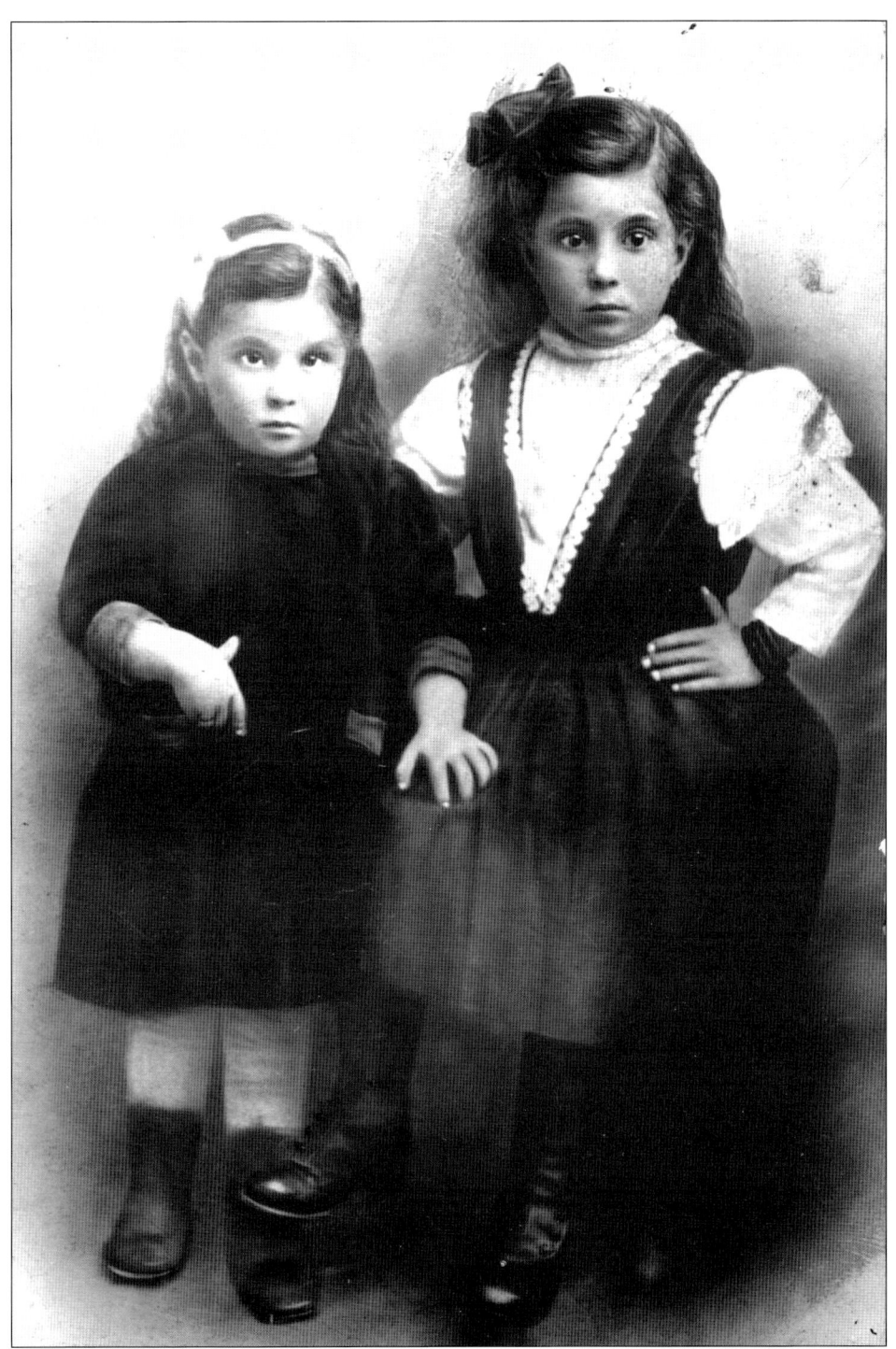

Railroad accidents do not always involve only equipment. Sometimes, tragedy strikes far closer to the heart. Sisters Emma and Rose DeCicco of East Kingston were killed at the Flatbush Avenue railroad crossing in November 1917. They are interred at St. Mary's Cemetery. May they rest in peace.

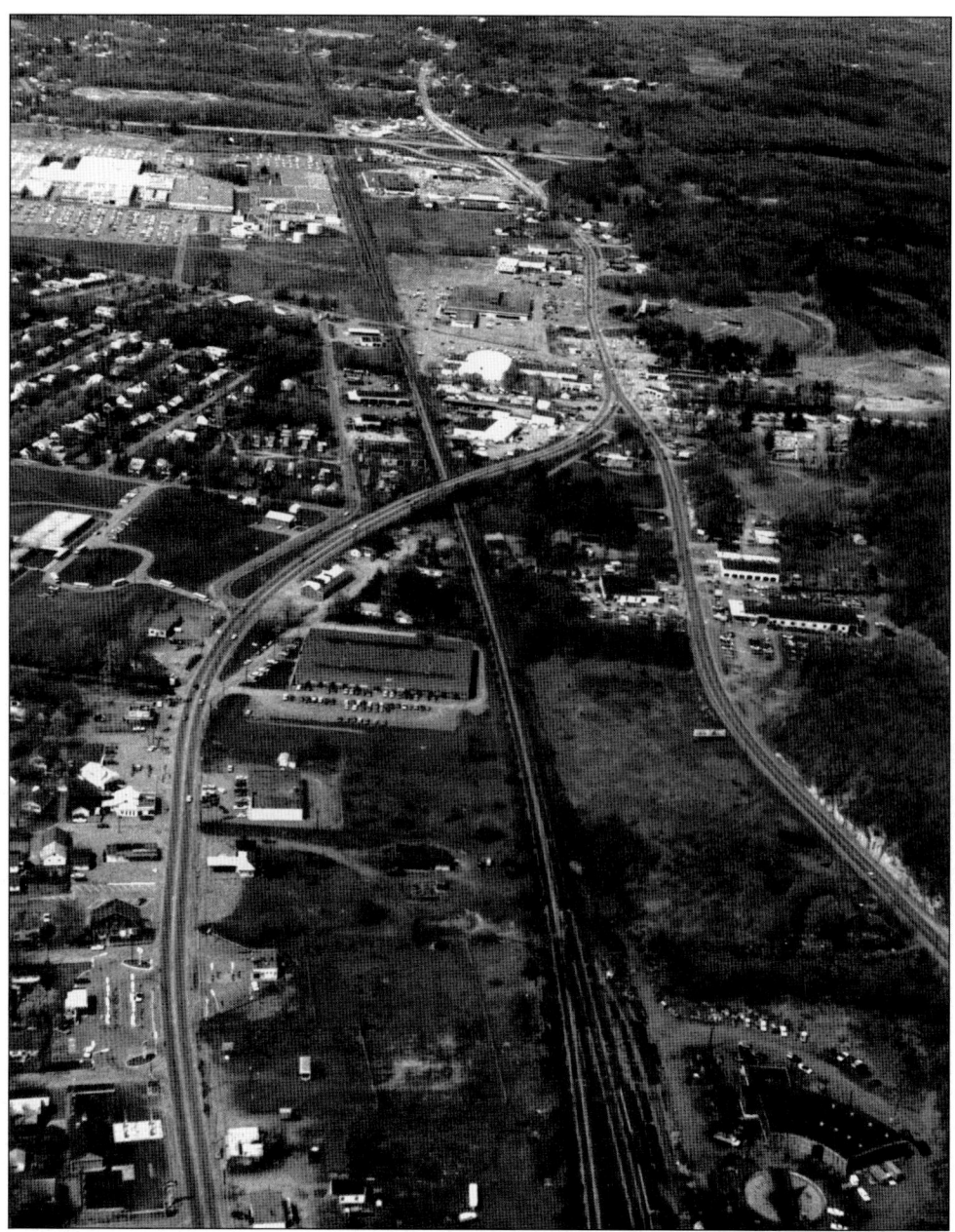

Footpath to Albany, Saugerties Road, Ulster Avenue, Route 9W, the name changes with each milestone on the road of progress. The commercial offerings do too. The business of hospitality evolved from in-house front-room taverns to accommodate post and stage travelers. By the 1890s, disorderly roadhouses such as Lake Katrine's Red House were offering illicit liquor, hanky-panky, and games of chance as attested to in a divorce action by a deputy charged with collecting the sheriff's rents. Then in roared the 1920s, and Mae and Harry Western were running the show. A falling out with Jack "Legs" Diamond found Harry gunned down shortly after writing out his will in 1930. The advent of a trend to incorporate brought a more professional and sober atmosphere to the business corridor as sole proprietors and partnerships were replaced with the corporations and conglomerates of today. (Bob Haines.)

Nine
CORRIDOR OF COMMERCE

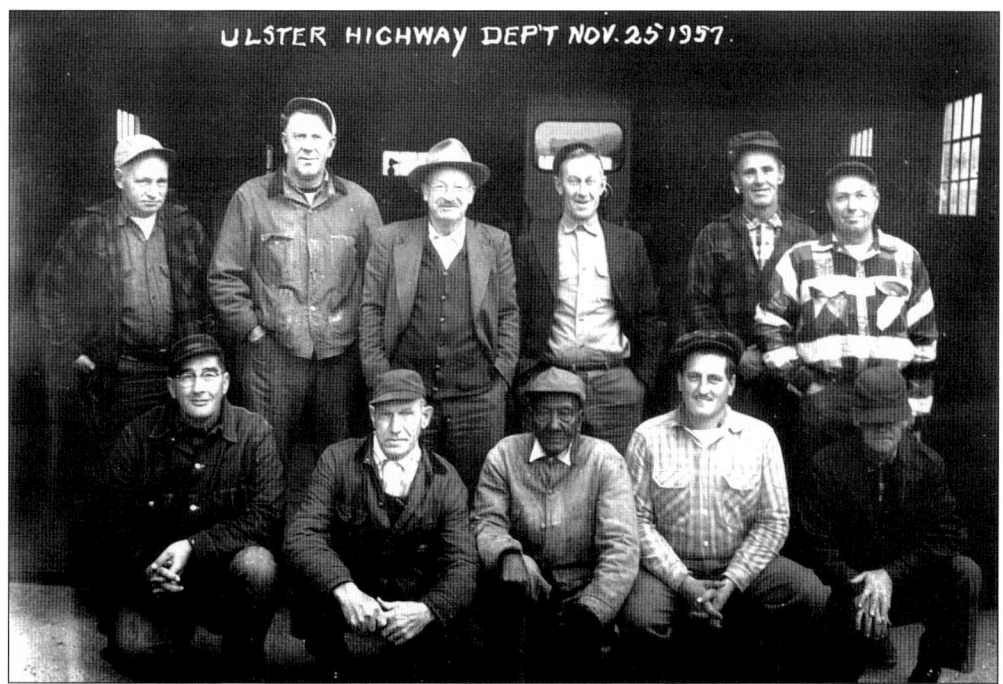

Amerindian trails, wagon paths, stage roads, royal highways, board and stone-slab turnpikes, macadam avenues, concrete thruways. Fords and ferries turned to bridges as a mad rush to modernization brought about the towns' highway departments. These are the men who served in 1957. From left to right are (first row) Bernie Lockwood, Ernie Schaller, Mr. Dardy, Griff Stoutenberg, and Joe Corcoran; (second row) Leighton Winchell, Norn Caunitz, superintendent Vern Felton, Harold Sutton, Bucky Scheffel, and Ralph VanKleek. (Town of Ulster Highway.)

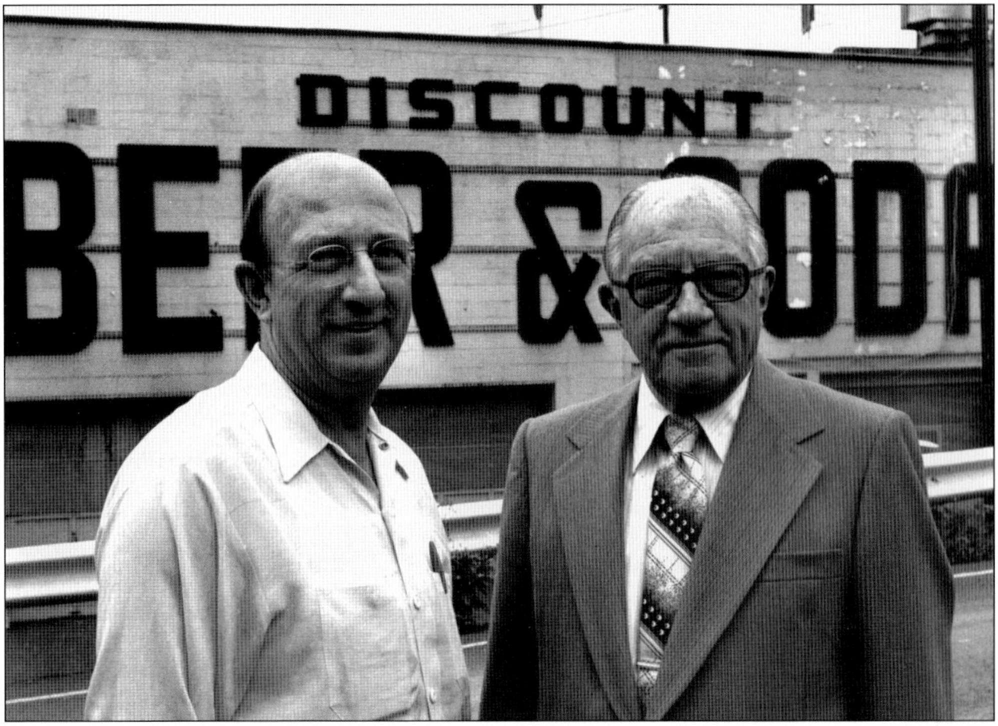

Chided by his peers as a foolhardy pioneer, J. Ellis Briggs (right) was the first retail entrepreneur to put his faith in the business future of the town of Ulster. In 1947, he plunked down $1,500 cold cash for a lot on the banks of the Bear Cat Creek. There with his eldest son, Donald E. Briggs I (left), he built an attractive appliance store. It thrived, as did successive businesses under the Briggs umbrella. (Donald Briggs I.)

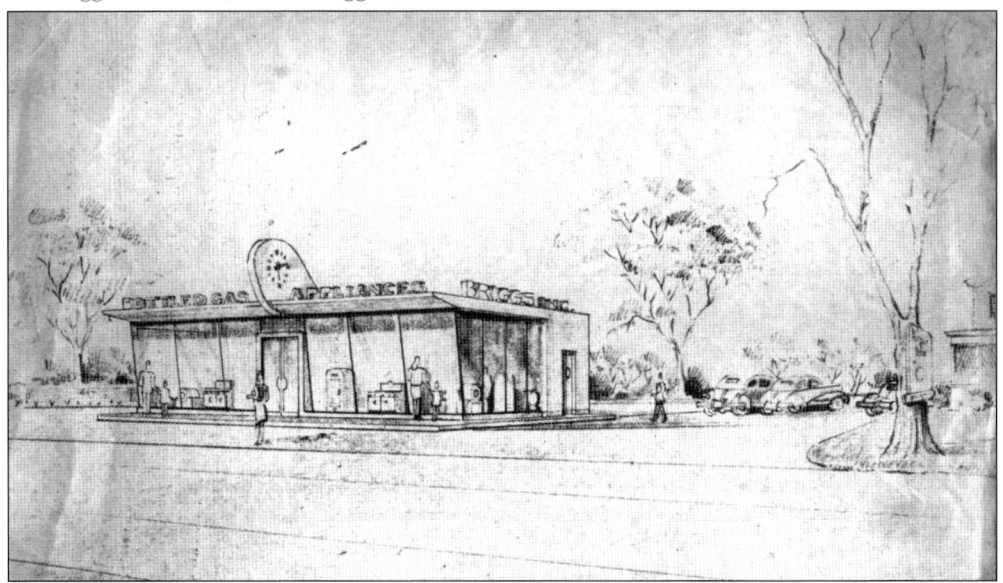

Working from a conceptual drawing and plans sketched on empty cement bags, scouring the countryside for scarce building materials in the post–World War II era, Don Briggs began building a future for his family using kegs of nails garnered from Ithaca. (Donald Briggs I.)

When International Business Machines chief executive officer Thomas J. Watson Jr. had a prior commitment for the night of the Ulster County chamber dinner, officers were bright enough to do the unthinkable. They changed their schedule to suit his. "You need to be flexible when you're courting economic success," the reigning president was heard to say. On January 25, 1956, the Ulster County Chamber of Commerce held its annual dinner at the Governor Clinton Hotel.

```
...PROGRAM...
       ↑↑↑↑
    CLARENCE H. BUDDENHAGEN
Banquet Committee Chairman, presiding

Invocation                    Rev. Kenneth N. Alexander
       President, Kingston Ministerial Association

Dinner

Welcome                              C. H. Buddenhagen

Greetings                            Frederick H. Stang
              Mayor, City of Kingston

Remarks and Presentation of 1956 Officers    J. Ellis Briggs
              Immediate Past President

Response                             George J. Silkworth
       President, Kingston Area Chamber of Commerce

Presentation of Guests  AND GUEST SPEAKER BY
                                   J. ELLIS BRIGGS
Guest Speaker                      Thomas J. Watson, Jr.
                  President,
       International Business Machines Corporation

Benediction                        Rev. Edward I. Farrelly
       Assistant Pastor of St. Mary's R. C. Church
```

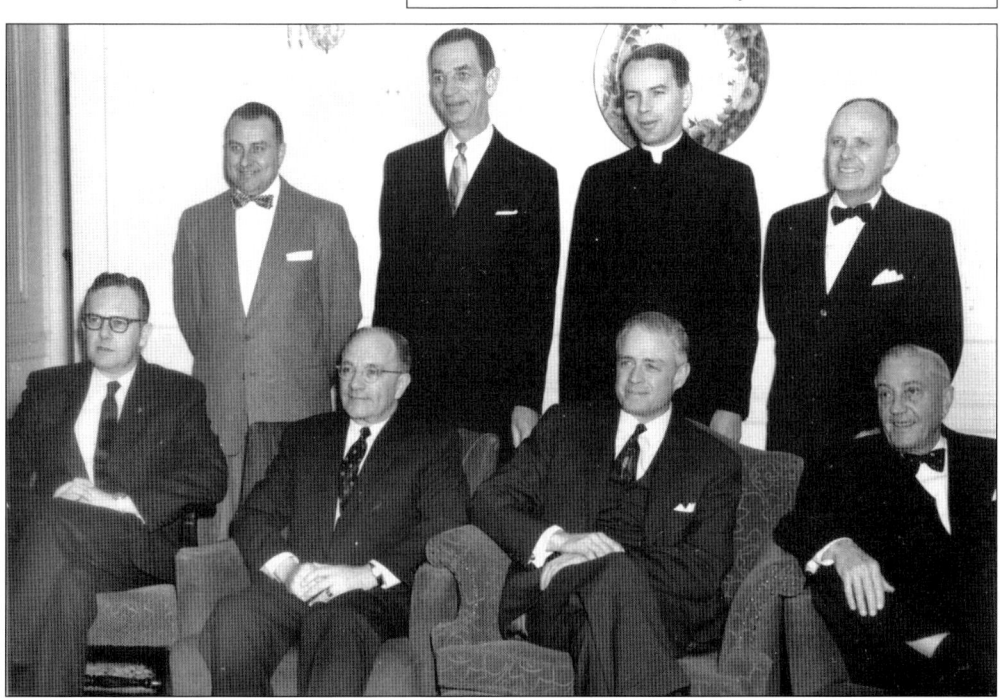

The guest speaker was Thomas J. Watson Jr. of the IBM Corporation. The large IBM plant became the centerpiece of not just the town of Ulster but the county as well and remained so for the next four decades. Seen here from left to right are (first row) George Silkworth, J. Ellis Briggs, Thomas J. Watson Jr., and Sen. Arthur Wicks; (second row) Clare Buddenhagen, Mayor Fred Stang, Rev. Edward Farrelly, and Rev. Kenneth Alexander. (Donald Briggs I.)

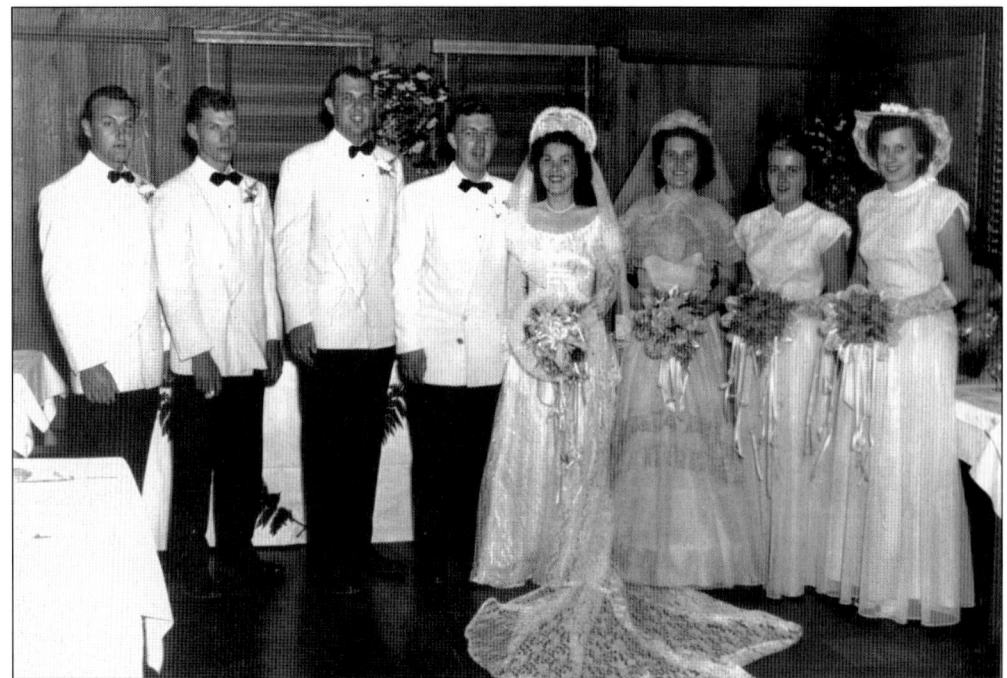

This is a wedding party at the Airport Inn in Lake Katrine in June 1950. Members of the entourage are, from left to right, Joseph Hill, Frank Codington, Joseph McAuliffe, Donald Briggs I, Shirley Ayers, Delores Ayers Cole, Jane Briggs, and Mary Countryman VanLaer. Twenty-five of the grooms Alpha-Zeta fraternity brothers serenaded the couple and the other guests. The inn was a favorite upscale establishment.

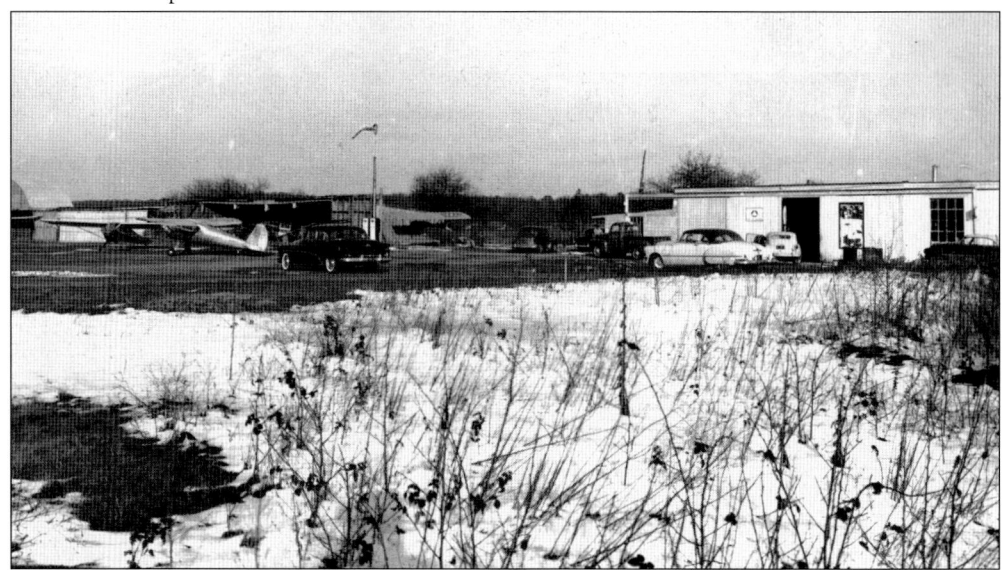

The Kingston-Ulster airport moved to a new location near Boices Lane after the thruway was constructed through its original Brabant Road location. This is a mid-1950s photograph of that location. The relocation was short lived, as the coming of the IBM Corporation forced yet another move, this time to Flatbush. The current airport remains in Flatbush and is a vibrant operation, hosting an average of 22 flights per day. (Bob Haines.)

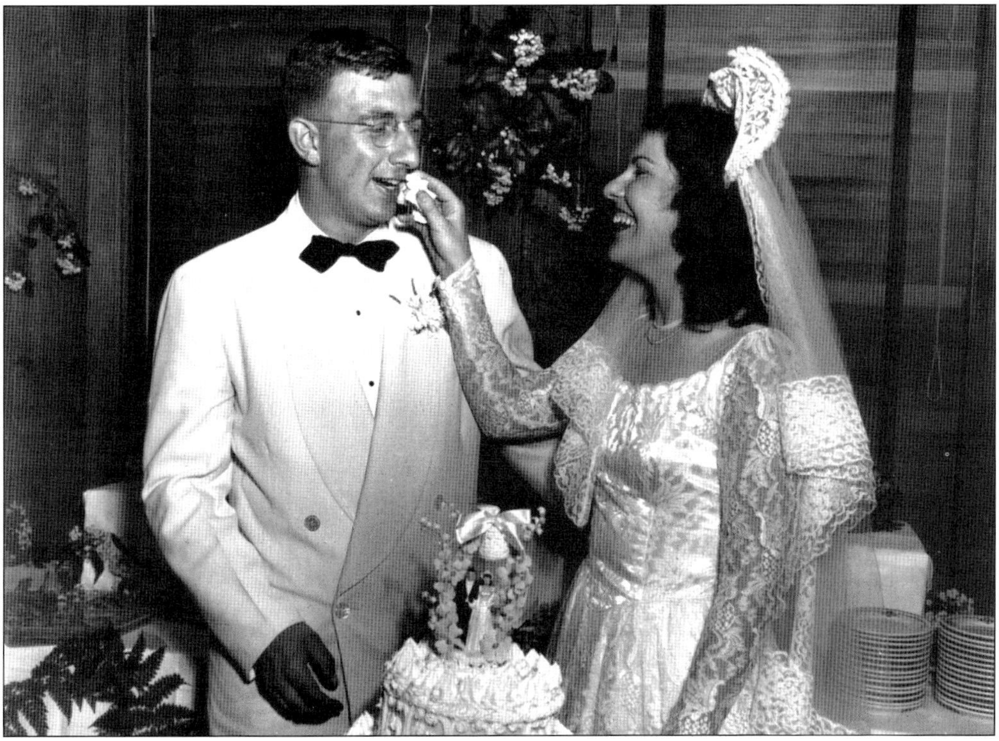

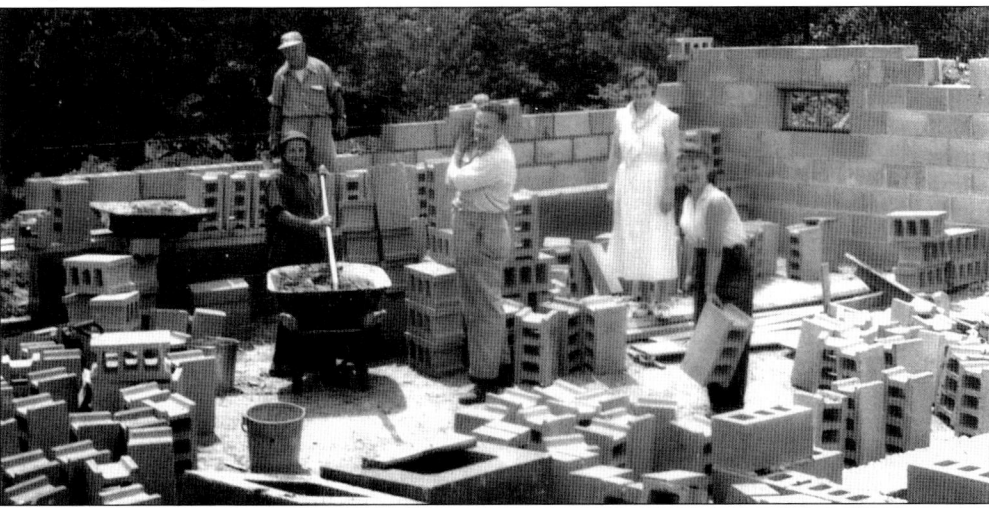

Bea Donell's Airport Inn sat on the corner of Route 9W and Boice's Lane providing elegant dining space for banquets and weddings in the 1940s and 1950s. A formal candlelight reception celebrating the marriage of Shirley Ayers to Donald E. Briggs I was held there on Saturday evening, June 17, 1950. After a honeymoon trip to Niagara Falls, Don and his Amerindian bride set up housekeeping in Lake Katrine.

Master mason Paul Teuber was one of many European craftsmen who came to the Kingston area to construct houses for the influx of new IBM employees. Before he could do this, he needed to build a home for his own family. He settled off Dug Hill Road and worked on many large projects including the Clinton Avenue United Methodist Church. Seen here from left to right are Emma Teuber, Paul Teuber, Horst Wick, Hilda Mack, and Monika Teuber Wick. (Emil Mack.)

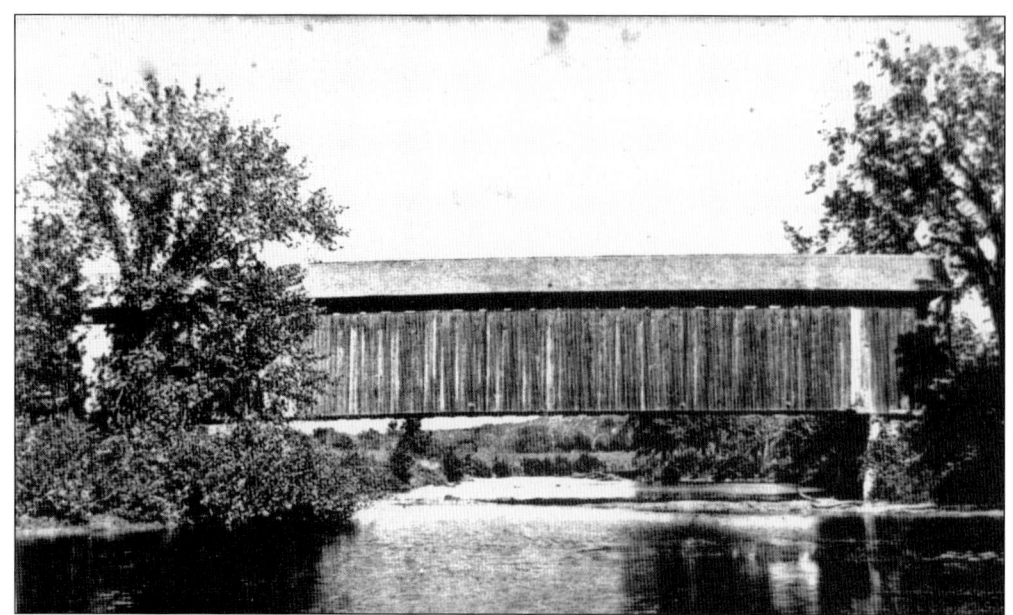

One of the early segments of the Corridor of Commerce was the covered bridge across Plattekill Creek in Lake Katrine. Even in this peaceful 1890s scene (now the site of a busy concrete bridge) a main roadway passed here. The town grew gradually over the years, until the coming of a large high-technology manufacturing company brought about an explosion of development.

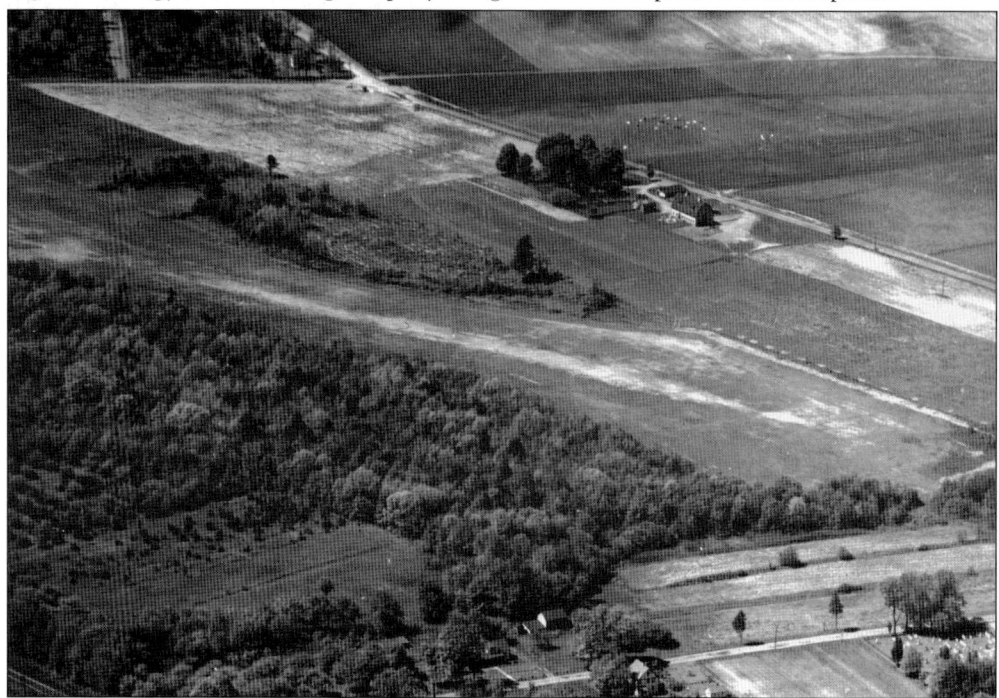

This is Lemuel Boice's farm in 1953, his cow fields are soon to be covered with an IBM complex. It opened in 1956 to the clickety clack of electric typewriters and had 1,000 black-suited employees by year's end. A boon to the local economy, IBM and its employees shouldered a large portion of the real property tax burden for 40 years. (Bob Haines.)

When the IBM Corporation came to the Kingston area in 1956 (opened in 1957), they needed a highly skilled technical workforce. The beauty of the Hudson Valley and the promise of secure employment at a decent rate of pay attracted many young geniuses from the New York City area. Horst Wick was one of these. Leaving a career with AT&T in July 1956, he relocated to the Kingston area. He started as a technician and quickly moved up to a position where he reviewed, and corrected where necessary, senior engineers' designs. After three years, he became a researcher in the experimental laboratory. His projects were top secret at the time. The most exciting years for the company were beginning.

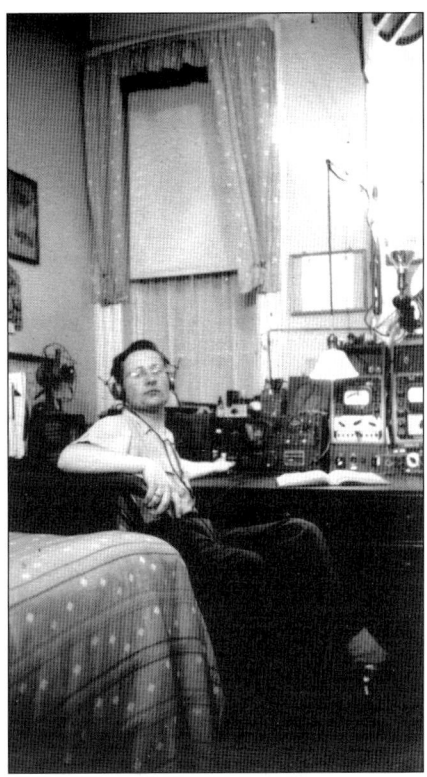

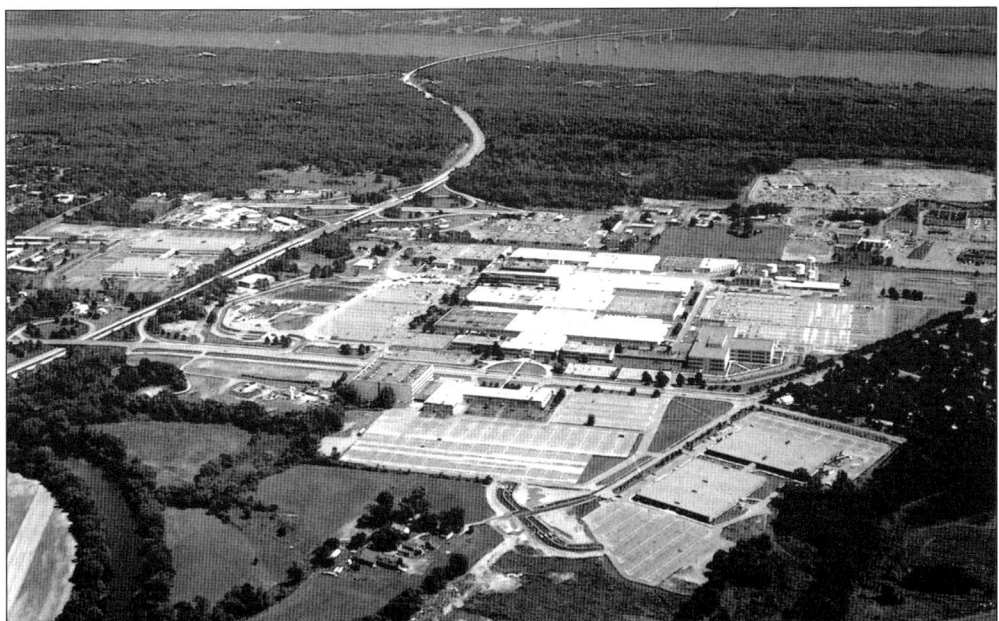

Terry Ramsey's dad worked as an engineer at "Big Blue" for 30 years. "It was all about security," she said. "Freedom from want. You were set for life with full company benefits . . . and job security so important to depression era babies. Dad was sent all over the world . . . and there were inspirational speakers to stimulate creative thought. It certainly could be stressful, but overall it was a good life." (Town of Ulster.)

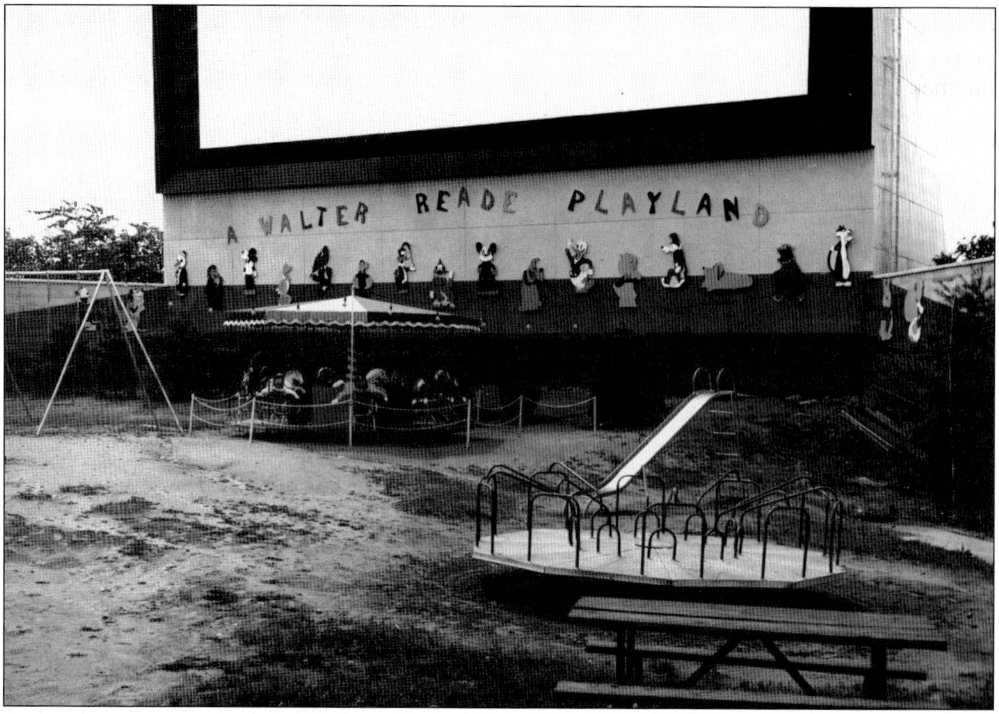

In the 1950s, 1960s, and early 1970s, a Saturday in summer meant a trip to the drive-in theater. The 9-W was the first. It had a snack bar, a playground for the kids, and the lively antics of auctioneer Bob Steele for predusk entertainment. Folks would bring everything from Christmas ornaments to used washing machines to put under the gavel. Steele was quite a pitchman, and by the end of the sale, every bit of merchandise had found a new home. Below is a 1965 aerial view of the area between Albany Avenue and Morton Boulevard showing Michael's Diner, Ulster Discount Beverages, and the original Shoprite Plaza. (Above, Bob Haines; below, Donald Briggs I.)

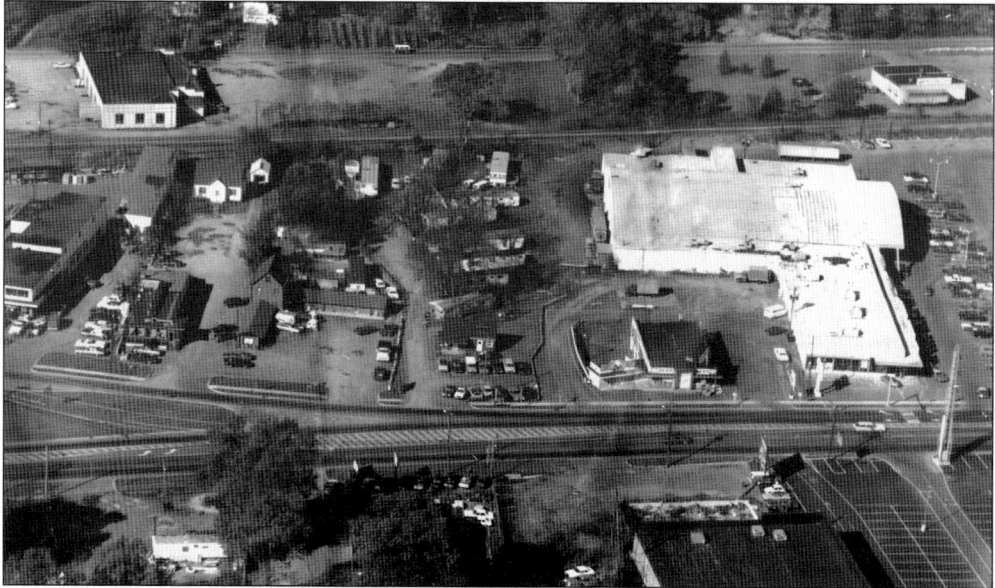

Highway superintendent Don "Mac" Tinnie (left) poses with Ulster town historian Bruce Burgher. Burgher, a retired sixth-grade teacher at Chambers Elementary School, was also Ulster County historian. He worked with Ken Hasbrouck of New Paltz on *The History of Ulster County*. When Burgher died in 2002, he left behind a nearly complete manuscript titled "The One Hundred Year History of the Town of Ulster." It was the product of a decade's work and a lifetime's love of history. The authors hope Bruce likes this book, as he was thought of along the way. (Mac and Peg Tinnie.)

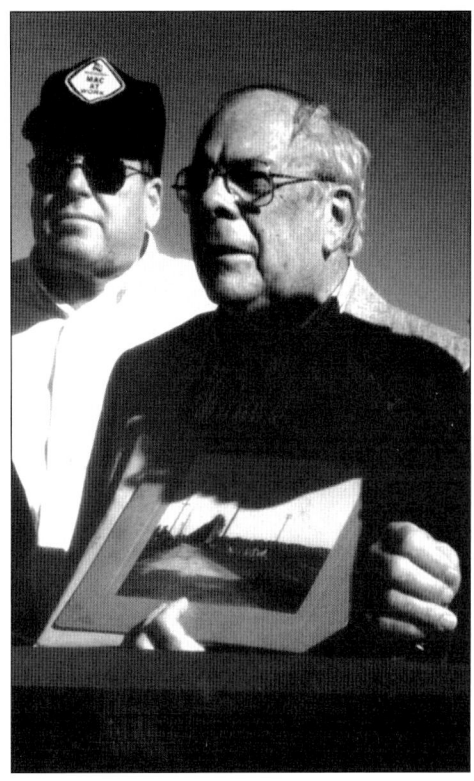

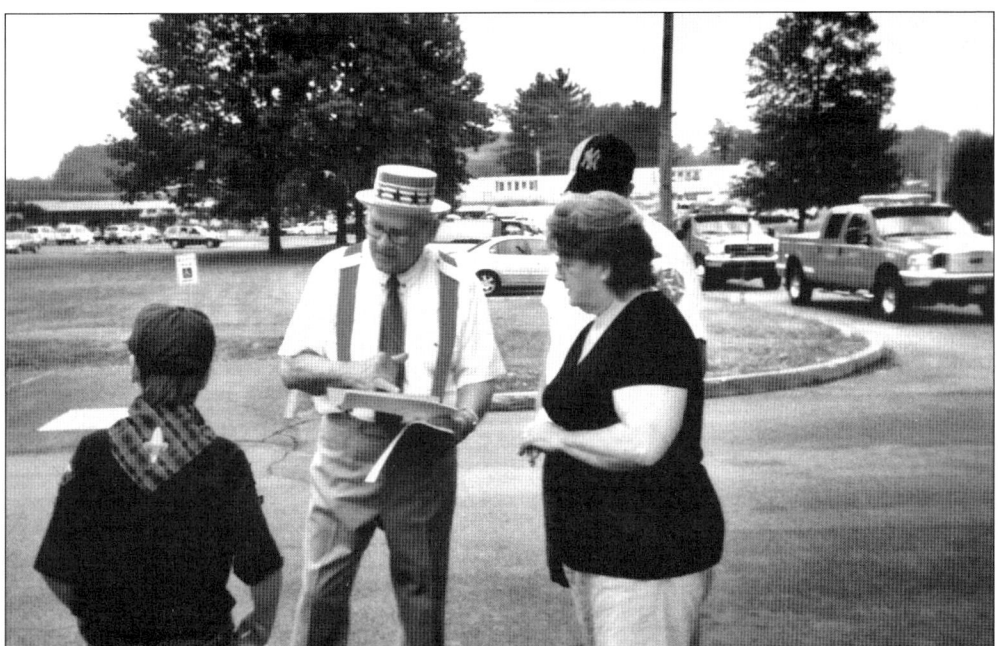

Orville Norman, radio host and local personality, is a hearty transplant to the Hudson Valley. He is well rooted in the town of Ulster, where with wife Ethel he raised a brood of children fed by his gardening expertise. Always ready to lend a hand, he is pictured here when he took the reins as parade master of the town of Ulster's 2006 Flag Day parade. (Dawn Wick.)

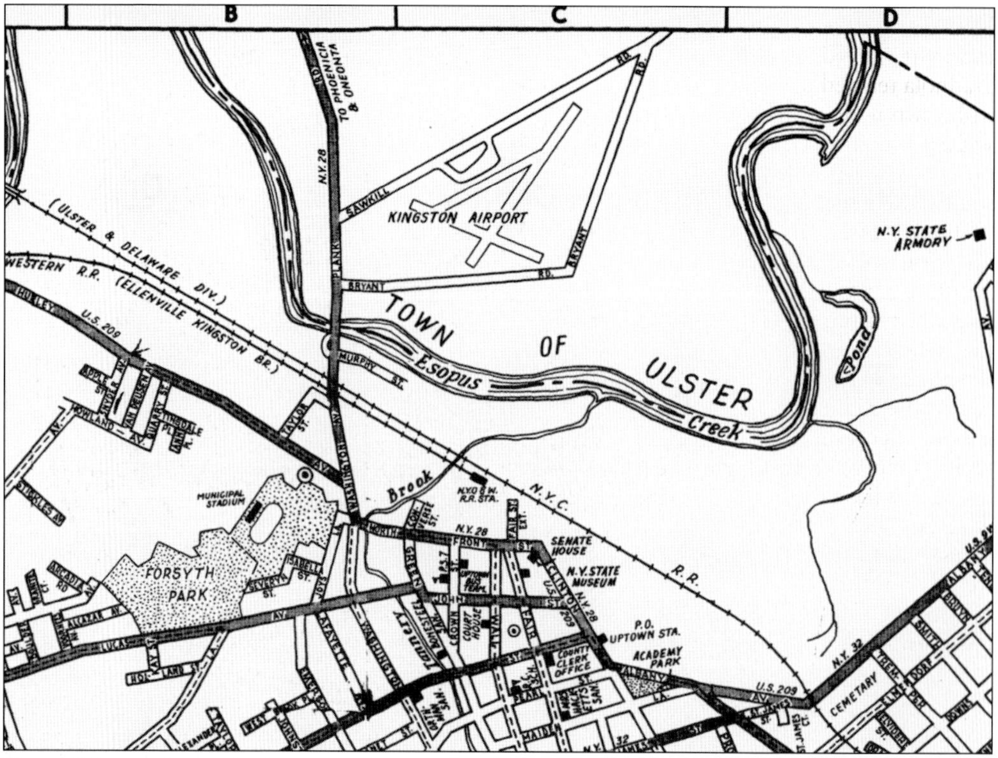

This 1951 map shows the location of the original Kingston airport nestled between Sawkill Road and Brabant Road in the township of Ulster. Brabant Road is no longer a through road, having been partially removed by the coming of Colonel Chandler Drive and the thruway interchange. The airport is perhaps best remembered for the surprise winter landing of two Douglas A-20 light bombers en route from Dayton, Ohio, to Mitchel Field.

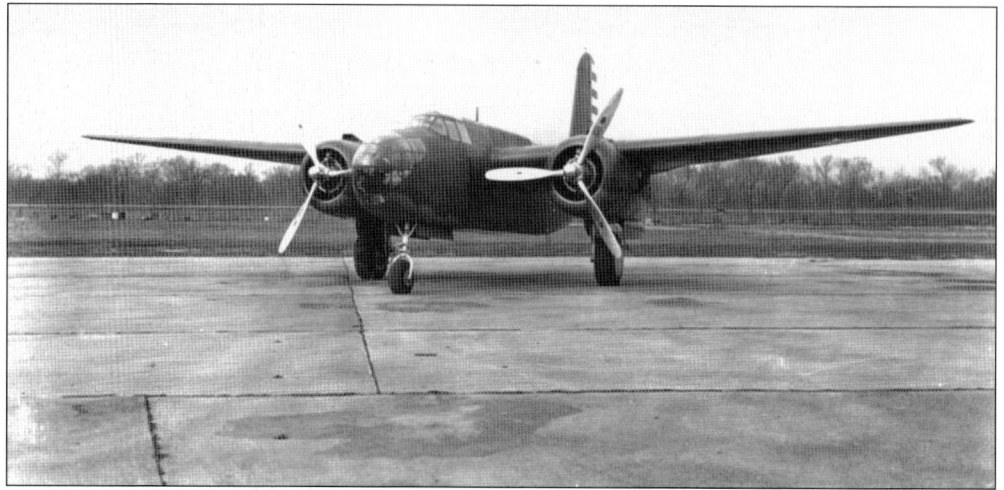

A-20s were configured to support troops on the ground. U.S. Army lieutenant Schurster said that the purpose of the flight was to "drop in at small fields to ascertain whether they were large enough to be used as emergency landing fields in case of war." Sawkill airport, as some called it, passed muster, except for some nearby electrical wires that posed a potential danger. The original hanger still stands.

In 1978, first-term councilman Fred Wadnola teamed up with town resident and art teacher Ann McCoy to create this seal for the Town of Ulster. Clockwise from the lower right, the arrowhead pays tribute to the Amerindians, the tractor represents the produce from farms past and present, electrons in orbit symbolize the township's future in progressing technology, and the last is a salute to the railroads and brickyards. (Ulster town clerk.)

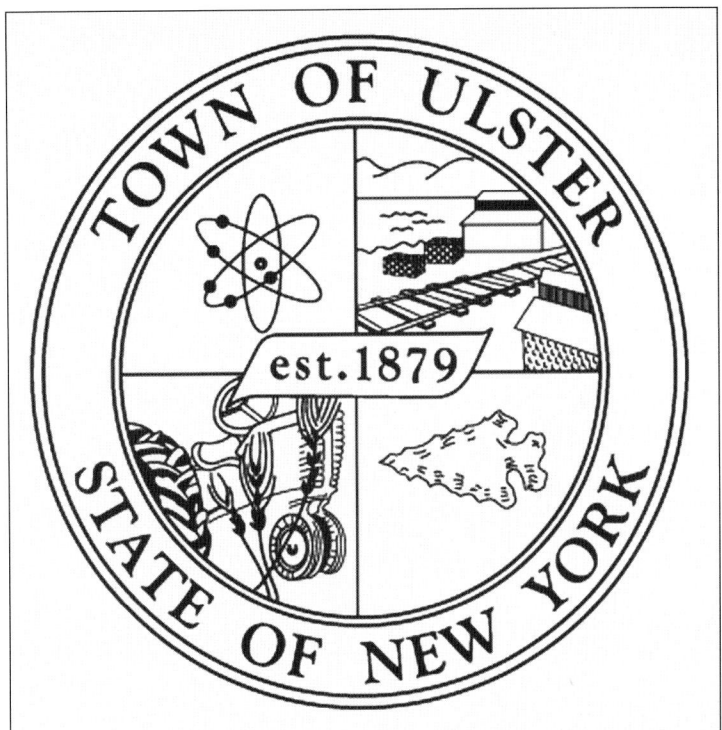

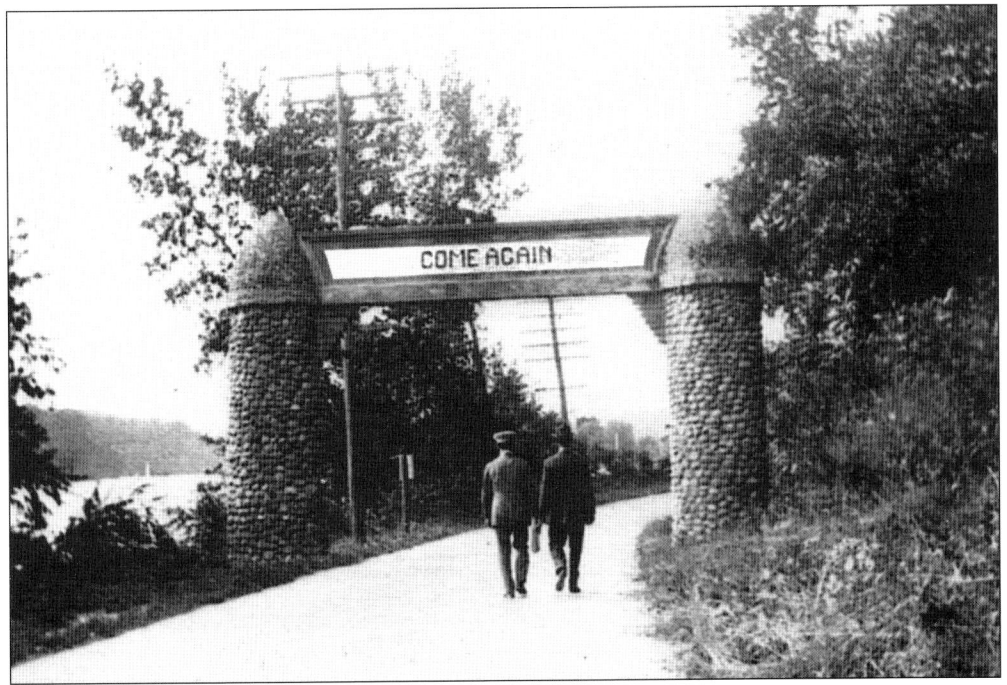

Now it is time for the authors to bid the reader a fond farewell. They hope that the reader has enjoyed this album of Kingston and Ulster. There are more pictures to see, and the authors invite the reader to visit their web site at www.stremy.net where they will list outtakes, corrections and further information. Farewell and please visit again. (Martin Jordan.)

Across America, People are Discovering Something Wonderful. Their Heritage.

Arcadia Publishing is the leading local history publisher in the United States. With more than 3,000 titles in print and hundreds of new titles released every year, Arcadia has extensive specialized experience chronicling the history of communities and celebrating America's hidden stories, bringing to life the people, places, and events from the past. To discover the history of other communities across the nation, please visit:

www.arcadiapublishing.com

Customized search tools allow you to find regional history books about the town where you grew up, the cities where your friends and family live, the town where your parents met, or even that retirement spot you've been dreaming about.

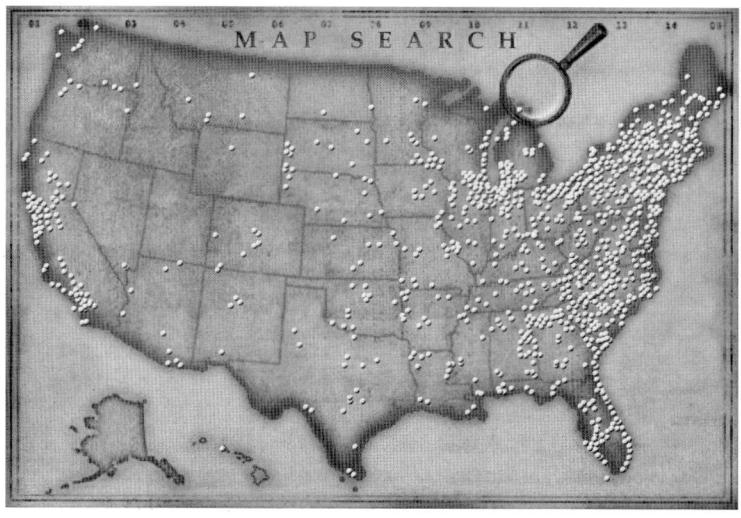